Céline
and the
Politics
of
Difference

Céline
and
the
Politics
of
Difference

edited by

Rosemarie Scullion

Philip H. Solomon

Thomas C. Spear

University Press of New England

Hanover and London

University Press of New England, Hanover, NH 03755
© 1995 by University Press of New England
All rights reserved
Printed in the United States of America   5   4   3   2   1
CIP data appears at the end of the book

Contents

Acknowledgments

▼

I WOULD LIKE to acknowledge the contributions of the Graduate College of the University of Iowa, which has supported my research in a number of crucial ways. Thanks also to the colleagues who offered encouragement and valuable critical and stylistic suggestions on the portions of this volume I authored, including: Cinzia Bloom, William K. Buckley, Alice Y. Kaplan, Andrea Loselle, Downing Thomas, and Steven Ungar. I am grateful to Janet Altman, Ora Avni, Kathy Heilenman, Laurie Hines-Munsen, Larry Kritzman, Sally Kenney, Sydney Lévy, Richard O'Gorman, Lauren Pinzka, Nathalie Rachlin, Diana Velez, and Sheila Zukowsky for the essential moral support they extended. Special thanks to Richard Golsan, who generously shared with me his expertise and experience as an editor and whose work on European fascism inspired me to undertake this project. I am especially indebted to my husband, Jalil Shirvani, who over the years has unfailingly and lovingly supported my intellectual endeavors and who has taught me much about the challenges and rewards of negotiating difference.

Rosemarie Scullion

I would like to thank Lehman College for a George N. Shuster Fellowship to assist us in the preparation of the manuscript. I dedicate my share of this volume to the memory of the eminent translator, Ralph Manheim (1907–1992), and to the memory of the innumerable victims of ignorance and "difference."

Thomas C. Spear

I would like to thank President Pye and the Faculty Senate of Southern Methodist University for awarding me a faculty research grant to assist me in the preparation of the volume. My thanks as well to Sue Sturgeon, Kimberly Lambeth, and Susan Weinberg for their help in corresponding with the contributors and typing the manuscript. Above all, I am grateful to my wife, Risa, for her unflagging support of my participation in this project. It is to her and to my daughters, Elycia and Cynthia, that I dedicate my share of *Céline and the Politics of Difference*.

Philip H. Solomon

Contributors

▼

PHILIPPE ALMÉRAS has written numerous articles about Céline and is the author of *Les Idées de Céline* 1987) and *Céline: Entre haines et passions* (1994). He is director of the French-American Study Center in Lisieux, France.

ISABELLE BLONDIAUX holds doctoral degrees in Literature and Medicine, with a speciality in psychiatry. She is the author of *Une Ecriture psychotique: Louis-Ferdinand Céline* (1985) and has also published articles on Mishima and Genet. She is a practicing psychiatrist in Paris and Amiens.

JENNIFER FORREST received her Ph.D. from Yale University and is currently assistant professor of French at Southwest Texas State University.

PASCAL A. IFRI is associate professor of French at Washington University in St. Louis. He is the author of *Proust et son narrataire* (1983) and *Céline/Proust: les correspondances proustiennes dans l'oeuvre de Louis-Ferdinand Céline* (forthcoming). He recently completed a study on Lucien Rebatet's novel, *Les Deux Etendards*.

ALICE Y. KAPLAN is associate professor of Romance Studies and Literature at Duke University. She is the author of *Reproductions of Banality* (1986), *Relevé des sources et citations dans Bagatelles pour un massacre* (1987), and *French Lessons* (1993), and co-editor, with Philippe Roussin, of "Céline, USA," in *South Atlantic Quarterly*, spring 1994.

CHARLES KRANCE is professor of French at the University of Chicago. He is the author of *L.-F. Céline: The I of the Storm* (1992) and has written extensively on twentieth-century French literature. He is series editor of the Variorum Editions of Samuel Beckett's Bilingual Works, for which he has edited *Company/Compagnie* and *A Piece of Monologue/Solo* (1993).

ANDREA LOSELLE is assistant professor of French at the University of California, Los Angeles. She has published a number of articles about Céline and currently is completing a book project entitled *Travel in the Works of Twentieth-Century French Writers: Tourism and War.*

ROSEMARIE SCULLION is associate professor of French at the University of Iowa. She has written on Céline, Marguerite Duras, Francis Ponge, Michel Foucault, and contemporary French cinema. She currently is completing a book on disciplinary power entitled *Rations of Constraint: Foucault, Céline and Modernity.*

PHILIP H. SOLOMON is professor of French at Southern Methodist University. He is the author of *The Life after Birth: Imagery in Samuel Beckett's Trilogy* (1975), *Night Voyager: A Reading of L.-F. Céline* (1988), and *Understanding Céline* (1992). He has published articles on Zola, Claude Simon, and François Mauriac, and is the editor of a special issue of *Yale French Studies* devoted to landscape and decor in modern French fiction.

THOMAS C. SPEAR is associate professor of French at Lehman College (CUNY). He has published articles on French and Francophone writers: Ben Jelloun, Condé, Confiant, Doubrovsky, Duras, Genet, and Robbe-Grillet. His translations include Leslie Kaplan's *Brooklyn Bridge*. He is completing a book on the "autofiction" of four French novelists.

PHILIP WATTS received his Ph.D. from Columbia University and is currently assistant professor of French at the University of Pittsburgh. He has published articles on Céline and Genet.

Abbreviations

Quotes from works not translated in English have been translated by the author or translator of individual chapters.

B	*Bagatelles pour un massacre*
BD	*Les Beaux Draps*
C	*D'Un Château l'autre*
	Castle to Castle
CC1	*Céline et l'actualité littéraire, 1932–1957*
CC2	*Céline et l'actualité littéraire, 1957–1961*
CC3	*Semmelweis et autres écrits médicaux*
CC4	*Lettres et premiers écrits d'Afrique*
CC5	*Lettres à des amies*
CC6	*Lettres à Albert Paraz*
CC7	*Céline et l'actualité, 1933–1961*
CC8	*Progrès, suivi de Œuvres pour la scène et l'écran*
CY	*Entretiens avec le Professeur Y*
	Conversations with Professor Y
D	*Mort à crédit*
	Death on the Installment Plan
E	*L'Eglise*
EC	*L'Ecole des cadavres*
F1	*Féerie pour une autre fois, I*
F2	*Féerie pour une autre fois, II: Normance*
G1	*Guignol's Band, I*
	Guignol's Band
G2	*Guignol's Band, II. Le Pont de Londres*
HER	*Cahier de L'Herne: L.-F. Céline*

J	*Voyage au bout de la nuit*
	Journey to the End of the Night
L	*Lettres à la N.R.F., 1931–1961*
LA	*Lettres à son avocat*
LHP	*Lettres à Henri-Robert Petit, 1938–1942*
LJG	*Lettres à Joseph Garcin*
Mea	*Mea Culpa*
MS	*Maudits soupirs pour une autre fois. Une version primitive de Féerie pour une autre fois.*
N	*Nord*
	North
O	*Œuvres complètes*
R	*Rigodon*
	Rigodoon
R1	*Romans, I*
R2	*Romans, II*
R3	*Romans, III*

Editors' Note: In quotations from Céline, the author's ellipses are kept as unspaced periods; deletions made by the writer of the essay are indicated by spaced ellipsis points.

Céline
and the
Politics
of
Difference

▼

Rosemarie Scullion

▼

Introduction

▼

CRITICS HAVE been actively engaged since the early 1980s in reevaluating works by French novelist Louis-Ferdinand Céline and their place in literary modernity. Semiotic, psychoanalytic, Bakhtinian, and historicist interpretations have greatly illuminated the aesthetic dimensions of Céline's writing and highlighted the linkage between purely literary concerns and the broader ideological and political issues his texts present.[1] These contributions have effectively shifted the focus away from the prevailing dichotomous view among Céline scholars that ritually lauded the novelist's literary talent and demonstrated his considerable influence on subsequent generations of novelists while treating his cluster of anti-Semitic pamphlets as a freak political sideshow in an otherwise stellar literary career.

Particularly in the American academic setting—rocked in recent years by intellectual and pedagogical clashes over issues of canon formation, multiculturalism, and identity politics[2]—inquiry into what Jacques Derrida had formulated philosophically as the problematics of "différance"[3] has also heightened awareness of the textual genesis of meaning and expanded the field of analytical objects of scholars investigating both extracanonical writings and "great works" by European male writers such as Céline. Deconstructionist and feminist thinking on marginality and alterity has further underscored the importance of sign systems in the production and dissemination of gender, racial, class, ethnic, and sexual differences. These cultural configurations, it is said, ensure homogeneity at the epicenter of power while perpetuating the oppression of identities that "texts" emanating from that hegemonic core have marked as "other."[4]

This volume of essays emerged conceptually from a confluence of these two trends: the advances in Célinian scholarship and contemporary philosophy's intellectual inquiry into the textual constructedness of all hierarchies of value ordering human existence. Informed by these intellectual insights, our primary objective is to bring into sharper analytical focus a range of social and cultural distinctions that are affirmed by an author, who, after decades of political scorn and ostracism, is now widely recognized as one of Europe's great literary modernists.

Believed in the early 1930s to be a left-leaning anarchist whose fiction assailed bourgeois literary norms and denounced a vast, dehumanizing complex of military, economic, colonial, and social powers, at the close of the decade Céline would leave his readers in an ideological daze by authoring a series of political pamphlets whose malicious anti-Semitism, racism, and pro-Nazism quite obviously endorsed authoritarianism and promoted the intolerance he appeared to disdain in his first two novels. In unraveling the essentialist, exclusionary notions that have—as an intelligible aggregate—remained largely invisible to Céline's critics, we hope to elucidate the ideological paradoxes and complexities of a writer who never shied away from declaiming in public space the discriminatory beliefs that Western culture has been muttering beneath its breath for centuries. In this undertaking, we aim not only to examine Céline's discourse on otherness but also to continue challenging the critical assumptions underlying more conventional author-centered, chronology-bound, and strictly formalistic interpretations of Céline's work. It thus seems appropriate to open the discussion of difference in Céline by mapping out the critical space in which we are inserting our readings; contributions, we hope, that will problematize the "great stylist"/"abhorrent racist" polarity that has so long constricted thinking and research on Céline.

Isabelle Blondiaux brings this distinction into forceful critical play in her discussion of the methodologies with which scholars have approached the topic of madness in Céline's writings. Introducing a slight twist into the standard dichotomous view of Céline, Blondiaux explores the rationale of critics who have grappled with the delirious aspects of Céline's literary and political texts, an often medically inflected discourse that acknowledges his immense literary talent while hypothesizing and diagnosing his insanity. One of the modern era's chief discursive mechanisms for enforcing normality and justifying the exclusion of what Michel Foucault has called "the unreasonable" other,[5] pathologizing discourses, such as those pervading interpretations of Céline, serve principally, Blondiaux asserts, "to distance and repress the outrageous, unassimilable" aspects of his writing. Tracing the critical discourse on Céline's dementia back to Milton Hindus's *The*

Crippled Giant (1950), the American critic's account of his meeting with Céline during his exile in Denmark immediately following World War II, Blondiaux foregrounds the identification and slippage taking place in this encounter between observing subject (Hindus the critic) and observed object (Céline the writer). Subsequent interpreters of Céline's writing have taken their cue from Hindus, saving the author's place in the pantheon of modern writers while either explicitly or subtextually according extenuating psychomedical circumstances for the most irrational (and disturbing) aspects of his literary and political texts. Blondiaux demonstrates how Céline did not hesitate to manipulate the diagnosis of madness for his own self-rehabilitative purposes, particularly following World War II when his contemptuous, vituperative pamphlets brought nearly universal reprobation raining down on him. Blondiaux's analysis underscores the need to critique the epistemological foundations of pathologizing discourses on Céline's (in)sanity and to project the discussion of his texts into the broader signifying arenas of ideology, politics, and culture.

Robert Young has noted that Jacques Derrida's reflection on writing and difference stemmed initially from his recognition of the ethnocentric foundations of Western civilization's philosophical traditions.[6] Similarly, the rabid anti-Semitism and ethnocentrism unleashed in Céline's political writings of the late 1930s and early 1940s, the most glaring form of othering he practices, was the springboard for our conceptualization of the problematic of difference. As such, these texts and their historical setting are the principal focus of a number of the essays that follow. Alice Yaeger Kaplan's investigation of Céline's sources for his first pamphlet, *Bagatelles pour un massacre* (1937), published here for the first time in English translation, firmly establishes the author's extensive involvement with France's anti-Semitic activists on the eve of the Nazi occupation of France. Producing a veritable "archeology" of the documentation the novelist amassed and manipulated in formulating and elaborating his anti-Semitic arguments, Kaplan uncovers the historical, political, and textual conditions of possibility that ultimately generated *Bagatelles'* protracted racist harangue. In another "unmasking" of sorts, Philippe Alméras reminds us that, at least in their substance, the anti-Semitism and racism pervading Céline's political writings, beliefs that so appall the relatively few readers who venture into the rare book rooms that are now their chief repository, were quite commonplace among French intellectuals and writers of his generation. Alméras's discussion further reveals the author's considerable finesse in dodging political attacks, in disingenuously inventing his literary and ideological self early in his career, and in reinventing himself during the purge of intellectuals and writers that came on the heels of France's liberation from Nazi rule.

Also anchored in the historical, Philip Solomon's intertextual analysis of Jean Renoir's 1936 classic, *La Grande Illusion*, and Céline's bashing of the film in *Bagatelles pour un massacre* a year later explores the intricate narrative emplotment of the novelist's perception of the film as an ideological weapon in a Jewish conspiracy to subjugate the Aryan world. Solomon's analysis further illustrates that Céline's discourse on race and ethnicity intersects with other discriminating and hierarchizing ideological constructs. Set in a German prisoner of war camp during World War I, *La Grande Illusion* imagines a world in which a constellation of differing identities speak across and begin to bridge the divides of class, race, ethnicity, and nationality that engender internal social strife and promote the most colossal form of human destruction: modern nationalist war. As he does throughout *Bagatelles*, Céline endeavors in his suspicion-laden attack on Renoir's compelling plea for social harmony, empathy, and tolerance to disperse the war clouds gathering over Europe in the late 1930s by deliberately fueling the xenophobic and sociopolitical hostilities that flared throughout French society in the final crisis years of the Third Republic.

Placing Céline in critical dialogue with another cultural icon of the period, Charles Krance examines the textual and ideological repercussions of a line Jean-Paul Sartre took from Céline's 1927 play, *L'Eglise*, and used for the epigraph of his first novel, *La Nausée* (1938). Sartre's choice is all the more ironic in light of Céline's vitriolic rejoinder to his postwar assertion that if the author of *Bagatelles pour un massacre* had espoused anti-Semitism before and during the war, it was because he had been paid by the Nazis to do so.[7] In historical hindsight, Sartre's seeming indifference to the intolerance of difference, that is, to the thinly veiled anti-Semitic slurs featured in Act III of *L'Eglise*, is quite astonishing. The inscription, which appeared in print four months after Céline's *Bagatelles pour un massacre* began circulating, effectively pays tribute to a writer whose militant racist convictions were by this time widely publicized. Moreover, the bonds linking Sartre and Céline go beyond *La Nausée*'s epigraph since one also finds a curious congruence between Sartre's estranged antihero Roquentin and Céline's Bardamu, the disaffected, bohemian narrator of *Voyage au bout de la nuit* (1932) who figured first as the protagonist in *L'Eglise*. How do we square Sartre's uncontested postwar aura of political correctness with his passing nod of approval for a work that is now seen as the first literary inscription of the anti-Semitic sentiments Céline was obviously harboring? Krance's reading of the literary and political implications of the Céline-Sartre "encounter" suggests that the well-delineated political differences established in the immediate postwar era between left and right, collaboration and resistance, conceal prewar affinities and empathies that blur those distinctions in rather unsettling ways.

But as any reader who simply skims Céline's pamphlets can attest, his angst about the other is even more ideologically tangled than the literary and political tensions specific to the history of France's immediate prewar and Occupation years might suggest. In an obsessive quest to homogenize northern European civilization into a milk-white race of Celto-Germanic peoples, Céline's pamphlets verbally bludgeon a grand sweep of Mediterranean and non-European cultures whose "contamination" the novelist-turned-racial-activist is determined to fend off. Following the discovery of the Nazis' genocidal horrors in Eastern Europe, Céline quietly, and without the slightest public rebuke, shifted the focus of his racist vituperation to "the Yellow Peril," a right-wing locution designating peoples of the Orient whom he envisioned steamrolling toward Europe, intent on annihilating the mass of Aryan dullards the author himself scorned but whose company he clearly preferred to that of the "other" biogenetic possibilities the human species offered. As is typically the case in modern anti-Semitic discourse,[8] Céline's ramifying constructions of racial and ethnic difference draw on a full repertoire of sexualized stereotypes and gendered polarities (subject and object, agency and inertia, mastery and submission) that serve to justify and legitimate the exclusion of devalorized, disempowered others.

Recognizing the synergy of racial and sexual difference in Céline's pamphlets, Thomas C. Spear observes that Bagatelles' narrator is as passionately engaged in fortifying phallic power as he is in countering what he believes to be the Jewish menace. In failing to oppose the nefarious influence of Jews, he asserts, Aryans in general and, more frightfully, Aryan males in particular, were being culturally, economically, and aesthetically emasculated by an increasingly aggressive and invasive adversary. Spear also notes that Céline's obsession with abject excretion, the central focus of Julia Kristeva's Powers of Horror (1980a), is bound up with the host of heterosexist fears and resentments his pamphlets so pruriently name. In an analysis of the narrative complexities of Céline's attempt to forewarn his oafish Aryan interlocutor of the Jews' destructive designs, Spear further illustrates the author's rhetorical skill in projecting the hateful affect of his incendiary speech beyond the diegetic limits of the political text.

Jennifer Forrest's discussion of the fabrication of femininity in *Voyage au bout de la nuit*, Céline's first and most successful novel, illustrates once again the author's reliance on the language of gender in signifying differences of human culture. Bardamu's predilection for American women springs not only from a fascination with the New World but also from his will to stem the oceanic tide of feminine viscosity, degeneracy, and formlessness with which European woman threatens to engulf his male self. Just as America's gargantuan industrial order appears to transcend the limits of nature, Forrest demonstrates how the American woman, in contrast to her European counterpart, is configured in Céline's literary imagination as a futuristic object of desire whose seductive charms derive as much from her steely, death-defying qualities as they do from her sheer exoticism. Prior to his sojourn in New York and Detroit, Bardamu imagines America as the legendary land of the rich and stalwart where he hopes to master its unmalleable woman and perhaps to partake in pleasures of the flesh without risking a feminine-induced dissolution of his male being. Although Bardamu's American adventure is fraught with frustration and disappointment, Céline's vision of the differences between the Old World and the New clearly conveys the hopes and the fears capitalist modernity generated in the early decades of the twentieth century, illusions and anxieties that phallocentric culture appears to have projected on to silhouettes of femininity that either served to inflate or threatened to efface the essential male subject.

My own discussion of style and gender in Céline focuses on the scopophilic economy within which the author obsessively lusts after female dancers, particularly the ballerina. Céline's extended—and distinctly gender-marked—commentary on dance and style in the postwar correspondence with Milton Hindus serves as a point of departure for my analysis of the tensions between what, in many respects, is an overtly feminized aesthetic vision and a more stereotypically masculine dominance asserting itself in the specular binding of the male voyeur and his female dancer. In Céline's discourse on dance, the sculpted body of the ballerina is perfection incarnate, an almost divine material presence that spiritualizes the artistic space it adorns, aesthetic virtues to which he aspires in his own writing. Not surprisingly, Céline's celebration of classical dance conceals the brutalizing exigencies of form that bend the human—and more typically the female—body into excruciating, gravity-defying contortions, a coercive dimension of the art that dance theorists have only recently begun to address. In occulting the enunciative apparatus that transforms such formal violence into a seamless, graceful flow of carnal movement for the spectators' delight, Céline not only naturalizes the aesthetic tyranny of his own male gaze but also effectively sublimates and artistically reconfigures the angst-ridden contempt for the female body and feminine identity discernible throughout his literary and political writings. Vacillating endlessly between rigidly dichotomized imagery of fluttering nymphettes and predatory piranhas, of ethereal lovelies and shriveled, matronly monstrosities, Céline's construction of gender is, oddly enough, as hackneyed in its substance as it is intriguingly ambivalent in its form. At the margins of his many scurrilously misogynist utterances loom the limits of phallic mastery that the surfeit of emotion Céline diligently sought to generate in his style strikingly marks. Despite Céline's vigilant attempts to affirm and uphold thoroughly conventional notions of sexual difference, the masculine/feminine polarity is, both in his aesthetic vision and writing practice, forever on the verge of collapsing altogether, thus constantly threatening to subvert the binary logic according and ensuring the primacy of male subjectivity, to whose prerogatives he steadfastly clings.

Configurations of class difference in turn-of-the-century France are the focus of Pascal Ifri's analysis of social distinctions in Céline. Telescoping the anxieties and resentments of the Belle Epoque's increasingly beleaguered lower middle class, craftsmen, and small shopkeepers, Céline's *Mort à crédit* (1936) can be seen, Ifri argues, as the sociological underside of the glittering aristocratic and upper-middle-class milieux his decidedly more genteel predecessor, Marcel Proust, depicts in *A la Recherche du temps perdu (Remembrance of Things Past)*. Unable to withstand the competitive pressures of the modern technologies and economic rationalities rendering their services and labor obsolete, *Mort à crédit*'s petty bourgeois world is haunted by the spectre of dispossession and, horror of horrors, of proletarianization. Ifri's historicizing analysis of the constructions of class difference in *Mort à crédit* underscores the uncanny similitude in Proust's and Céline's keen awareness of the Belle Epoque's profound structural mutations, seismic shifts in which historically stable features of France's social landscape were being rent, folded in on, and covered over by new class formations.

Bringing considerable depth to the interlocking themes of race, ethnicity, and nationality raised in the preceding essays, Andrea Loselle's study of the German trilogy deconstructs Céline's postwar literary assertion of ancestral Aryan kinship bonds between Franks and Gauls, fanciful historical affinities that are ideologically consonant with the Franco-Nazi alliance he had openly advocated in his prewar political writings. Well after the war had ended and the Nazi regime had been reduced to charred rubble, Céline remained intensely preoccupied with issues of bloodlines and heredity, continuing to enunciate in his chronicles of war a more historiographically embedded but still thoroughly "unrepentant racism." In fact, Loselle argues, when he sporadically harps in the trilogy on the "Yellow Peril" mounting in the East, statements that have signaled for some critics an evolution or permutation in his racial views, Céline obscures the actual continuity of his pre- and postwar commitment to ensuring that the vestiges of Europe's Nordic race remain genetically unsullied by contact with mongrel peoples. In elucidating Céline's literary use of racial legends and their fictitious historical underpinnings, Loselle demonstrates that the novelist's aims in the German trilogy were not simply to chronicle for posterity the spectacular destruction he had witnessed while trekking across the crumbling Reich in the closing months of the war. She effectively debunks the notion that after the war Céline abandoned the racist passions and biological activism of his pamphlets and wartime journalism. In its deep-seated ideological ambitions, Loselle illustrates, the trilogy participates actively, though with far greater subtlety and political deftness than in earlier polemical writings, in the postwar revisionist crusade to denounce the order of the victors, to challenge the legitimacy of its juridical institutions, and, above all, to reimagine in the wake of the Nazi defeat a social word governed by the logic of the "same" and infused with the spirit of like racial origins.

In his essay on the postmodern theoretical turn in Célinian studies, Philip Watts echoes Loselle's concerns with respect to the hypervaluation of the aesthetic dimension of Céline's postwar novels. Although the contributions of Philippe Sollers, Julia Kristeva, Henri Godard, and Robert Llambias have fostered a heightened awareness of its linguistic complexity and destabilizing semiotic force, their somewhat single-minded focus on the pluralizing, fragmentary, and desemanticizing effects of Céline's postwar writing generally "obviates both the historical context and the political discourse manifest in [this] literary production." In demonstrating, for instance, that Céline's radically decentered subjectivity subverts post-Enlightenment rationalities and teleologies, Kristeva shuffles consideration of his "provocatively bad and irresponsible politics" off to the theoretical side, an analytical maneuver similar to that used by Sollers (1986), Godard (1985), and Llambias

1986). Céline's poetic forms, Kristeva asserts, tower semiotically over their objectionable political content, doggedly resisting ideological recuperation of any sort. This position is oddly congruent, Watts notes, with Céline's own postwar claims that the import of his writing was, in the final analysis, aesthetic rather than political. Watts further demonstrates that Céline's apocalyptic imagery of the levelling of German cities and the pulverizing of its civilian populations at the end of the war signify much more than humanity's eternal, compulsively reenacted propensity for self-destruction. Céline's representation of the bombing of German cities and the attack of their civilian populations is, in the context of postwar France, far from politically neutral. Indeed, Céline's highly poeticized postmodern writing of that history is driven not simply by an all-encompassing rage against the Symbolic and its myriad monologic institutions, as Kristeva suggests, but also very specifically by a deep and abiding revisionist contempt for the Allied victors and their triumphant postwar order. Céline's later literary works — their polysemic, logos-shattering aesthetic notwithstanding — are, then, not substantively different from the prewar and wartime political writings in which he zealously champions a totalizing authoritarian vision of racial, ethnic, and cultural unicity.

Watts identifies the various developments that prompted a new generation of critics in the late 1960s to begin once again poring over Céline's prolific œuvre, significant portions of which had gone untreated in the post-Liberation era. Among the factors he sees contributing to this revitalization of Célinian studies were the slackening of Sartrian existentialism's hold on postwar France's intellectual and literary culture and the waning of the purges that had channeled anticollaborationist political passions after the Occupation. Céline's critical appeal has no doubt also been enhanced by the broader revival of interest in the strife-ridden prewar and Occupation years in which he became a literary celebrity, a period in which French society was reeling from economic crisis and internecine political struggles that directly contributed to the vituperative tone and combative substance of the political writings that were to become the principal source of his postwar ostracism.

The critical attention given to French fascism, fascist aesthetics, anti-Semitism, and the politics of Collaboration has in fact expanded over the last decade into a veritable cottage industry of literary and historical scholarship that has begun lifting taboos and erasing the clichés obstructing possibilities for a more complex view of Céline, of the discourses on difference he uttered and of the times in which he

wrote.[9] In one of the most provocative studies of these studies, Henri
Rousso frames the discussion of the late interwar and Vichy era in
Freudian terms of psychic trauma, unconscious repression, and 'the
inexorable return of that which has been repressed.[10] The profound
antagonisms generated by Vichy's collaborationist pact and the lasting
wounds it inflicted on a French body politic already mangled by the
prewar crisis and Nazi invasion were, Rousso argues, hastily patched
over in the immediate postwar years, largely in a Gaullist-inspired
attempt to foster national reconciliation.[11] Knee-jerk political indigna-
tion saw that high-profile collaborators or Nazi fellow travellers, in
many cases intellectuals and writers such as Céline, were tried, judged,
and condemned, while prominent institutions and the complicitous
wartime conduct of countless bureaucrats overseeing their operations
largely escaped juridical scrutiny. In the end, however, the purge process
failed to resolve the underlying tensions or to remedy the deeper
societal afflictions whose lingering symptoms have periodically erupted
out of the interred past to trouble the seemingly unrelated present.

In broader cultural terms, Rousso's psychohistorical model helps to
explain the vicissitudes of Céline's literary fortunes since the Liberation. Implicated textually—and therefore quite publicly—in the prewar
and wartime traumas, Céline's identity became closely entwined with
an agonizing past that begged forgetting. As memories of the conflict
and its horrors receded in the decade following the war, so did Céline's
literary presence and prestige. His obsessive focus on the war in four of
his last five novels (*Féerie pour une autre fois, II* [1954], *D'un Château
l'autre* [1957], *Nord* [1960], and *Rigodon* [1969])—a pesky reminder of
the very events and circumstances the collectivity was striving to
forget—could not help but reinforce the identification between an
author tarnished by his compromising prewar and wartime political
stances and French society's own deeply conflicted relationship to that
past.

According to Rousso, Marcel Ophuls' 1970 film *Le Chagrin et la pitié*
tripped the mnemonic mechanisms that returned the repressed historical material to the public fore and have since driven the vast intellectual and artistic inquiry into its meanings and effects. Anticipating
Ophuls' cinematographic encounter with the Vichy past by several
years, Patrick Modiano's *La Place de l'Etoile* (1968) also became a
reminder of the collaborationist regime's far-from-commendable achievements. Nearly a quarter century after the last train of Jewish deportees
pulled out of Drancy en route to Auschwitz, Modiano's "anti-Semitic
Jewish" narrator, Raphaël Schlemilovitch, mordantly revived the issue

of Vichy's involvement in the Nazi's "Final Solution" of Europe's "Jewish Problem." Céline's anti-Semitism, a frequently ignored aspect of his literary saga, is recurrently invoked and his racist wrath prominently displayed in Modiano's masterful pastiche of *Bagatelles pour un massacre*.[12] Appearing roughly at the same moment the author was returning to favor in aesthetically preoccupied and theoretically oriented literary circles, Modiano reminds the public of the postpurge era, particularly untractable youths whose generalized rebellion might draw them to Céline's anarchistic writing, that the author of *Voyage au bout de la nuit* belongs as much to France's heritage of ethnic and racial discrimination as he does to its illustrious literary tradition. In resituating Céline's anti-Semitism in cultural context and correlating it with more self-restrained—yet essentially like-minded—literary and intellectual figures of the modern era, Modiano openly allies Céline's presumably marginal racist thinking with the ethnocentric impulses of the mainstream society that shunned him after the war. His pastiche of the pamphlets further draws attention not only to their textual constructedness but also to their endless reconstructability from the signifying materials proffered by ambiant cultural norms, values, and practices, thus providing the semantic props for a potential reenactment of the tragedies of the Vichy era.

France is, of course, not the only society with a history of injustice and prejudice toward racial and ethnic minorities.[13] In fact, although the cadence and timbre of Céline's voice of intolerance are emphatically French, the substance of his bigotry is fully consonant with the homogenizing logic governing a host of Western societies whose modern wealth and grandeur owe much to generations of racist pillaging of colonies where paradoxically—or perhaps hypocritically—its own "foreign" minorities reigned supreme. The cultural wars currently being waged across the postcolonial and post–Cold War landscape over issues of racial, ethnic, and national identity indicate that the questions of human diversity that so riled Céline in the 1930s and 1940s are still very much before us. Although the equivalence between the 1930s and the present should not be overstated, there are striking parallels in the crisis-induced population shifts occurring today and the refugee crises of the 1930s, where in France, historians recall, a sudden influx of "stateless peoples" (apatrides), produced a significant rise in antiforeign and anti-Semitic feeling, resentment on which Céline clearly capitalized in his pamphlets.[14] With refugees fleeing both the chaos of Eastern Europe's disintegrating nation-states and the desperate poverty of the former colonies, the West is facing increasing pressure to adapt to the presence of linguistically and culturally distinct communities in its midst, demands for inclusion that are being met in certain quarters with hostility and malice of the type sanctuary seekers and other minority groups encountered a half century ago. On her eastern borders, Europe's ancient ethnic rivalries are spawning the sorts of enmities with which students of Céline's pamphlets are only all too familiar.

This resurgence of overt public expression of ethnic and racial animus[15] that led to such human devastation in the 1930s and 1940s makes the following essays particularly timely. At this project's inception, our principal aim was to foster understanding of the dark energies and animosities spilling over the fault lines of a variety of social distinctions configured in Céline's texts: chiefly the racial and ethnic differences foregrounded in the pamphlets, but also those involving discourses on rationality, gender, and class. It has since became evident that insights into the historical and cultural roots of the difficulties of the present might well be garnered from our efforts to bring the bleakest aspect of Céline's *œuvre*—his naked aggression against whose who were different from himself—to the analytical fore. Rather than couching his prejudice in insidiously naturalized forms that occult their essential violence, Céline swaggers in his misogyny and white supremacy, rendering his exclusionary utterances unrecognizable to a dominant culture averse to such unseemly expression of verbal and political rage. Yet, perceptive readers of his texts will observe that Céline's surly, often outrageous discourses on human difference mirror the hierarchies of value and relations of dominance, that have historically structured Western patriarchy and ideologically underwritten its acquisitive adventurism abroad. An oddly conformist stance indeed for a self-styled maverick such as Céline who prided himself on his seditious literary practice and his defiance of all institutional authority. Rather than bringing closure to the discussion of the relationship between Céline's literary subversion and his more tradition-bound, Eurocentric politics of exclusion, the essays that follow point to the substantial amount of analysis and reflection that remains to be done and invite, we hope, further reflection on a subject of importance not only in understanding Céline but also in comprehending the barbarities of his times and the cultural matrix from which they sprang.

Isabelle Blondiaux

▼

Céline:
A Clinical
or a
Critical Case?

▼

SINCE 1932 when his first novel *Voyage au bout de la nuit* appeared in print, Céline's critics have recognized the morbid character of his writing.[1] Following the publication of his deliriously racist pamphlet *Bagatelles pour un massacre* five years later, one critic, H. E. Kaminski, was indeed adamant in his claim that Céline's madness had a basis in concrete reality and was inseparable from the author's political involvement—which had to be considered in any discussion of his social responsibility. Although Kaminski's provocative assertions fell largely on deaf ears and were subsequently ignored in Célinian scholarship, some sixty years later his statements retain their validity and significance: "Is he insane?... Quite probably. But there are dangerous madmen who are all the more menacing in historical circumstances in which madness is readily universalized. . . . As such, the case of Céline is of compelling interest not only to psychiatrists, but also, indeed especially, to society at large" (Kaminski, 1938, 83–84).

In the literary arena, however, the notion of madness does not generally connote mental illness, whose function and meanings belong to an entirely different sphere of understanding. Rather, the term designates, as Shoshana Felman has shown in *La Folie et la chose littéraire* (1978), a constitutive and differential relationship between writing and reading that highlights the inassimilable, outrageous character of a given work. Felman argues that this relationship generates important ideological ramifications. An instance of autofiction,[2] which itself claims to be a *praxis* of madness, Céline's writing is a prime example of the theoretical postulations Felman advances in her psycho-analytic interpretation of literary modernity.

The intolerable aspects of Céline's work stem principally from its ideological content, the most extreme expression of which is found in the political pamphlets *Bagatelles pour un massacre* (1937), *L'Ecole des cadavres* (1938), and *Les Beaux Draps* (1941). Prior to being localized in a given work, the designation of madness can therefore be viewed as the product of the act of reading. In other words, the madness of the writer in question derives essentially from the reader's own resistance to the production of textual meaning. This would explain why, when faced with the "crazed" Céline, there is a virtual absence in Célinian scholarship of a critical discourse analyzing the position from which such psychiatric judgments are enunciated. In other words, in the court of "popular psychiatry," as Sigmund Freud called it, the writer's "madness" can be ascertained no more readily than the "normality" of his commentators.[3] Medicalized readings of Céline have served princi-pally to distance and repress, by way of banalizing, the unassimilable meanings his texts present. Thus, critics tend either to account for the author's textual "excesses" or to justify their partial or wholesale repudi-ation of the man and his works. In other words, the recourse to psychiatric and/or psychoanalytic discourse (the "psy" alibi, as it were) in producing a clinical profile of Céline's works involves a conscious or unconscious repression of the ideological issues at stake in his writings. The end result is an elision of the central critical problems raised by the author's political argumentation.

The idea that Céline suffered from a paranoid disorder can be traced to *The Crippled Giant* by Milton Hindus (1950).[4] This hypothesis has since enjoyed wide currency, becoming one of the most oft-invoked clichés in the critical assessment of his works. Certainly, Hindus, who could be reproached for authoring a text that reveals more about himself than about Céline, was not completely unaware of the ideological ramifications of his critical approach, nor was he blind to what it implied for him personally. "Conscious," to use his own term, that "it may seem incongruous for me to go to the length I have to reveal the life and thought and work of an enemy of my people" (1986, 2), he states that if he decided to introduce himself into the discussion, it was because he recognized that the idiosyncrasies of the observer shape his vision, transforming it into the perspective of "[t]he Jew in me, massacred generation after generation" (2). To some extent, Hindus's psychiatric presupposition—which itself confers on the critic's hypoth-esis a diagnostic and *symptomatic* value it lost in passing into the public (or rather, lay) domain—forced him (perhaps in spite of himself) to play the game of madness. In this respect, Hindus's account of his sojourn at Korsör is of crucial importance and, from a clinical perspective, still holds great significance. It demonstrates quite well that the insanity Milton Hindus attributes to Céline—in, one might argue, Hindus's own troubled state of mind—must be understood as the privileged mode of expression in the dynamic between the two men. Hindus's journal further illustrates that traces of madness are present throughout their relationship, not as a trait belonging to one and/or the other[5] but, rather, as a function vacillating between them, working to some extent as a mediating force in their emotionally charged encounter.[6]

Hindus recognizes this dynamic of madness in his own way by assuming a tone that is at once *persecuted* and, if not paranoid, at least highly projective. On August 9, 1948, for instance, Hindus writes: "To borrow an image from Céline's section of *Journey* dealing with his experiences in the madhouse, there is nothing between Céline and myself except *his madness*, and therefore when we pass each other I had best keep my eye on him to see that he doesn't let go with a good kick at me. He apparently feels the same way about me" (39, Hindus's emphasis). This reciprocity results in an oscillating (and mirroring) effect between the symptoms Hindus attributes to Céline and those he discovers in himself, psychological traits that are clearly perceptible in any reading of his journal. Thus, when Hindus locates "something petulant in the naive expression of his grudges and resentments, for there is much of the spoiled child about him" (17), he can not refrain from adding, "I should know; I'm one too" (17). And once again, when he elaborates on July 26 his hypothesis regarding Céline's "anal complex," he supplements it several days later, noting: "the difference between Céline and me is that I'm emotionally constipated and he has emotional diarrhea" (31). Similarly, Hindus begins to feel a bout of depression coming on, which closely parallels what he observed in the novelist from the moment of his arrival. Furthermore, to the degree he finds Céline "crazier than ever" (39), Hindus himself increasingly exhibits symptoms of emotional distress that, at the very least, testify to the considerable interpersonal tensions that surface during the encounter between the two men:

I myself have developed a nervous tic in my eye that is quite annoying. (40)

The nervous tic in my eye is really bothering me, and I have unaccountable pains in the muscles of my leg and in the fingers of my hand. I wish I were well out of this. (42)

He's made me as crazy as himself. My eye twitches, the muscle in my right leg pulls and gives me pain. This afternoon I could hardly stand on my left foot because I had such an itch in the sole of the foot, and the forefinger of my right hand is almost paralyzed. (44)

Reading these passages, one might (with a bemused grin) conceivably ascribe the detection of Céline's paranoia to a paranoid reaction on the part of Hindus himself or, again, to a shared delirium, *une folie à deux*. There are, however, sparks of paranoia flickering in the chasm between the text and its interpretation. As such, it is more compelling, from an analytic perspective, to determine how this diagnosis has become, for Hindus and the critics who have followed him, a given on which subsequent readings of Céline's work have been built.

For Milton Hindus, the hypothesis of a paranoid element in Céline's personality is an intellectual contingency. In fact, paranoia seems to be the only logical explanation his argument presents for "the content of important segments of his work, such as the Admiral Bragueton episode in *Voyage*, which portrays a persecution mania" (HER, 377). His evidence: Céline confided to him that this was one of the few episodes in the novel "*completely invented* and without naturalist models [drawn] from his lived experience" (377; emphasis added). Hindus does not even momentarily consider the possibility that Céline, who, after all, was a physician, might have had extensive knowledge of paranoia as a medical phenomenon.[7] Beyond his effort to take into account the "hallucinatory quality" of Céline's writing—which had so "struck Gide's fancy" (377)—Hindus's "demonstration" is more understandable if one remembers that it, too, is also subject to ideological constraints[8] and to Hindus's need "to explain without excusing" what he terms the "fanatical" nature of Céline's anti-Semitism (377).

His personal convictions notwithstanding, Hindus appears to be somewhat hesitant when he pronounces his diagnosis. After assembling the fragments from the journal he kept in Denmark (most apt to convince us of Céline's insanity), even while taking note in his August 12 entry of Lucette Destouches's thoroughly alarming confidences ("She fears that Céline is on the verge of a complete breakdown. He awakens her in the night screaming, 'I'm going mad. I can't sleep anymore'" [1986, 45]), Hindus finds "that [Céline] behaved not so much like a madman as a *prima donna*" (46). A week and a half later in Paris when he attempts to take stock of their meeting, Hindus assures himself, in a similarly waffling fashion, that he is indeed dealing with a "borderline" case (58), a psychic game in which the writer appears to be toying with madness just as madness appears to be toying with him. Hindus writes: "There is something fictitious about these nightly performances of Céline. As a screamer he is something of a virtuoso. Still, there is always a bit of madness in this desire *to play* at it too" (57, emphasis added); this despite the fact that, in other respects, the American critic stands firm in his conviction that the novelist "is still on the same side of the boundary line as we are" (59):

> Yet I hesitate to call Céline mad. I am as conservative with this diagnosis as most comfortable, confident, conventional, securely normal people tend to be with the opposite. Especially do I hesitate with regard to people who seem to deserve the epithet, those on the border line. . . . I have seen in my life only a few cases of people who I should be willing to grant were crazy. . . . Céline is in no similar case. When his eyes meet mine, even at the moment that he is being most stubborn, spoiled, hysterical and hateful, there is rapport and communication possible. He is still on the same side of the boundary line as we are, although closer to it perhaps and full of impulses, threats, intentions and fears of crossing over momentarily to the other side. (58–59)

Employing a different metaphor, Hindus argues that Céline had "tottered so long on the brink that he has perhaps achieved a sense of balance in unbalance" (62). Despite a definite confusion in the American critic's mind (though elegantly expressed in the notion of the "border line" case), Céline finally emerges in Hindus's account as an individual whose paranoid tendencies would surely drive him insane were they not fettered by his obvious "power over an artistic medium" and were the writer not savvy enough to limit their expression to paper alone.[9]

Over twenty years later (1974), another literary critic, Albert Chesneau, once again advanced the claim that the novelist suffered from paranoid delusions. He supported this assertion by way of a sort of *vox medicali*: "One might thus wonder if this isn't a case of paranoid delusions provoked by professional failure. This is the opinion of several doctors I happen to know" (256). Chesneau had invoked this same argument in his 1971 *Essai de psychocritique*, based on what he termed Céline's "capricious" character, which he saw as the reflection of an infantile personality trait in the writer, held sufficiently in check by other, more adult propensities: "The paranoid hypothesis is, nonetheless, invalidated by the shifting character of his obsession. He does not completely sink into a persecution mania, far from it. Due to the fact that his adult personality is more forceful than its mythic infantile counterpart, Céline proves to be perfectly capable of using the latter to his own advantage, be it for political purposes (as in the pamphlets) or for literary fame (as in *Voyage au bout de la nuit* and *Mort à crédit"* (1971, 90–91).

From Chesneau's perspective, Céline is not, in the final analysis, truly paranoid. Rather, he can be seen as a situational paranoid or, perhaps more accurately, a paranoid through self-indulgence, depending on whether the expression of his paranoia serves his own personal self-interest or is the product of an inability to censor the pernicious manifestations of the writer's "personal myth" (to borrow a term from the psychocritical method developed by Charles Mauron). Chesneau sees as a manifestation of Céline's paranoia, a modern incarnation of an inner demon the writer must ceaselessly repress lest it possess and overpower him completely. According to Chesneau, Céline's "submission" to his adult personality is threatened by the contagion of the paranoia embodied in that myth:

In all likelihood, it is possible that in Céline's case this particularly bleak personal myth is one of truly paranoid proportions: it is the myth itself which is insane, by virtue of its relentless persecutory imagery. . . . Céline thus ran the risk of becoming too acquainted with his myth: more vigilant censoring would have prevented it from fully manifesting itself. This is what I meant when I asserted that Céline should never have indulged in writing *Mort à crédit*, which revived the monster in a far too dynamic and even dangerous form; in visiting a paranoid too often, you become one yourself. (1971, 91)

The notion that Céline suffered from paranoid tendencies, which manifested themselves only under special circumstances (and which he more or less curbed), has close affinities with Dominique Durette's view that, particularly in *Bagatelles pour un massacre*, the author was actually feigning a paranoid disorder (1972, 30). Substantively, Chesneau and Durette's arguments are comparable: both are based on the assumption that the novelist had the ability to maintain a distance between himself and his discourse, and both claim that his anti-Semitism was circumstantial and mercurial. It should be noted that the latter view has been outmoded since Philippe Alméras (1987) and Marie-Christine Bellosta (1990) clearly established the continuity in the novelist's anti-Semitic and racist ideas from, or even before, *Voyage au bout de la nuit*. If Durette places greater emphasis on its ludic aspects and underscores the manipulation and pleasure at play in Céline's "paranoia," and although it remains for him "a feigned, to some extent aestheticized delirium" (1972, 31), both he and Chesneau find in the pamphlets alone a distinctive body of texts exhibiting what they have termed "persecutory imagery."[10]

Although it is exemplary of the type of criticism practiced throughout the 1970s, this approach now seems decidedly superficial and simplistic. Because of the very absence of a clinical foundation, this sort of reading nonetheless clearly illustrates that the issues raised by the hypothesis of Céline's "delirious frenzy" are more a literary than medical phenomenon and that such claims are ultimately only an "aestheticizing"—perhaps even delusional?—effort to seize the unnameable that underlies the novelist's anti-Semitic pamphleteering.

The position taken by Jean-Claude Ollivier, a physician as well, is altogether different. If in his view, Céline does indeed have a paranoid personality, Ollivier immediately qualifies this assertion by stating that the novelist is a "sensitive paranoid" in the Kretschmerian use of the term.[11] He is thus a sort of "benign" paranoid who would likely do more harm to himself than to others. On the other hand, from Ollivier's perspective, Céline can be considered paranoid only at the level of his personality structure. Ollivier establishes a basic distinction between the core personality and the presence of a mental disorder expressing itself in the form of delusional episodes. Céline, he writes: "does not give free rein to his fantasies. . . . He retains enough awareness to assume responsibility for himself and his actions. Consequently, he does not become delirious" (1970, 61). Thus, in line with Jean Delay's (1956) studies concerning the cathartic function of literary creation, Ollivier interprets Céline's writing activity as an effort to ward off psychosis. Writing, he asserts, "plays a marvelously cathartic role by allowing the 'liberation' [and 'actualization'] of a delirious frenzy churning in Destouches" (1970, 52).

Whether their initial frame of reference is medical or literary, proponents of Céline's paranoia find in the basic diagnostic category of the paranoid personality disorder ample "proof" of a pathological predisposition evinced both in the author and in specific works, most notably his pamphlets, traits that contribute to understanding his entire œuvre. In this tautological reasoning, various critics demonstrate that it is because Céline was paranoid that he wrote the pamphlets and that because he wrote the pamphlets, one can prove he is paranoid. Furthermore, these same critics concur that if paranoia is indeed discernible either in his writings or in facets of the novelist's personality, it can only be, to use Durette's words, "simulated' or, at most, only partially mastered and manipulated with some degree of artistry. Pointing out the stumbling block common to each argument, there is no need to dispute the theoretical relevance of the various, somewhat misguided, approaches that made it possible to arrive at the minimal diagnostic hypothesis of this personality disorder: the notion that if a paranoid disorder is discernible in Céline, the novelist appears to have been in control of it much more than it was in control of him. If such a conception skirts the contentious issue of granting the writer diminished responsibility for the ideological content of his writings, it is, along with the simulation hypothesis, of analytical interest because it raises the possibility that this writer-physician was versed in prevailing psychological concepts regarding mental pathology rather than actually suffering personally from it. This possibility, oddly enough, has been consistently overlooked by critics.

In fact, Céline's penchant for "transposing" reality, even beyond the realm of fiction writing, has been widely acknowledged by critics, most notably his biographers, for whom, aside from any pathographic concerns, it has presented thorny problems of interpretation. The difficulty of grappling with this facet of Céline's writing is highlighted in the analyses of two ideologically opposed critics. The first, Marie-Christine Bellosta, approaches Céline's often wild distortion of truth with a categorical word of caution: "We know that Céline was a mythomaniac and a liar, and that falsehood and truth are mingled, especially beginning with *Mort à crédit* [where we find] all sorts of lies: through omission, distortion, intricate invention, an obsessive fear of revealing his creative secrets or of fueling conspiracies, and a megalomanic desire (especially following his exile in Denmark) to mold a certain self image for literary posterity" (1983, 12). Nicole Debrie, whose ideological stance is, as noted, diametrically opposed to Bellosta's and who energetically disputes the use of the terminology of falsehood, which she considers excessively moralistic, is no more capable of circumventing the standard warning label and seeks, as does Bellosta, to avoid, "if at all possible, falling into the traps the author did not hesitate to set for his future biographers" (1990, 348).

However, if the novelist's "fanciful imagination" (as François Gibault puts it) is recognized by all, critics have reached no consensus regarding its source. It is seen alternately as the product of moral vice (for Céline the liar), of a psychological disorder (for Céline the pathological liar), or simply of a personality quirk in a writer well known for his antics and talents as provocateur.[12] But here again, it is important to remember that the central issue involves not so much the judiciousness of either a value judgment or a nosographic label as it does the implications of invoking a medical diagnosis or a moralistic assessment of the novelist. If the moral admonition of Céline is perfectly compatible with the grim view of the writer (liar, anti-Semite, racist, fascist supporter, traitor to his country, etc.), the most obvious effect of the diagnosis of mythomania, with all the ludism this evokes for the novelist's commentators, is to refute claims of the author's paranoia, thus calling into question the entire body of critical and ideological interpretations on which that diagnosis has been based. It should be noted that ludism and paranoia are mutually exclusive phenomena. It is well known that there is no one less playful than a paranoid. Beyond the fundamental absurdity of a dual diagnosis of this sort, a Céline who is simultaneously paranoid and mythomanic effectively confirms, if this were still at issue, the validity of Kaminski's claim that Céline's case is more a critical than a clinical matter.

If the notion of madness involves a censoring of the ideological content in Céline's work, the writer himself did not hesitate, either by impugning or invoking it, to bring into literary play the duality of madness and ideology. Two central problems emerge from this maneuver. First, if the "sphere of madness"[13] is accorded primacy in the discussion of Céline's literary project, then the novelist's own conception of the relationship between madness and the creative process must be closely examined. Whether deemed the product of pathology or simply abject excretion, Céline's literary creations appear to have derived both from a hereditary flaw (the anxieties whose origins he attributed to his parents) and from the sickly expression of mythomania, a tendency shared, as it were, by the entire human species. This latter trait is also relevant to an inquiry into the artist's cultural status as viewed alternately from the perspective of the histrion and/or genius, a problematic that, as the study of Nietzsche's thought has shown, is not without anti-Semitic implications. Second, the manner in which Céline either endorses (as in his postwar interviews) or disputes (as in *Bagatelles pour un massacre*) pathologizing approaches to his works is closely linked to his own ideological aims. The literary investigation of madness in Céline's writing leads to a consideration of his anti-Semitic views; it also invites a reassessment of the ideological import and significance of a style such as Céline's that strives to privilege the sensate over the intelligible and emotion over words.

Céline's own understanding of the recourse to delirium as a means of privileging the emotive is evident in his earliest statements regarding madness in which he makes frequent reference to pictorial works of art such as those of Bosch, Breughel, and Goya. In this regard, his first letter to Léon Daudet, written toward the end of 1932, is particularly suggestive: "You are no doubt familiar, sir, with P. Breughel's monumental *Fête des Fous*. It's in Vienna. For me, therein lies the essence of the problem. I am willing to understand something else. I understand nothing else. I can't. My delirium takes this direction and I scarcely have other deliriums. I take pleasure solely in that which is grotesque and situated at the limits of death. For me, all the rest is meaningless" (HER, 63, 92). In the pamphlets, the converse approach—favoring cognition over emotion—is presented as a trait specific to Jews. It is also seen as the method adopted by critics and, of course, by psychiatrists (perhaps because they are delirium "killers"), "super-critics" (B, 305) who apply a reductionist, (i.e., explanatory) interpretation to the work of art.

In interviews with journalists, Céline suggests other direct ties between his creative process and the realm of madness. In the following segment of a December 1940 interview with Max Frantel, the author makes this linkage explicit:

M. FRANTEL: Come on now! You're the only one who writes like that! With such originality! With a truculence that cuts right to the bone!

CÉLINE: Writing! Writing! Glorious wonder! What's this obsession with writing? Hysteria!

M. FRANTEL: You? Hysterical?

CÉLINE: And why not?

M. FRANTEL: Then you agree with psychiatrists who believe that genius... [Louis-Ferdinand Céline has a subtle, evasive smirk on his face: a paradisiacal echo of his irony.]

CÉLINE: Genius? A pedant's invention! Pff!...

And he falls silent. Bardamu's creator amuses himself by electing to say no more. (CC7, 99)

Céline shares this same view in more explicit terms with Francine Bloch when she questions him about his fundamental pessimism:

Madam, I believe that... clinically, the matter is much more simple, as soon as you... begin babbling tales, it means there is something wrong with your nervous system. It's obvious I have a birth defect. . . . I was in a bad position, my mother was high-strung, my father was high-strung, they were both innately skittish. Undoubtedly, I've inherited their anguish and congenital anxiety. So I transformed this innate anxiety into babble but I would have preferred to have done better in medicine. (CC7, 443–44)

One can see parallels between this 1959 interview and his response to a 1960 *Tel Quel* survey that asked various authors: "Do you think you are a gifted writer?": "Hedonists don't need to write. Asking such a question of a writer! You write because you're unhappy. Your world devours everything else. You're completely alone. And sustained by style. Poets have no inner life. Writers are usually babblers" (CC2, 168).

It is apparent that the novelist had a fixation on what he deemed the unhealthy character of "the obsession with telling stories" (CC1, 101). In fact, when he describes literary creation as the product of a transformation "into babble" of the anguish and innate anxiety he claims to have inherited from his parents ("I was born . . . obviously, to write books, a defect, in short" [CC7, 444]), Céline's stance closely resembles that of Jean Delay who has examined the relationship between neurotic and creative activity, placing particular emphasis on anguish, which he sees as the *primum movens* of both neurosis and artistic creation. Delay explains: "When a man suffering from internal problems finds himself driven by a sort of compulsive need to express himself, the very act of expressing himself can alleviate his anxiety or anguish and, in some cases, is enough to free him from it. Between the effort and its fruition, there is an uninterrupted chain of intermediary steps" (1956, 59). The affinities in their thinking become more apparent if one compares Delay and Céline's descriptions of the process of literary creation. Again, for Céline, "It's a defect, guided with considerable *self-will*. Basically your *will* sees to it that you don't completely fall apart. Otherwise, the only thing that's left is chatter, babbling on about your defects" (CC7, 444; emphases added). While Delay proclaims, "What is admirable is that [writers] have known how to make good use of the ailment and find a solution to internal difficulties which might drive others to *failure*. The same neurotic conditions which we in pathology typically see lead to *ruin* can, in fact, lead to creation for those gifted enough to transform their basic needs into original works and to convert their weaknesses into strengths" (1956, 58; emphases added).

In contrast to Delay, however, Céline finds no cathartic value in creative activity. In his mind, literary creation remains the symptomatic by-product of an unbalanced mind and is by no means viewed as a cure. The image of secretion to which he sometimes resorts explicitly describes this activity. One can recall, for example, Bardamu's declarations in *L'Eglise*, speaking of photographs taken of writers seated at their desks: "I can't think of anything more aggravating than photographs like that. Do you think it's glamorous, someone writing? Have you seen the great Daradada at his work table, [working on] his last novel? There he is, Daradada, like a legless amputee, prose in hand, frozen in his seat for the hundred thousand readers he's hoping for... In the first place, it's disgusting to write, it's a secretion.... Do you get photographed doing your business?" (E, 111–12). At the same time, if this secretion is for Céline an abject excretion, he is not unaware of its grotesque nature. In his postwar correspondence with Albert Paraz, Céline writes: "You know, I write in the same way psychics make tables rotate—with horror and disgust. I don't like and I have never liked to write. First of all, I find the posture grotesque. This guy crouched, as if over the john, squeezing his head in order to force out his precious thoughts! What vanity! What stupidity! Revolting! I'm no exception!" (CC6, 136).[14] Because Céline sees literary creation as a basically unhealthy activity (it involves, even when highly elaborate, the pathological notion of mythomania[15]), he is highly sensitive to what he calls the "vanity" of literature and of writers. Hence, as early as January 1934, the notion of literature he proposed (in response to Louis Aragon's questionnaire asking, "Pour qui écrivez-vous?") generated considerable controversy: "If you were asking why men, all men, from birth to death, have the mania, drunk or not, to create, to tell stories, I would understand your question. It would then (as with any profound question) require several years for an adequate response. But, Writer!!! biologically makes no sense. It's a romantic obscenity, the explanation of which is necessarily superficial" (CC1, 101).

In his 1955 interview with Robert Sadoul, Céline tries to explain his activities as a pamphleteer by recourse to this same argument.[16] Yet, Delay cautions us against "mistaking a manifestation of the illness for a reaction to the illness itself" (1956, 56). Céline conceives of literary creation both as a reaction to illness (anguish) and as a manifestation of illness (vanity, grandiosity). Literature is thus simultaneously the pathological, although fully elaborated, product (i.e., "it's a defect, guided with considerable self-will" [CC7, 444]), of inborn torment and the morbid expression of a "phenomenal 'self'" in *mal du siècle* proportions, thereby justifying its equation with the mythomania he finds so pervasive: "The essential truth of this world is that it's paranoid!... Yes! paranoid! it has presumptuous madness!... paranoid sickness lays waste fields and cities! the phenomenal ego swallows everything... stops at nothing!... demands everything!" (CY, 39–41) If Céline refused in 1954, to be identified as a writer ("I am not a writer. I am anything you want, but not a writer. I have no pretensions of conveying a message. No, No, and NO" [CC1, 157]), it is undoubtedly because he renounces the "grotesque play-acting" that had driven and still drove him to send messages to the world; he did not want to be taken for a buffoon.[17] A few months prior to writing his first anti-Semitic pamphlet, Céline had already proclaimed to literary journalist Noël Sabord: "No theater trestles! I don't want to be a buffoon. They'll not make me reveal myself, get up on stage. They'll not see my face, or even, from now on, the color of my ink. They haven't even dared publish the few letters I've already written to them" (CC1, 107).

In Céline's work, the process of striving to articulate the relationship between madness (or delirium) and literary creation is indissociable from ideological aims. This occurs both when he rejects madness, as he does in the context of his anti-Semitic writing where he claims it is incapable of accounting for his genius, and when he invokes it as he does in postwar interviews in attempting to explain his "misguided actions" prior to and during the war. In the following passage, from *Bagatelles pour un massacre*, Céline expresses, in the rawest manner possible, his view of the pathographic enterprise and of efforts to apply it to his own person:

I no longer know what clumsy little Yid (I have forgotten his name, but it was a Kike name) went to the trouble, in five or six issues of a so-called medical journal (in reality, Jewish shit), to come crap all over my works and my "obscenities" in the name of psychiatry. This coward's racist rage, his craze of envy, were dressed for the occasion as scientific vituperation. This foul infection slobbered over with insults in his delirious, pluri-moronic psycholo-Freudian gibberish. . . . I have no idea by means of what mental or physical defects... this buggered low-life of pedantry was explaining all my books; but, in any case, never has a pus-filled toad (my noggin), oozing with poisonous droppings, been more hideous, more unbearable in the eyes of the pristine white, flawless dove (himself, of course). (B, 305)

Ten years later, Céline would do a 180° turn. Contrary to the declaration just cited, he himself (during a period of his life in which he was no doubt seeking to muffle the repercussions still resounding from his earlier political stands) encourages critics to pursue an interpretation of his ideological texts as "crazed literature," or "folliterature":[18]

The very meaning of my writings is radically and perfidiously betrayed. They turn a word of caution or a prefatory warning into a call for murder. God knows I'm open to criticism. A hundred times, a thousand times, I know they accuse me of madness, they see my way of judging things outlandish, they say: "Ferdinand is loony, Ferdinand is spouting drivel, he's losing it, he doesn't get it" and so on. But why charge me with vile intentions when everything is crystal clear to anyone who cares to take a closer look. (CC7, 291)

The advice Céline offered his German friend Erika Irrgang long before the war could be readily summoned in this context and is particularly fitting: "You are of an excellent and courageous nature—a bit perverse and that's just fine—but all this must be done logically—genius is an amalgam of madness and ruse" (CC5, 43). And yet, this was precisely the crux of the views expressed in a 1936 essay, "Les thèmes scatologiques en littérature," by Nina Gourfinkel,[19] the psychiatrist on whom Céline heaped abuse in *Bagatelles pour un massacre)*: "Céline's hero is a typical case of the unbalanced individual. A state of mental defect discernible in his confessions is compounded by physical infirmities. . . . Ferdinand's delusions, his fits of ferocious hatred, his instability, his inability to adapt to life, all of these are irrefutable symptoms which Céline, deliberately or not, has chosen for his hero: if not literally a madman, at the very least a characterization of an obvious kook" (1936, 51). It is safe to assume that given the astuteness of Gourfinkel's allusion and her confidence in the opinion of experts, Céline would not have tolerated the confusion of Ferdinand, the character in the novel, and his creator. All the same, the author did not hesitate to play on this confusion, as the opening pages of *Bagatelles pour un massacre* clearly illustrate:

I was recently confiding in a good buddy of mine... Léo Gutman, about this more and more intense craving... which I have developed for dancers...: "Ah!" he retorts, "there's a new vice for ya! . . . Tell me, you wouldn't by any chance happen to be a poet?"... he asks me abruptly. . . . "I don't think so. . . . The critics would have told me so." "The critics haven't said so?"... "Ah, not at all!... They said you couldn't find a better treasure of shit." . . . "Mr. Céline is not at all insane... That hysteric is a crafty devil... He takes advantage of all the malarkey and gullibility of the connaisseurs... his style, as twisted and as contrived as you can get, is nauseating, perverse, a pathetic and dismal extravagance." (B, 12–14)

Do these statements indicate that Céline manipulated the concept of madness only to camouflage the ideological dimension of his works? Or do they illustrate that this so-called genius was merely a "crafty devil" who, behind the mask of madness and a literary representation of delirium, duped critics preoccupied with aesthetic merit into elevating to the pinnacle of literary greatness an entire *œuvre* whose intolerable ideological content is somehow seen as comparable to the excesses of other "delirious" artists of genius? Given the bad faith and deceit Céline so obviously displays in the commentaries just cited, both questions can be readily answered in the affirmative. Yet, reducing Céline's use of madness to a mere desire to conceal an ideological intention serves little more than to support facile moral judgments.

What is actually at stake in Céline's resorting to an exercise in delirium is no doubt more abstruse. Surely, it is not by happenstance that the diagnosis in *Bagatelles pour un massacre* ("Mr. Céline is not at all insane... That hysteric is a crafty devil") invoking a nosographic category that appears time and again in the pamphlets and his postwar correspondence[20] offers, in fact, one of the most strikingly explicit tropes for the expression of Céline's anti-Semitism. In *Powers of Horror*, Julia Kristeva focuses considerable attention on aspects of the delusional thinking that congeals in Céline's writing in the identification of the Jew with a "desired and envied brother" (1980a, 216).

Nor is it mere coincidence that in his recourse to the notion of hysteria Céline introduces a diagnostic category whose distinguishing features include its legacy of having called into question the late-nineteenth-century's burgeoning corpus of psychiatric knowledge, with all this implies in cultural and historical terms for the problem of dissimulation. Charcot's two disciples, Freud and Babinski, had differing conceptions of hysteria and of its relation to dissimulation. In forging his conception of the unconscious, Freud described hysteria—in his view a reflection of intrapsychic conflict—as the product of unconscious dissimulation-imitation manifesting itself in somatic disturbances. Babinsky comes to understand these same disturbances as deriving from willfully self-serving and deceitful dissimulation. The latter view prevailed during World War I and became one of the justifications for treating hysterical paralysis with electroshock therapy. It is this conception and treatment of a feigned hysteria that are foregrounded in the representation of pathology-inducing war traumas in the opening passages of Céline's *Voyage au bout de la nuit*.

Seen at the dawn of the new century as one of the privileged modes for expressing the anguish humanity was experiencing in relation to the modern world, hysteria was interpreted as a symptom of civilization's malaise, quickly gaining status as a term of reference not only in the clinical terminology but, especially, in broader cultural discourse. It is from this vantage point that hysteria attests to the crisis of human identity engendered by modernization; it becomes a defining moment for both society and the individual, indissociable from the problem of sexual difference.[21] Ultimately, all inquiry into artistic endeavors passes through this consideration of hysteria.

Nietzsche's thought supports this claim in exemplary fashion. The philosopher assimilates woman and Jew by way of the question of dissimulation, a term signifying forms of histrionism, or play-acting, in which both artist and hysteric are said to indulge.[22] The peril connoted in the notion of the artist itself in fact stems from a dual menace of "Jewification" and feminization. Drawing parallels between the artist and "little hysterical women," Nietzsche concurs with his contemporaries that hysteria is indeed a symptom of modernity: "[a]nd our artists are only too closely related to little hysterical women. But this is to speak against 'today' and not against the 'artist'."[23] Commenting on this fragment from *The Gay Science*, Jacques Derrida establishes a distinction between the histrionic and the hysterical artist.[24] But, for the clinician, if all hysterics are essentially histrionic, not all histrions are hysterical. The hysterical artist's "something extra," a surplus of meaning discernible chiefly in modern artists (the pejorative connotations evoked by the very idea of modernity confirm this), also seems, paradoxically, to signify "something less," something specific to "little hysterical women," that is, to the problem of sexual difference and castration. Hysteria is thus presented as a symptom of modernity because it expresses the modern artist's vulnerability to demasculinization (éviration).

At the core of Céline's writing, this gender-marked problematic—inherited from Nietzsche—signals neither the text's nor the author's pathology. Rather, it illuminates the very function of a form of writing that both plays with and works against all binary oppositions, the foremost being the masculine/feminine dualism. The symptoms presenting themselves in Céline's artistry derive, then, from a game of mastery in which the feigning of a number of disorders serves, in the final analysis, only to illustrate the very impossibility of simulating pathology. Beyond the narcissistic vanity and passion for telling stories, the symptoms exhibited by the writer-histrion-hysteric ultimately succeed—though at the horrendous price of his anti-Semitism—in defying literary institutions, just as the "hysteria of culture" of La Salpêtrière effectively challenged the medical wisdom of its day.

Translated by Dory O'Brien and Rosemarie Scullion

Alice Y. Kaplan

▼

Sources and
Quotations in
Céline's
*Bagatelles pour
un massacre*

▼

BAGATELLES POUR un massacre, the first anti-Semitic pamphlet bearing Céline's actual name, Louis-Ferdinand Destouches, is readily distinguishable from his novels of the same period as it was here that the author began the systematic use of a narrative trait that was to become the hallmark of his postwar chronicles.[1] Described by Henri Godard as "a discourse in the making" (1985, 203), this newly adopted narrative mode is characterized by constant reference to current events and circumstances—to a minor detail of everyday life, to an image glimpsed or, as is often the case in *Bagatelles*, to texts that the narrator claims to have just read—that appear to have driven him to take up his pen. And because *Bagatelles* aspires to be an "anti-Semitic document" rather than a work of fiction, Céline provides (rather carelessly, as he is working at a feverish pace) just enough data so that a half century later the bulk of his original sources can be identified. Aside from his references to daily and weekly newspapers (*Le Journal, Paris-Soir, L'Univers Israélite, L'Humanité*) and to recently published works (Maurice Thorez's *Le Fils du peuple,* Jean-Richard's *Espagne,* André Gide's *Retour de l'URSS,* Georges Duhamel's *Défense des lettres*), Céline crams his pamphlet full of quotations with slightly modified names that are, by and large, cannibalized from other authors' pamphlets. With these recovered source materials in hand, it is possible to situate *Bagatelles pour un massacre* in its proper historical setting and to appreciate fully that any future republication of this text, which seeks to draw its readers into the most demented racist furor, carries, even for scholars, some degree of risk.[2]

The original editions of *Bagatelles pour un massacre*, now generally available only in libraries, continue nonetheless to be read, studied, and quoted. They have served in recent years as the point of departure for ambitious, theoretically oriented studies of critical endeavors that have not been based on any systematic documentation. Believing that the sources of the pamphlet could not be located, critics have tended to attribute to the language Céline uses in *Bagatelles* an originality it does not possess. With its authentic sources all too easy to find, we can now address in a rigorous manner the ideological issues dogging Céline's work. For example, in composing *Bagatelles*, did Céline distort secondary sources or did he read the Talmud himself in the 1930s? Is Céline's language as raw in the novels as it becomes in *Bagatelles*? Who are the real individuals he is attacking, and how does his text deform their names and identities? Was his aggression directed toward a specific Jewish community or the same one targeted in run-of-the-mill pamphlets? And does Céline's highly acclaimed "style" in *Bagatelles* remain as striking when his racist tirades are contrasted with their actual sources? To provide a material basis for this type of discussion, it has seemed to me fundamental to constitute an archeology of sources and quotations found in *Bagatelles pour un massacre*. In this endeavor, I owe much to Georges Zérapha, whose 1938 article, published in *La Conscience des Juifs*, was a compelling point of departure for my own investigation.[3]

In the first of the secondary sources referred to in *Bagatelles*, Céline narrates the scene where he discovers an incendiary text:

Toward the end of that summer, I was still in Saint-Malo . . . from afar, a lady, running at top speed, flags me down... she runs up to me waving a newspaper.

"Hey!... com'ere a minute, take a look at my newspaper... look at how they're treating you. You haven't seen this yet?"

She points out the passage... "Boy! you've sure been smeared!" She was thrilled about it, happy as a clam...

"You're Céline, aren't you?"

"Why yes, of course it's the name I show off with, my *nom de guerre*... Whose newspaper is this, what paper have you got there?..."

"Just read what they've written, why it's the Journal de Paris! the newspaper 'Journal'... 'Renegade'!... They're calling you.... Yep, it's right there in black and white... 'Renegade'!... like André Gide, they've added.... Like Mr. Fontenoy and a bunch of others...."

Furious! my blood runs cold!... I jump up... leap forward.... I've been called a lot of things in my day... but never before a "renegade"! Me, a renegade?... who's a renegade?... what renegade?... renegade, no way!... But I've never renounced anyone... the insult is outrageous. Who is this snot nose who thinks he can torment me about Communism?... Some guy named Helsey.... But I don't [even] know him!... How did he come up with such insults?... Where's he from, this twisted, hateful creep? Has he got nerve or what?... It's right here in the middle of the page in huge print... no mistake about it... the lady's right....

"Of course, the opinion of renegades is of no importance, the Gides, the Célines, the Fontenoys... etc.... They torch what they once worshiped."

He's full of it, this clod!... What right does this dimwit have to slander [me] in this way?...

But I've never renounced anything!... But I've never worshiped a thing!... where did he see that written? (B, 44–45)

In this passage, all of the information needed to locate the original publication is furnished. Céline insists on these details, even when he appears to be providing them in a totally fortuitous manner: we are given the date ("towards the end of that summer"), the name of the newspaper (the daily *Le Journal*), the article's author ("a guy named Helsey"), and finally the topic of the article ("On Communism"). With these cues, we can easily locate Helsey's reference to Céline in an article dated June 15, 1937, part of a series Helsey had written on communism entitled "Partisans of the Hammer and the Sickle,"[4] that was published by *Le Journal*. In this particular segment, Helsey is lamenting the dearth of objective reporting on the Soviet Union: "Let's not take the word of repentant observers," he writes in the original, "of an André Gide, a Céline, or of a Fontenoy, since it will surely be claimed that such contradictory accounts cancel each other out, and that one is discredited by retracting earlier statements."

Helsey's text allows us to assess the degree to which Céline distorted the attack directed against him, since we have before us the criterion for linguistic evaluation, that is, for studying his mode of reading. The expression Helsey uses, "an André Gide, a Céline, a Fontenoy"—which is rendered approximatively by the woman in the Saint-Malo incident ("like an André Gide, they've added")—is altered when it is reported and pluralized by the narrator Ferdinand: "les Gides, les Célines, les Fontenoys." More surprising and indeed significant is Céline's transformation of Helsey's key word "repentant" (repentis) into "renegade." The lexical shift is in part a displacement from *L'Ecole du renégat*, the title of Fontenoy's book on the Soviet Union, which was published in October 1936, just after Céline's return from Leningrad, the period during which, *Mea Culpa,* his first pamphlet, was undoubtedly taking shape.[5]

If not the actual catalyst of *Bagatelles pour un massacre,* Helsey's attack on Céline might be considered the initial trauma that compelled him to write the book. Céline assures his reader ("I guarantee you") that he has written one, two, if not three letters to the editor of the *Journal* in response to Helsey's article and states that they were never published. The editor's dismissal of Céline's response produces the ideal pamphleteering reflex for the writer: "I say to myself: 'Well then, I'm going to bug the hell out of them!' I reach for my shiny pen and take down one of these notes" (B, 48). One has the distinct impression that Céline, having just seized his pen, begins immediately to write, and this rapid response to the daily news helps us to date precise passages of his text. Frequently, Céline furnishes indices in passing, as if he presumes that his reader, too, has happened upon them as did the "jubilant" woman in Saint-Malo.

At times, Céline asserts that he is writing at the very moment events are taking place. For instance, when he derides Maurice Thorez's book, *Le Fils du peuple,*[6] Céline indicates that the time of his writing corresponds to that of the event—in this case, the book's publication ("Currently, that fine fat head, the handsome Thorez" [B, 302]). Although he does not mention the title of Thorez's book, he describes its jacket blurb, noting "on the cover [of] 'My Life'." This lack of precision is significant in that the reference "My Life" is gleaned from the advertisement for *Le Fils du peuple* that was running at the time in Parisian newspapers. Next to the article quoted by Céline, whose source can be traced to the October 25, 1937, issue of *Paris-Soir,*[7] is one such ad that reproduces the cover of *Le Fils du peuple* and proclaims: "Thorez speaks to you about his childhood, his life, and his life in the [Communist] party. On sale everywhere October 25." Knowing Céline's habits, it is safe to say that he had not read the book and that he did not even know its title. A glance at the advertisement was all he needed to commence writing.

Indeed, one can identify a range of quotations and dates Céline mentions in *Bagatelles pour un massacre,* beginning with the article by Helsley published on July 25, 1937. The epigraph attributed to Béla Kun on page 309 of *Bagatelles* appears, for instance, in the December 9, 1937, issue of *Candide.*[8] The references Céline makes to specific events, such as the June 3rd marriage of Edward VIII to Wallis Simpson (B, 135) or the awarding of the Nobel Prize to Roger Martin du Gard on November 11 (B, 183),[9] are from this same time frame and give the pamphlet the feel and texture of a personal diary spanning a period of six or seven months.

Two articles Céline quotes from *Paris-Soir* clearly illustrate the passion for detail with which he read the daily press on the lookout for allegories that might lend credence to his anti-Semitic vituperation. In his duplication of "The Career of Careers," an October 25 installment of Jean Barois's society column, Céline changed nothing but the proper name "Lévy de Tact," which replaces the name "Alphand" from the original article.[10] Charles Alphand was the French Ambassador to the Soviet Union and to Switzerland during the 1930s; at the time, his son Hervé (who was to become the ambassador to the United States) was a fledgling member of the government agency in charge of foreign trade negotiations. In actuality, the Alphand family was not Jewish, even though Céline associates the name Alphand with the Jewish names Alphen, Halphand, Alphand. This article on the Alphand family could not help but trigger a surge of anti-Semitic thoughts in Céline, via the added element of song in the Alphand profile. Claude Alphand had performed vocals for the 1937 International Exposition's radio broadcasts; anyone remotely tied to the entertainment presented at the Expo automatically became Céline's foe. Moreover, this singer's diction, Céline asserts, "is comparable to that of Yvette Guilbert." Claude Alphand's husband, Hervé, delighted in entertaining his friends by imitating French songs. Céline encourages his readers to establish links between Alphand's imitations of "true" French singers and the claim he advances throughout *Bagatelles* that mimicking robots—and Jews— have invaded French culture.

Céline's second quotation (dated "the day after" the preceding article) is taken from Jean Barois's October 28 society column.[11] Once again, Céline faithfully reproduced the article except for altering the names: "Le Baron de Cahen" replaces the Baron Emile d'Erlanger; "The Baronesse of Cahen, née de Grand-Bey" is substituted for the Baronesse d'Erlanger, née de Rochegude; Ysabel and Arielle de Faucigny-Lucing, the baron's grand-daughters, become "Sarah, Esther and Rachel." The Baron Emile d'Erlanger belonged to the Erlanger family, an important banking concern. French by birth, a naturalized British citizen, the Baron participated actively in French cultural life. In Barois's article *Paris-Soir* announces the upcoming private performance of the Baron's play, *Sapho or the Academy of Lesbos*, at the Odéon Theater, as well as his scheduled lecture on *Abraham* being sponsored by the Franco-British Association. Worse yet, from Céline's perspective, is a fact concerning the Erlanger family of which the article makes no mention but that Céline adds in a sentence that seems to come from other, as yet undiscovered, sources: "In his Moorish harem, from Sidi-bou-Saïd to Carthage, his brother Alexander gathered melodies from Arab folklore, while the other brother, Samuel, composed the music for 'A Thousand Kisses,' successfully staged not long ago at Covent Garden during the Russian Ballet season." (B, 264). Emile d'Erlanger's brothers, Camille and Rodolphe—whom Céline calls Samuel and Alexander—both moved in artistic circles: Camille (1863–1919), an opera composer, was known for a work entitled *Polish Jew* (1900) that the Opéra Comique had reprised in 1933. Rodolphe, a musicologist and oriental painter who died at Sidi-bou-Saïd in 1932, was known for his voluminous history of Arab music. For Céline, the history of the Erlanger family becomes an allegory of Jewish cultural domination: the Jewish capitalist with cultural pretensions sees his play performed at the Odéon Theatre before a private audience, and his brother's ballet is staged at Covent Garden. Conversely, Céline's own ballets are everywhere being rejected out of hand. For Céline, the other Erlander brother, Rodolphe, has lapsed into Africanism; Céline reiterates the theme of the "negroid Jew" on which he places such great emphasis in the most delirious passages of *Bagatelles pour un massacre.*

The distortion and "revelation" of names is a common practice in anti-Semitic writings that target the name changes of assimilated Jews. Following the lead of Jean Boissel, author of *The Jew, Deadly Poison,* Céline renames Erlanger as "Cahen,"[12] whereas Céline's transformation of "Alphand" into "Lévy de Tact," though still anti-Semitic, is of a more bantering, literary nature. In each of these cases, Céline's central aim is to unmask the true identity of those whose names are not immediately identifiable as Jewish, in order to make them easily recognizable as such. For instance, in quoting an anti-Semitic pamphlet seeking to illustrate that the pseudonyms adopted by Bolshevik leaders always efface their Jewishness, Céline chooses the wording "Lenin, whose real name is Oulianoff" (B, 282).[13] He also replaces the word *name* itself with the slang term *blase,* which he will introduce once again in *Nord*[14] to designate his own pseudonym. This is one of the rare instances in *Bagatelles* in which Céline enriches conventional anti-Semitic language through recourse to slang, which gives his insults much greater linguistic density; the French slang term *blase* signifies both *name* and *nose,* recalling the pun "un juif bien nez" (a play on the French expression *bien né* signifying to be born into privilege or a good family, and *bien nez,* suggesting a prominent nose), a classic anti-Semitic joke of the period.

Céline's will to know "all of the real names" (B, 250) is but one aspect of *Bagatelles*'s sociological ambitions. The Jewish community he targets specifically is not essentially that of the immigrant or even the religious Jew, but, rather, the entire international assimilationist Jewish community whose activities in the arenas of commerce, literature, and the arts he is obsessively monitoring, particularly in his quotations from *L'Univers Israélite*, a very conservative—and very French—periodical of the time.[15] However, the most grievous and insidious attack on Jewish assimilation one finds in the pamphlet takes the form of a quotation from a *Readers Digest* article by Maurice Feuerlicht, entitled "Children of the Martyred Race," that had appeared in an American magazine. Maurice Feuerlicht was a young lawyer when he sent his original essay, "Where the Jews Fail," to *Forum Magazine*, a publication that, after the stock market crash in 1929 and ensuing economic crisis, had begun purchasing the work of amateur writers.[16] The great distance Feuerlicht takes from the Jewish community in general and his family in particular is no doubt attributable to what American historians term "the assimilationism of second generation immigrants." The desire on the part of the second generation to become "American above all" leads it to retreat more or less consciously from its heritage and to renounce its Jewish identity. For Feuerlicht, this involved establishing an enormous distance between himself and his father, Morris Feuerlicht, a Rabbi, professor of Semitic languages and member of the Central Congress of American Rabbis. Motivated by a desire to become a "normal citizen," the younger Feuerlicht denies the importance, indeed the existence, of any social anti-Semitism in the United States and accuses American Jews of suffering from a "persecution complex." When *Readers Digest* reprinted Feuerlicht's article in October 1937 in condensed and simplified form, it added the following caption: "The son of a rabbi asks what responsibility Jews themselves have in the perpetuation of prejudice." *Readers Digest*'s appeal to an anti-Semitic readership could hardly be more blatant. It is not the article from *Forum Magazine* but the version in the *Readers Digest* that Céline opts to cite in its entirety in four pages of *Bagatelles pour un massacre* (B, 255–58). How Céline stumbled on this article remains unclear. One can only surmise that one of the anti-Semitic pamphlet mills he frequented had come across the article and was waiting for the opportunity to publish excerpts. In fact, the organization of Nazi Propaganda known as the Welt Dienst (World Service), or in French, the Service Mondial, succeeded in producing their own tract from another

Jewish-authored article in the American press. Céline cites an entire paragraph of this essay just two pages before quoting Feuerlicht.

Céline's second American source cited in *Bagatelles* is Marcus Eli Ravage, a Jewish-American journalist who happened to be working in France in the 1930s.[17] Ravage parodies anti-Semitic writings by giving so-called "friendly advice" to budding anti-Semitic writers. It was evident to the American reader of the *Century Magazine*, in which two of his articles appear in 1928, that the butt of Ravage's jokes was the anti-Semitic industrialist Henry Ford. To cite Ravage: "If you really want to accuse Jews of disrupting civilization," he quips, "talking about Jewish influence on cinema, etc., isn't enough. What you really need to do is examine Jewish influence on the entire Western tradition, beginning with Jesus-Christ." Taken out of context, Ravage's statements can be construed as a warning to Gentiles: "We are intruders, we are destroyers, we have taken over your wealth, your ideals, your destiny." The Welt Dienst circulated Ravage's articles in the form of pamphlets in England, France, and Germany. During the 1930s, numerous anti-Semitic documents quoted Ravage in French; three of these documents served as sources for Céline.[18]

Very little is known regarding how Céline located his sources or became impassioned by them, but it is certain that the work of minor pamphleteers appealed to him more than the urbane anti-Semitic essays of sophisticates such as Marcel Jouhandeau or Robert Brasillach. We know that Céline did an apprenticeship of sorts in the history of the genre by reading a five-volume collection of tracts published by the right-wing bibliophile and book collector John Grand-Carteret.[19] In *Bagatelles*, Céline borrows from Grand-Carteret a passage concerning the financial relations between the Jews and the kings of France (B, 300).[20] More important for the understanding of Céline's pamphlet, however, is the fact that Grand-Carteret's book provided the author with the following literary and, quite exceptionally, non-anti-Semitic epigraph taken from Agrippa d'Aubigné: "What can I hope for amidst these degenerate souls, if not to see my book cast in the rubble" (B, 185).[21] As he is presented in Grand-Carteret's account, Agrippa d'Aubigné's ordeal runs surprisingly parallel to the myth surrounding Céline's life in subsequent years—lore that Céline himself helped to create: the myth of poet and historian caught up in events and of the literary martyr of religious wars, doomed as a result of his eccentric style to be misunderstood and ostracized by his contemporaries.

Céline was not content to remain an admirer of the pamphlet genre; he became a collector and collagist of pamphlets that were manufactured for the most part in two or three centers by a band of anti-Semites of a variety of persuasions (anti-Masonic, right-wing anarchists, National Socialists). The sources for a significant number of the anti-Semitic commentaries (concentrated in pages 200–300 of *Bagatelles*) can be found in texts published between September and October 1937, the period immediately following Céline's return to his Parisian apartment on the rue Lepic after a summer in Saint-Malo and Le Havre.[22] An article written by Georges Zérapha in 1938 indicates that pamphlets bearing Henry-Robert Petit's signature, and published at Darquier de Pellepoix's headquarters on the rue Laugier, provided Céline with many of *Bagatelles'* "gems."[23] Céline's manipulation of quotations reminded François Porché, writing in *L'Epoque* on February 28, 1938, of the "slapdash, grab bag type of work" carried out by the "long-haired dodderers lugging briefcases crammed with papers" he encountered during his youth at the Sainte-Geneviève Library.[24] Close analysis reveals that *Bagatelles* is but a hastily compiled collection of references that lend the text an erudite veneer that is pure simulacrum.

At this point, it is important to distinguish between what I call the *quotations* and the *sources* in *Bagatelles pour un massacre*. In some instances, Céline places his text in quotation marks when citing an author, and in others he borrows from writers without acknowledging their contributions, presenting the material at times with, and then again without, quotation marks. The "quotation" category typically includes popularized works of anthropology (*Sémites et Aryens* by Charles Picard) or of history (*Les Gallois* by Albert Grenier and *L'Histoire— La Vie—Les Mœurs* and *La Curiosité par l'image, le pamphlet et le document*—by John Grand-Carteret), quotations from Jewish writers taken from newspapers such as the *Univers Israélite* and from books such as Arthur Ruppin's *Les Juifs dans le monde moderne*. Along with "anti-Semitic versions" of quotations from the Talmud, the "sources" category also contains direct quotations from racist pamphlets and books published in 1937, particularly in the fall of that year, signed by Coston, Petit, Santo and De Vries. But the distinction between "attributed" and "nonattributed" citation tends to become blurred when, for instance, Céline quotes anti-Semitic witticisms, which a Santo or a De Vries attributes to "Fourrier," Bakunin, or Cicero. Céline does indeed invoke writers of this stature but neglects to name the authors and the titles of the pamphlets from which he draws the citation. If Céline does not always specify the source of his materials, the fact that he lifted passages from others rather frequently is signaled in his own book through the excessive use of quotations marks, so typical of the pamphlet genre.

The most direct source of material for Céline's quotations was very likely Henry Coston's Office de Propagande Nationale (Office of National Propaganda) situated on the rue du Cardinal Mercier to which Céline had easy access from his rue Lepic apartment. From a document entitled "The Jewish Conspiracy" bearing Henry Coston's signature, Céline transcribed, more or less verbatim, a total of twenty-six pages that were incorporated into pages 277–288 of *Bagatelles*.[25] Céline did not have before him the alleged primary sources, texts such as *The Discourse of Rabbi Reichhorn*, *The Protocols of the Elders of Zion*, the *Report of the American Secret Service*, or *The Surrender of an Empire*. He lifts an entire series of quotations from "The Jewish Conspiracy," even going so far as to plagiarize Coston when he introduces certain documents. Coston's "This is not the result of a fleeting arrangement between Jews and Bolsheviks. It was thus everywhere" (11) is rendered in *Bagatelles* as: "All of this is not the result of a fleeting arrangement between Jews and Bolsheviks. It was thus everywhere" (B, 283). At times, Céline animates Coston's dry, academic prose. "The Jew Blumenthal was, then, justifiable in writing that the 'Judisk Tidskrift'" becomes, in Céline's words: "I think this all jibes, coincides, quite admirably with current events. So that it be known, the Jew Blumenthal was thus perfectly correct in writing in the 'Judisk Tidskrift'" (B, 281). This is a prime example of what Céline would later call an anti-Semitic discourse rendered "plebian," "crude," "stylized."[26]

An oblique statement of Céline's methodology of quotation can be found in the following remark he makes in *Bagatelles* about modern art: "You photograph an object, just any object, a chair, umbrella, telescope, bus, and then you cut it up into a puzzle... You scatter the morsels, these scraps, over a huge sheet of paper, green, ivory, orange. Poetry!" (B, 221). Similarly, Céline carves out portions of texts that he scatters as epigraphs throughout his pamphlets. For example, in the case of one of his sources, Picard's *Sémites et Aryens*, Céline extracted three segments—containing two quotations from the Bible along with a bit of commentary—and turns them into three epigraphs that appear to have been taken directly from the Bible (B, 49, 53, 56). It is not until page 86 that he attributes a fourth epigraph from *Sémites et Aryens* to Picard and gives the book an incorrect title, *Histoires des sacrifices*, (taken from the chapter that had provided the first three quotations, but not the fourth). It is well known that Céline's works contain numerous such "scraps" and "morsels": those of the demented Doctor Semmelweis, who, in a suicidal frenzy, sticks his hands into the intestines of a cadaver, or those of the clergyman in *Mort à crédit*, who thrusts his into the papers and innards of Courtial des Pereires after the latter commits suicide. Céline uses quotations in *Bagatelles* in a strikingly similar fashion: just as his fictional characters sift through documents and plunder body parts, in *Bagatelles pour un massacre*, Céline lifts morsels of text, such as those of the works cited, butchering their authors' names—a practice that ultimately contributes to the massacre of his own literary reputation.

In a more direct fashion, Céline describes the composition of *Bagatelles* in *L'Ecole des cadavres*, a second major anti-Semitic pamphlet published a year later. He first acknowledges his own lack of originality: "If I may be so bold as to quote myself: Bagatelles pour un massacre will, I believe, instruct you rather well regarding the importance of this issue, its timeliness, the fate awaiting us all. This has all been written. I have discovered nothing. No pretentions. Simply virulent, stylized vulgarization" (EC, 33). He goes on to specify that "Judeology," a "science of plagiarism," is also a discipline that is "intricate, finicky, facetious, tragic, contradictory, treasonous" (B, 34). He graciously provides readers with a list of specialists:

Some Judeologues master their discipline completely, they've got it at the tip of their fingers, the rudiments, the History of Jews, of the Jewish conspiracy, from an ethnographic as well as a biological perspective. Their works are renowned, indisputable, essential. All Aryans should read Drumont. More current: De Vries, De Poncins, Sombart, Stanley [sic] Chamberlain; closer to home: Montandon, Darquier de Pellepoix, Boissel, H.-R. Petit, Dasté, H. Coston, des Essards, Alex, Santo, etc... You can find a well-stocked French library at the Centre Documentaire, 10 rue d'Argenteil [sic], [or] at the Anti-Jewish Mobilization, 12 rue Laugier. Certain newspapers, journals, follow the Jew rather closely. At the present time [these include]: "La France enchaînée," "La Libre Parole," "Je Suis Partout," "L'Action Française," and on some days... "Gringoire," some weeks rather sheepishly, and that's about it. I cannot overemphasize the importance of reading Dasté's admirable book: "Marie Antoinette and the Masonic conspiracy." (EC, 34–35)

There is no direct trace in *Bagatelles* of Drumont's *La France juive*; Céline is inspired only by Drumont's mode of formulating arguments by pasting together quotations (a very common practice among pamphleteers) and published statements made by several of Drumont's disciples—most particularly Lucien Pemjean. Among the authors Céline quotes after the fact in *L'Ecole des cadavres*, De Vries, De Poncins, H.-R. Petit, Coston, and Santo have furnished *Bagatelles* with countless citations. Louis Darquier de Pellepoix ran the anti-Semitic Centre Documentaire that published Santo's and Petit's pamphlets. Boissel collaborated with Pemjean, Petit, and Santo at the *Grand Occident*— one of Céline's indirect sources. Darquier founded and managed *Le Réveil du peuple* from March 1936 to August 1937, and then again between 1939 and 1941. The publication appears to have given Céline but a single direct quotation, which originally came from Joseph Goebbels.[27] Beginning in May 1936, R. des Essards codirected La Nation Réveillée: Organe de l'Union des Comités de Défense des Jeunesses Françaises Ouvrières et Paysannes with J. Chevillard. Houston Stewart Chamberlain, the racist theoretician who influenced Nazi racial ideologue Alfred Rosenberg, is not mentioned in *Bagatelles pour un massacre*; neither are Alex and des Essards. Dasté's production of pamphlets dates back to 1899 (*L'Armée et la Franc-maçonnerie*) but ends in 1912 (*Les Sociétés secrètes et les Juifs*); Céline does not directly quote any pamphlets published prior to the 1920s. Finally, Céline refers to a particular author, Werner Sombert,[28] who did not write pamphlets. Sombert was a renowned German intellectual who had incorporated anti-Semitic thinking into his economic theories during the 1930s. Although he is not explicitly mentioned in *Bagatelles*, Sombert is nonetheless quoted in the Canadian pamphlet *La Clé du mystère*, a work that, along with "La Conspiration Juive" (a gallicized variant of the same text), constituted Céline's basic source.

We know from the existing manuscript for *L'Ecole des cadavres*[29] that Céline liked to cut out his favorite quotes and affix them directly to his text. Although the manuscript for *Bagatelles* has not been found, one can well imagine that it was done partially with pasted clippings that the copyeditor later distinguished from Céline's text by inserting quotation marks. There are also numerous spelling errors in *Bagatelles* that suggest a hasty typographic transcription of source-texts rather than recourse to collage. When it is pointedly a question of mistakes in the transcription of proper names, it is quite feasible that such errors sprang from a conscious design by the author to attack his enemies by distorting their names. Céline was no doubt delighted to see André Gide's name appear in *L'Univers Israélite* as "André Gode." It spared him extra work![30]

Bagatelles pour un massacre proposes an "anti-Semitic pedagogy": an instructional method that, as noted, is first and foremost onomastic, seeking to "know all of the true names" (B, 250). To this end, Céline includes a list of the members of the Paris Consistory[31] and catalogs the "true names" of the leaders of the Bolshevik Revolution, viewing both groups as operatives in the "Jewish Conspiracy" (B, 286–87). The statistics he produces regarding the crisis of literacy in France, followed directly by figures on alcoholism, have the goal of demonstrating— another "pedagogy" of sorts—that Jews endeavor to "alcoholize" Aryans in order to prevent them from reading. For if Aryans actually read Jewish writings, he asserts, they would come to realize fully that there exists a Jewish plot to dominate the world. "Jews," Céline observes, "are the greatest readers in the world" (B, 199). In turn, he counsels Aryans to read the Jews so as not to be snared in the trap *they* have set: "It is Jews who instruct you the best about the state of Jewish demands, who allow you to gauge their hate and racism" (B, 245–46). On a more sophisticated level, one must also become adept at reading "assimilated Judaism" between the lines of text "managed" by Jews in newspapers such as *Paris-Soir* and *L'Humanité.*

It is, however, to "authentically Jewish" sources such as the *Talmud*, *L'Univers Israélite, The American Hebrew*, and so on that Céline often appeals in supporting his racist claims. He explains his reasons for this in *L'Ecole des cadavres:* "I'm not going to go over this again, all of it's been told by Jews themselves, since the Talmud, in numerous, copious works that some Aryans, too few, have bothered to read, analyze, summarize for you" (EC, 33). The organization that contributed most during the 1930s to the dissemination of this pseudo-"Judeology" was the Welt Dienst. This German propaganda agency, subsidized by the Nazis, began publishing its newsletter in France in 1933 under the title *Service Mondial.* It was the February 15, 1937, issue of *Service Mondial* that recommended De Vries' book, *Israël: son passé, son avenir*, one of Céline's unacknowledged sources in *Bagatelles.* The *Service Mondial* reports that, because De Vries "availed himself exclusively of material taken from Jewish sources, it can be said that it is a book written by Jews rather than by an Aryan." The article concludes with: "The study of the Talmud should be included in the curricula of all schools, from the lowest grades of primary school right up through the universities and military academies! Only when this measure has been adopted will non-Jews be able to know the mind of Juda. Only he who knows the weapons and designs of this world enemy can undertake to combat it with some hope of success. No exams without a composition on the Talmud!"[32] An attempt at humor is part of the pseudo-recognition of "Jewish domination": the anti-Semite claims to have been "already invaded." Céline does not fail to surpass the *Service Mondial* in this comedic genre. He went much further; so far, in fact, that a number of critics, among them André Gide, found it hard to take his racism seriously.[33] For Céline considered himself the model writer for Jews: "Personally, it would no doubt be possible for me to defend myself for some time to come, thanks to my enchanting style, my bawdy, vociferating, accursed lyricism, in this very special style, rather Jewish in some respects, I do better than Jews, I can give them lessons. This redeems me. American Jews think I'm mentally gifted. Let's hope it lasts!" (B, 204).

In his response to the Helsey article of June 1937, Céline proclaimed: "I have never micronized [taken up the microphone] at meetings," and "I have never signed petitions" (B, 45). It is true that Céline's name does not figure on the list of "friends of the *Grand Occident*," one of France's most virulently anti-Semitic newspapers, that appeared in its September–October 1937 issue. Jeanine Roy's March 1938 article in *Esprit* asserts that Céline had ferreted the documentation for *Bagatelles* out of brochures "of the type sold at subway entrances along with lists of the latest winning [lottery] numbers and pornographic illustrations."

My research leads me to believe that the brochures Céline used in composing *Bagatelles* came not from a random subway kiosk he might have come across but from the Office de Propagande Nationale (OPN) situated on the rue du Cardinal-Mercier not far from his apartment. This office was one of a series of several rather unstable organizations that operated in the 1930s, in the years preceding the *Décret Marchandeau*.[34] Although their headquarters changed, the personnel, their publications, and readers clearly overlapped. By 1938, leaflets nearly identical to those of the OPN were being reproduced by the Centre de Documentation et de Propagande located on the rue Laugier. Citations from both propaganda factories were reprinted in *Le Grand Occident*, *Le Réveil du peuple*, and *L'Anti-Juif*. These publications benefited, as did the *centres* themselves, from the financial support and advertising revenues of the *Service Mondial*. Boissel, Darquier, Coston, Petit, and Santo, the managers of these anti-Semitic organizations and publications, knew one another well and collaborated at various moments. Petit, for example, first ran his own research center on the rue Troyon and then joined Coston on the rue du Cardinal-Mercier. He later teamed up with Darquier at the rue Laugier institute, diffusing the very same documents and quotations under separate titles with differently designed covers. It was at one of the *centres*, the one located at 10 rue d'Argenteuil, that H.-R. Petit founded the anti-Semitic newspaper *Le Pilori* in July 1938.

I found only two specific traces in the anti-Semitic press of the period of specific activities organized by these groups. A propaganda meeting at Petit's previous "research center" on the rue Troyon is mentioned in the March 1, 1936, issue of the monthly *La Libre Parole*. The report describes a public reading of two texts that Céline will later quote. The first was a forerunner of *The Protocols of the Elders of Zion* entitled *The Discourse of Rabbi Reichhorn*. The second was an anti-Masonic passage taken from Petit's *Drame Maçonnique*. According to the report, the public reading by one of the *centre's* "technical consultants" took place in an atmosphere of "religious veneration." This published report provides evidence that the texts Céline used as sources circulated within this specific community as early as 1936.

A similar group headed by Darquier de Pellepoix met on April 20, 1937, to form the "French Anti-Jewish Committee" (also referred to as the "Anti-Jewish Mobilization"). Because he had been a city councilman from the Ternes district of the 17th Arronissement since 1935, it is quite possible that it was Darquier de Pellepoix who set up the group's meeting place, a Gothic building in the 17th Arrondissement at 10 rue Laugier. It is also in this neighborhood, at the Salle Wagram, that the committee chose to hold its first public meeting on May 11, 1937. Newspapers quoted Darquier's concluding remarks to the meeting: "We must, therefore, with great urgency, resolve the Jewish question, that Jews be expelled or slaughtered [massacrés]." Was Darquier's exhortation already known to Céline, a writer in search of a title?[35]

That Céline failed to attribute his quotations to Coston or to any of the numerous other local anti-Semitic writers whose works he appropriates in *Bagatelles* might suggest that he was not yet working closely with them or was simply not ready to acknowledge that he was. At the beginning of 1938, the official position of the anti-Semitic groups toward *Bagatelles* seems to have been fairly ambivalent. In a meeting held at 10 rue Laugier on February 10, 1938, about a month after the publication of *Bagatelles pour un massacre*, Darquier recommended his cohorts read the pamphlet, "in spite of its crudeness."[36] Jean Drault[37] acknowledges in the March issue of *Le Grand Occident* that he is slightly envious that a carpetbagger from the lofty world of literature had succeeded in attracting readers, given the exorbitant price of his work as compared to ordinary pamphlets (averaging 3 francs): "Rarely do you see one of our boys . . . treating themselves to a book that costs 27 francs" (3). In this case, Céline finds himself treated merely as a repentant philosemite: "Before this book, Céline, an avowed anarchist, was praised to the high heavens by Jews. His *Voyage au bout de la nuit* even found favor with the Goncourt brothers." Like Darquier, Drault tempers his enthusiasm for Céline: "I call him a precursor because he is one, considering the rather Jewified milieu in which his literary career skyrocketed, a milieu which indulged his defective syntax and his penchant for obscenities which prohibit the reading of his book by the few remaining Frenchmen who are still finicky about morality and decency"(3).

Reservations of this sort notwithstanding, from the month of February on, *Bagatelles* had been on sale at the Centre de Documentation et de Propagande on the rue Laugier. It is probably in the summer of 1938, while working on *L'Ecole des cadavres*, that Céline first wrote to Henry-Robert Petit.[38] His first letters to Petit are essentially requests for new pamphlets. Then, in correspondence displaying a growing familiarity, Céline ridicules the *Esprit* article accusing him of having plagiarized Petit: "Of course, I don't kid myself about having sifted through your writings, I ground them up, lifted parts from them, as I wished" (LHP, 10). Finally, in a letter that appears to date back to the month of September,[39] Céline puts Petit in contact with Georges Montandon, the racist ethnologist. His letter takes the form of literary advice: "Dear friend, . . . He [Montandon] will give you the best doctrine but all of this will have to be rendered *popular*"; and in another letter, written just before the publication of *L'Ecole des cadavres*, he notes: "It seems to me that this is not a very propitious angle, not very clever of us" (LHP, 12). On December 3, 1938, Céline attended a meeting organized by *La France enchaînée*.[40] His relationship with Parisian fascists, at the start textual, takes an epistolary turn and ultimately becomes public. With its June counterattack against Helsey as a point of departure and the plagiarism of Coston's *Jewish Conspiracy* in July 1937, the range of sources in *Bagatelles* illustrates a process of reading and quotation that led Céline to this new community. It is thus possible to see *Bagatelles* as an encounter between two textual worlds and the confluence of two literary markets: the great daily newspapers on the one hand, and the minor pamphleteer literature on the other. In attending the meeting at Darquier's headquarters, Céline openly declared his support for the pamphleteers. This act is, I would argue, the logical outcome, rather than the origin, of an anti-Semitic allegiance with textual foundations.

In researching Céline's sources, I found myself facing an ever-widening abyss of propaganda, a veritable "anti-Semitic international." The quotations Céline uses in his pamphlets can be traced to those that provoked the pogroms in Russia at the turn of the century; they can be followed to the United States where they carry Henry Ford's signature, then to Canada, under the emblem of an anticommunist women's movement, to South Africa with an Afrikaans title, and to Germany, where they animated Nazi meetings. These sources allowed me to take stock of a virtual anti-Semitic culture, whose father, in France, is Edouard Drumont. One can distinguish among three great "families" of French anti-Semites. The one with the deepest cultural roots is Catholic and anti-Masonic. The second claims to be anarchist, and a third, the most recent in origin, has been inspired by neighboring National Socialism.

Paradoxically, anti-Semitic propaganda, by virtue of its obsessive quality, seems to parody that on which it has declared war: the "perversity" of the Jewish mind. The vast corpus of literature alleging the authenticity of the *Protocols of the Elders of Zion* is written in a style one might be tempted to call "Talmudic," given the fervor with which editions and variants make reference to this text. The conventions of the anti-Semitic pamphlet have now been impeccably established thanks to Norman Cohn's research on the *Protocols*: the same story of conspiracy repeated in numerous countries throughout the ages comes to present itself in pamphlets as absolute proof of that conspiracy, becoming a substitute for argumentation.[41]

When one stops to think that we are dealing in *Bagatelles* not with a garden-variety pamphleteer but rather a great literary talent, what is perhaps most curious is that actually believing, as Céline clearly does, in the *Protocols of the Elders of Zion*, in the Rabbi's *Discourse*, and in the vaguely conspiratorial statements attributed to Disraeli is tantamount to believing not in the power of Jews but in the power of fiction. Originally, the *Discourse of Rabbi Reichhorn* was a chapter in a popular novel that was translated, circulated, and presented as real. The quotation of the "Jew Mirès," a statement that was supposed to have been related by a general at a dinner party, is subsequently reiterated in the Goncourts' *Journal*, quoted in *La Clé du mystère*, attributed to the Goncourts themselves, and finally reprinted, out of context, in Petit's *Le Règne des Juifs*. (Jules-Isaac Mirès was a flamboyant Jewish banker during the Second Empire and was portrayed in several dramas of the period. He is reported to have stated: "If in fifty years you haven't hanged all of us [Jews], then you Christians won't have enough left to even buy the rope to do it with.") The French text of the *Protocols of the Elders of Zion* was quite probably taken from a French pamphlet entitled *Dialogue aux Enfers entre Machiavel et Montesquieu* whose chief aim in 1864 was the denunciation of Napoleon III's despotism. Disraeli's quotation, undoubtedly the one that was most rehashed in this literature, came not from his official political statements as prime minister but from his novel *Coningsby* (1844), in which a remark regarding the world being governed by hidden powers was interpreted by anti-Semites as referring to Jewish machinations. Whether dealing with quotations or pseudo-documents, what counts most for the anti-Semite is not their actual source but the number of signatures they carry and the extent of their circulation. Hence, the instructions at the end of Santo's pamphlet: "let this document be passed from hand to hand"; or the notice found on the first page of *Service Mondial*: "Reproduction authorized and even solicited."

If Céline excels in this ritual transgression of copyright, he is not content simply to reproduce quotations verbatim. He attaches his famous "three dots" where Henry-Robert Petit or Henry Coston had placed a semicolon, where Grenier placed a full stop, thereby pointing to the necessity to go beyond the ordinary pamphlets, to read "between the lines." For instance, one quotation evoking the Roman defeat of the Gauls should be read, in Céline's view, as a warning to modern France, a country on the brink of falling into Jewish hands: everyone—be it Racine or the Pope—was to be suspected of being, if not Jewish, then "Jewified." Moreover, Céline surrounds his often pointed and pseudo-scholarly epigraphs with highly personal complaints and accusations. He tirelessly gallicizes anti-Semitic clichés in a kaleidoscope of proper names and minutia relating to daily life in Paris, explaining in a letter to Petit: "I could have focused on science or biology in which I am a master craftsman. I could have fallen prey to the temptation to be pompously correct. I didn't want to. I wanted to goof off a little, a lot, to stay in the popular realm" (LHP, 10).[42] However, right in the middle of an exemplary passage pilfered from "La Conspiration Juive," Céline allows a smidgen of doubt to filter through his scheme for popularizing anti-Semitism: " I myself am sensitive enough when it comes to what's preposterous." He nonetheless persists: "But just the same, there are names... people, events... this inevitable, irrefutable, sudden, implacable, the most squawking, virulent, zealous, voracious Jewish regrouping over each of our catastrophes... like a thousand crows from hell taking flight, on the very site of all our disasters. This can't be invented" (B, 284). With his "squawking" crows, Céline seeks to give a literary twist to his anti-Semitic discourse. But with the proviso: "This can't be invented," which echoes "the names... people, events...," he immediately rushes to deny any innovation, offering instead of a deeply personal racist passion the pseudo-objectivity of documentation.

Translated by Rosemarie Scullion

▼

The Plot as
Conspiracy:
Céline's Review of
Renoir's
*La Grande
Illusion* in
*Bagatelles pour
un massacre*

▼

IN MAY 1937, at Saint-Malo, the city on the Brittany coast where he spent many of his vacations, Céline began work on the first of the three anti-Semitic pamphlets[1] he would eventually write, *Bagatelles pour un massacre*. He wrote it hastily, completing the volume in September of that year. It was published on December 28, 1937.[2] In January 1937, Jean Renoir began shooting *La Grande Illusion (Grand Illusion)*. He finished filming in April, and the movie premiered at the Marivaux Theatre in Paris on June 4, 1937.[3] One could say that these two works had been on a collision course. That collision took place when Céline saw the film (one assumes he actually viewed it) and decided to include a critique of it in *Bagatelles*.

The attention that Céline devotes to *La Grande Illusion* and the issues he addresses in his review belie any mere annoyance on the part of the anti-Semitic pamphleteer that a successful film by a well-known director would portray a Jew sympathetically. I hope to demonstrate in this essay that Céline's review of the film reveals a perception of *La Grande Illusion* as a work that calls into question several of the premises underlying the writing of *Bagatelles*. For Céline, *Bagatelles* is a counterdiscourse, opposing a Jewish hegemonic discourse based on an assumed social, cultural, economic, and political domination by Jews, in France and throughout most of the world. Céline writes: "[The Jew] owns everything... the Press... the Theatre... the Radio... the Parliament... the Senate... the Police" (B, 45). A manifestation of that dominance, of the menace posed by international Jewry, was the coming to power in France in 1936 of a Popular Front government, headed by a Jew, Léon Blum, and supported by the French Communist Party, a party that Céline links to the Russian revolution, which he claimed was funded and led by Jews for the benefit of their own interests. If Blum's assumption of political power is one of the events that sanctions the writing of *Bagatelles*—Céline describes Blum as the "leader of a Jewish army invading France" (96)—the other is Hitler's ascendency to the German Chancellory in January 1933. "I would like to make an alliance with Hitler," Céline notes, "he does not like the Jews and neither do I" (317). "I would prefer twelve Hitlers," Céline concludes, "to one omnipotent Blum" (318).

In order to discredit Renoir's film, Céline will attempt, as my analysis will demonstrate, to show that its positive treatment of the Jew is a politically motivated deception, that the plot of the film is, in reality, but a ploy to conceal the advancement of an underlying plot: a Jewish conspiracy to achieve worldwide domination. As a means of deconstructing Céline's argument, I will place it within three interrelated contexts. First, I will briefly describe the conditions under which the Popular Front government arose, its concerns, and some of its accomplishments. Second, I will situate Renoir with respect to his ideological orientation and provide an analysis of *La Grande Illusion* that will serve as a necessary background for Céline's review of the film. Third, and most important, I will examine Céline's critique of *La Grande Illusion*, his attempt to decipher its plot as Jewish conspiracy, within the framework of the anti-Semitic tenets that shape *Bagatelles*.

My treatment of *Bagatelles* will perforce be partial. As Paul J. Kingston has noted in his *Anti-Semitism in France during The 1930s* (1983), what distinguishes *Bagatelles* from the abundant anti-Semitic literature of the period is its criticism of the French character and of French institutions (103). Such elements are not relevant to my demonstration, nor does their presence alter the essentially anti-Semitic nature of the pamphlet (Céline implicates the Jew in all of these criticisms, as a contributing factor or as a beneficiary of such deficiencies). Alice Yaeger Kaplan has shown in her *Relevé des sources et citations dans* Bagatelles pour un massacre (1987) how extensively

Céline borrowed from existing anti-Semitic literature (a literature that is, by definition, highly intertextual), to which he had access at various documentation centers that were clearing houses for anti-Semitic materials.[4] Finally, as a Jew, I should acknowledge that I may be biased in my reading of a work such as *Bagatelles*. I will leave that judgment to the reader.

Greeted with revolutionary fervor by its adherents, the Popular Front government was a short-lived experiment that lasted but two years: June 6, 1936, to April 8, 1938. Blum's resignation as prime minister on June 22, 1937, after just a year in office, marked the rapid decline of the Popular Front's effectiveness in governing the country. When Blum returned as prime minister on March 11, 1938, he was unable to form a Popular Front ministry similar to that of 1936. He resigned three weeks later, leaving the remnants of the Popular Front to fade away in the face of the new and more intractable economic and political crises that would beset France in the late 1930s.

The Popular Front came to power for two reasons. One of these was economic. Although France had initially seemed able to weather the effects of the Great Depression, by 1932–33 there was a major downturn in the economy, along with labor unrest and a massive flight of capital. A succession of governments, most under the control of the Radical Socialists, had been unable to arrest the slide. The second reason, one that is of more immediate interest with respect to Céline and the writing of *Bagatelles*, was ideological. There was a rapid growth of French fascism in the 1930s, inspired, initially at least, more by the Italian model than the German one. Various fascist "leagues" (the Jeunesses Patriotes, Croix-de-Feu, Action Française, among others) supported by right-wing veterans groups and by a strident right-wing press, became increasingly prominent. In general, they were nationalistic, anticommunist, antiparliamentarian, and anti-Semitic. For such organizations, democratic republicanism was politically and morally bankrupt, The Stavisky affair (that Céline recalled in his review of *La Grande Illusion*) provided additional grist for their mills. Stavisky, a Ukrainian Jew and naturalized French citizen, had been involved in a variety of fraudulent financial schemes, apparently with the connivance of important political figures. In December 1933, he was implicated in the issuing of phony bonds to finance the Municipal Pawnshop of Bayonne. When he supposedly committed suicide in January 1934, the Right claimed he had been killed by the police to cover up the complicity of government officials in the scandal. On February 6, 1934, various elements of the leagues attacked the Chamber of Deputies in an ill-planned effort to seize control of the government. In the ensuing street battles, involving the police and combatants drawn from across the political spectrum, several people were killed and hundreds injured.

The growing fascist menace in France and elsewhere had led to a change in the policy of international communism, which enabled local communist parties to cooperate with other political groups in their struggles against that danger, thus making possible an alliance between socialists and communists. In June 1935, ten leftist organizations met to plan an antifascist march for Bastille Day. Following the success of that demonstration, a Comité National du Rassemblement Populaire was formed to prepare for the elections of 1936. In that election, the three principal parties on the Left, the communists, the socialists, and the radical republicans, easily won the majority of seats. Léon Blum, the parliamentary leader of the socialists and again, a Jew, was called upon to head this coalition Popular Front government. The communists refrained from taking any of the cabinet posts in order to oppose the government if necessary and to assuage fears that the election of the Popular Front government would be the first step in a communist revolution.

Most of the major social legislation of the Popular Front was passed during the first months following its accession to power. The Matignon Accords put a temporary end to labor unrest by raising salaries and establishing collective bargaining procedures. Workers were granted a forty-hour work week as well as a two-week paid vacation (reforms that Céline will condemn in *Bagatelles* as leading to a further aggravation of France's problem with alcoholism). The Popular Front government also nationalized war-related industries and restructured the Bank of France.[5]

One of the goals of the Popular Front government was to restore a sense of republicanism to the country and, notably, to the working class. One means of creating that support was to bring French culture to the masses. The central role in this effort was played by the Communist Party. In *The Popular Front in France: Defending Democracy, 1934–38*, Robert Jackson notes that "to the extent we can talk of a Popular Front cultural doctrine, it was largely the creation of the Communist Party" (1988, 118). Nowhere was this notion of a Popular Front cultural ideology, as filtered through the organizations established by the Communist Party, more manifest than in the domain of the cinema, the vehicle par excellence of popular culture. The chief spokesperson as creator and propagandist in this cultural arena during this period was Jean Renoir.

"Saint Renoir does not exist, has never existed," Claude Gauteur has commented in *Jean Renoir: La Double Méprise* (1980, 9). The image of Jean Renoir that emerged in the years following the war as a disinterested humanist, disseminated by many of his critics and by the director himself, is blatantly false for the mid-1930s. Renoir was politically involved with the Left as a critic and as a director—and perceived as such. "In the eyes of the Right," Gauteur notes, "he was the official film director of the Communist Party" (45). In *The Social Cinema of Jean Renoir*, Christopher Faulkner concurs. During the period 1936–38, in film as well as in print, Renoir was, according to Faulkner, a "known and energetic supporter of the [Communist] Party" (1986, 79). Hence, one can argue that in the heated, divisive political climate of France during the years in question, to attack Renoir's films was tantamount to opposing the political ideology with which he was most closely identified—in our context, the Popular Front government of Léon Blum, with its Communist Party support.

Renoir was never a member of the Communist Party, despite his participation in such communist-supported publications as *Ciné-Liberté* (the magazine published by the organization that had helped to produce *La Vie est à nous* [*The People of France*] in 1936; Renoir was president of its cine-club), *Ce Soir, La Commune,* and *L'Humanité.* Georges Sadoul wrote in the September 24, 1936, issue of *L'Humanité* (the official communist daily): "The people of our country deeply love Jean Renoir because they know that this great artist is their . . . sincere devoted friend. . . . We are happy that Renoir is one of us."[6]

Before analyzing Céline's critique of the film, it would be useful to look briefly at *La Grande Illusion*, focusing our attention on those aspects of the film that are emphasized in the review. In its depiction of French soldiers and aviators captured and interned by the Germans during World War I, the film centers on two sets of relationships. One of these pairs consists of a French aristocrat, Captain de Boeldieu (played by Pierre Fresnay), and his German counterpart, Captain von Rauffenstein (Erich von Stroheim). The second couple involves an aviator—a mechanic in civilian life—Lieutenant Maréchal (Jean Gabin) and a Jewish soldier, no rank given—a member of a wealthy family, himself the owner of a superb country manor, Rosenthal (Marcel Dalio). Von Rauffenstein, an aviator, shoots down the plane Maréchal is piloting, from which de Boeldieu, a member of the General Staff, had been observing the front. When the Germans seize the Frenchmen, von Rauffenstein and de Boeldieu find they have much in common as fellow members of European aristocratic society. This acquaintanceship will be renewed when, after spending time in several German prison camps owing to his repeated attempts to escape, de Boeldieu finds himself in a camp run by von Rauffenstein. The latter, much to his chagrin, has become a "policeman" after several plane crashes have rendered him unfit for further service as an aviator. His burned and broken body is encased in a neck brace and steel corset. At this same prison camp Maréchal, who had also made several attempts to escape, will be reunited with Rosenthal whom he had met earlier.

The two aristocrats represent a world of privilege and mannered elegance from which men like Maréchal and Rosenthal are excluded. Appropriate to the location of the camp, the medieval fortress of Wintershorn, von Rauffenstein's medical accouterments, which further stiffen his aristocratic Prussian demeanor, resemble the suits of armor housed in the chateau. They, like he, are anachronisms in the modern world. Indeed, as the film indicates, and as de Boeldieu recognizes, aristocrats will have no place in the new society that the changes effected by the war are producing. Because officers were traditionally drawn from the nobility (warfare has historically been a proper aristocratic activity), both men are the bearers of a military tradition that is assumed to be disappearing with them. There is, however, a crucial difference between von Rauffenstein and de Boeldieu. The latter is aware of his obsolescence and of what Maréchal and Rosenthal represent for the future, whereas von Rauffenstein clings to the old order. Thus, when he is searching the prisoners' quarters for materials that could be used in an escape attempt, von Rauffenstein is willing to accept de Boeldieu's "word of honor" that he is not hiding anything.[7] But when de Boeldieu asks him why he would not accept similar verbal assurances from the other prisoners, von Rauffenstein scoffs at the notion of the "word of honor of a Rosenthal or of a Maréchal."

De Boeldieu validates his point of view by sacrificing himself so that his two comrades can escape. He creates a diversion, and, in so doing, forces von Rauffenstein to shoot him. His last words to von Rauffenstein indicate that his death has been consonant with the responsibilities of their class: "For a man of the people it is terrible to die in war. For you and me, it's a good solution."

If, in Renoir's view, individuals such as von Rauffenstein and de Boeldieu have become an anachronism in a new society that values achievement rather than privileged birth, in which there is no class antagonism—and one can think of the Popular Front government as attempting to foster this democratic ideal—Rosenthal is, paradoxically perhaps, their heir. He shares the food packages his wealthy family sends him, packages that reveal his sophisticated tastes in food and drink. He is proud that having been French for only one generation, he has already acquired the kinds of properties that were once identified with the aristocracy.

One might object to the film's portrayal of Rosenthal as verging on the sort of stereotypical image in which the anti-Semites trafficked— the wealthy Jew, protected by his money from the harsh realities of the war, who has assumed the guise of a French aristocrat. What saves the depiction of Rosenthal from becoming an anti-Semitic cliché is that Rosenthal himself makes no effort to hide his religion and expresses a critical self-awareness of his Jewishness and his privileged position. As such, he is accepted as an ordinary person by the others, and notably Maréchal, the typical ordinary Frenchman. When Maréchal thanks Rosenthal for the food parcels he has shared with his fellow prisoners, the latter both avows his Jewishness and apologizes for his coreligionists: "The crowd [i.e., non-Jews] believes that our great fault is avarice. A serious error! We are often generous. Alas, Jehovah has amply bestowed upon us the sin of pride." But Maréchal insists, without mentioning religion, that Rosenthal is a "great guy" and a "good buddy," a judgment that is based strictly on merit.

Maréchal is, however, a product of his society and not without anti-Jewish prejudice. When, in the course of their escape, Maréchal and Rosenthal are crossing the German countryside on their way to the Swiss border, Rosenthal sprains his ankle and thereby slows their progress. The two men quarrel and separate. As Maréchal walks off, he tells Rosenthal that he has become a "ball and chain" that he can no longer drag about, and then he adds, "I've never been able to stomach Jews." Rosenthal, surprised by his friend's comment, can only reply, "it's a bit late to realize that." But Maréchal returns to help his companion, and together they manage to drag themselves to a nearby farm, where they are sheltered by a German war widow. Rosenthal helps make a *crèche* for the Christmas celebration, commenting that Jesus is his "racial brother." Later, when the two men resume their journey to Switzerland and are faced with the imminent prospect of being separated, Maréchal tells Rosenthal, "goodbye, dirty Jew," and the latter affectionately replies, "goodbye old chap." It is obvious that Maréchal can playfully use a common anti-Jewish epithet with Rosenthal as a sign of their genuine friendship.

The viewer may wonder whether the relationship between Maréchal and Rosenthal is no less an illusion than the disappearance of class conflict, of artificial national boundaries, of the need for war. The experience they have shared has perhaps been utopian, a moment outside of time, outside of history. Once they return to the reality of the war—or of peace—will traditional class and religious differences irremediably separate them? Will they no longer perceive themselves as united by what Renoir calls in *My Life and My Films* the "common humanity of men" (1974b, 148)?[8]

Why did Céline write *Bagatelles pour un massacre*? He had given relatively limited expression to his anti-Semitic views in his earlier writings. The publication of a 379-page "pamphlet" that denounces the Jews as responsible for the social, political, economic, and cultural decline of Western civilization, as a parasitic race insinuating itself into an otherwise healthy Aryan social body and weakening its host in order to enslave it, as the masterminds of an international conspiracy bent on world domination, represents the author's public commitment to and expression of an ideology that was, at least implicitly, an incitement to persecution and destruction. Céline would subsequently claim that he had never "urged anti-Semitic persecution" but, rather, had protested "against certain Semitic clans who were pushing us into war" (HER, 483). Such self-serving protests are at best a grand delusion to which even the most cursory reading of *Bagatelles* readily attests.

François Gibault, Céline's principle biographer, writes in his preface to the seventh volume of the *Cahiers Céline* that Céline was prompted to write *Bagatelles* by two related factors. One of these was a "failure of inspiration." Céline had exhausted the autobiographical materials—except for his London experiences, which would be reflected in *Guignol's Band*, published in 1944—that served as a necessary point of departure for his fictions and had been dejected by the harsh critical treatment accorded to his second novel, *Mort à crédit* (1936). The second factor that Gibault posits is political rather than literary in nature—Céline's desire to take part in the ideological struggles that were polarizing France: "Witness to a world struck by insanity, he was consumed by the desire to take part in the struggle of ideas, not as a member of a party or a group but, as he was wont to do, as a solitary figure, as a lone knight." Gibault notes that Céline had traveled to "fascist Italy" in 1925, to a "decomposing Germany" in 1932, to Nazi Germany in 1935, and, finally, to the Soviet Union in 1936 (CC7, 6–8), choices that reflect a growing involvement with an increasingly turbulent political world.

Although Gibault may be accurate in his account of some of the circumstances that may have precipitated the writing of *Bagatelles*, his remarks suggest the absence of any continuity between Céline's earlier writings and the pamphlet in question. A number of Céline's critics, among them Philippe Alméras, Patrick McCarthy, and Nicholas Hewitt, have demonstrated various connections between the earlier works and *Bagatelles*.[9] One can, of course, readily point to the "farce" that constitutes the third act of *L'Eglise* ("farce" means "stuffing" in French and recalls the practice, dating from the middle ages, of inserting a comic interlude into an otherwise serious play). That segment of the play depicts the League of Nations, the international agency for which Céline had once worked, as directed by and used for the profit of the Jews.[10] In *Bagatelles*, he refers to the League of Nations as the "greatest Synagogue in the greatest Masonic Temple of the universe" (98),[11] an instrument of the worldwide Jewish conspiracy.

One can also recall *Mea Culpa*, Céline's "report" of what he observed during his 1936 trip to the Soviet Union. *Mea Culpa* makes a passing comment about the Jews having benefited from the revolution. However, as Nicholas Hewitt notes, in *Bagatelles* Céline "transposes" *Mea Culpa* into a "personal account" (1987, 141–42), discoursing at length about his experiences in a Soviet Union run by the Jews after they had successfully masterminded and led the revolution. It is Céline's image of the Jew that links Blum, Hitler, and the Soviet Union,[12] a connection that plays a crucial role in Céline's condemnation of Renoir's *La Grande Illusion*. In terms of Céline's anti-Semitic politics, "Jew and Communist are synonymous" and "democracy is a screen for Jewish dictatorship" (51).

The point of the departure for *Bagatelles* is the refusal to produce two of Céline's ballets: *La Naissance d'une fée* ("The Birth of a Fairy") by the Paris Opera and *Voyou Paul, Brave Virginie* ("Hoodlum Paul. Good Virginia") by the Paris International Exposition of 1937, an exposition that served as a showpiece for the Popular Front government. In both cases Céline blamed the Jews for this rejection of his works. In the first instance, he supposedly could not find a "well-connected Jew" (27) to furnish the music. As for the second instance, he claims that his ballet was turned down by the "racist Jews" (40) running the "Jewish Exposition" (29). "Nothing is for the French," he states, "everything is for the kikes" (40). These refusals were presumably anticipated by the Jewish critics—"criticism is a famous undercover agency of the Jews" (15)—who had excoriated the author of *Mort à crédit* "as a plagiarist of bathroom graffiti" (14). There is a third refusal, one that is recounted later in *Bagatelles*, after Céline's review of Renoir's film. During the course of his stay in Soviet Russia, Céline submits *La Naissance d'une fée* to the Marinski theatre in Leningrad. The ballet is rebuffed supposedly because it is insufficiently "sozial" (sic, 351)—not an example of social realism. However, Céline has already noted that the front rows of the theatre are occupied by "Jews with glasses" (346) and that the director of the theatre is a "weasel-faced Jew" (349). The reader of the pamphlet cannot help but draw the obvious conclusion that, once again, Céline has been a victim of the Jews—thus linking Paris and Leningrad in terms of Jewish influence. It should be noted that there is no supporting documentary evidence to substantiate that the author ever submitted his ballets to any of the entities in question, thus opening to question his claims of persecution stemming from these presumed three rejections. As if to reinforce for the reader that he has been a target of Jewish prejudice as well as to assert the value of his ballets, Céline frames *Bagatelles* by placing the two rejected ballets close to the beginning of his text and closes it with a third ballet, *Van Bagaden*.

Céline's point of departure serves two important functions. First, he portrays himself as personally victimized by the Jews and thus justifies the writing of the pamphlet as a counterattack against his oppressors. As Paul Bleton, reading Céline's mind, notes: "My suffering is exemplary in that it is not only an *illustration* of the maliciousness of the Jews but it legitimizes my anti-Semitism" (318). Second, Céline distinguishes himself from Jean Renoir, who, he implies, succeeded in having *his* work produced by virtue of his support of the Popular Front's pro-Jewish ideology. In his review of *La Grande Illusion*, Céline never mentions Renoir's name as the director of the film and coauthor (with Charles Spaak) of its scenario: It is the Popular Front, he claims, that is "the creator of this thing" (270). His use of the denigrating term "thing" (chose) suggests that *La Grande Illusion* is some ill-conceived piece of propaganda and that its very existence is a product of the larger Jewish conspiracy that turned down the ballets.

As I have noted, the cinema, given its mass appeal, was perceived as an excellent vehicle for the dissemination of Frontist ideology. *Bagatelles* is replete with derogatory remarks about cinema, particularly in the section of the text that precedes the review of *La Grande Illusion*. Although Céline's vituperations are directed for the most part against Hollywood, they are meant to serve as a condemnation of cinematic culture in general as a propaganda weapon in the hands of the Jews. Suffice it to say that Hollywood is an easy target for such attacks given the well-known presence of Jews in the film industry. It is not surprising that Céline fails to mention his own visit to Hollywood in July 1934, when he sought to have *Voyage au bout de la nuit* made into a film. Nor does he mention the publication of a short story that he conceived as a potential film scenario, *Secrets dans l'île* ("Island Secrets") in 1936. In *Bagatelles* he speaks of "Jewish Hollywood" (52); of Jews as the "origin of all cinema" (222), controlling every aspect of the industry; of the use of movie stars as instruments for the "colonization of the world by the Jews" (222). "All films," Céline concludes, "French, English, American . . . exist and are propagated for the greater glory of Israel" and to "stupefy the goy" (222), and thus they show the faults of the non-Jews but fail to reveal the true nature of the Jews as "voracious, larval, and vulturine" (226).

Having condemned the cinema in general as an instrument of Jewish propaganda, Céline begins his review of *La Grande Illusion* with a justificatory statement that he restricts to the French situation. Given that the Jews have "doubled their exactions since the coming to power of the Popular Front" (268), it is not surprising, Céline asserts, that there has been a concomitant increase in anti-Semitism, which has then prompted a pro-Jewish counteroffensive from the Jewish-controlled cinema. *La Grande Illusion*, Céline argues, is part of that offensive. As proof of the audacity of that effort—and what in his view most distinguishes the film—Céline offers the presentation of the "Jew as such . . . as a real, textual Jew . . . as Rosenthal" (268).

The notation "textual" suggests a problem of reading—of Céline's reading of the film and the sociopolitical text that serves as its (con)text. He contrasts the term "textual" with "symbols," "insinuations," "allusions," (268) as well as with "shadow" and "disguise" (125). One of the assumptions underlying Céline's reading of both texts is that they must be deciphered for the unenlightened; their figurative language ("symbols," "allusions," etc.) must be properly interpreted so that their real—"textual"—meaning can be revealed. What must be shown is the occulted presence and dominance of the Jews. As Céline puts it: "To signal the mark, the trace, the ascendancy, the initiative of the Jews in all the upheavals of the world . . . to pierce . . . through all the labyrinths of the phrasemakers . . . behind all the grimaces [so as to demonstrate] the implacable, conquering Jewish megalomania" (125). Hence, Céline the writer-turned-reader must discern the "figure" (in Genette's sense of the term) of the Jew, collapse its "space" (between signifier and signified) and, in so doing, reveal its "motivation" in terms of an underlying plot, a Jewish world conspiracy.[13] Both *Bagatelles* and the sociopolitical text are thus palimpsests. It would seem, therefore, that *La Grande Illusion*, by presenting the "textual" Jew, endangers the pamphleteer's task and menaces the rationale for his writing/reading. If that is indeed the case, then Céline must somehow recontextualize the Jew, so that the latter can be reinterpreted as figure.

Céline must therefore question what sort of Jew the film presents and, in particular, whether the friendship between Maréchal and Rosenthal can be predicated, as the film implies, on the assumption that the Jew can be "a man like any other man" (271). Such a question (and the negative answer it implies) touches on one of the dynamics of anti-Semitism. In *Toward a Definition of Anti-Semitism*, Gavin Langmuir has analyzed anti-Semitism in terms of cognitive group relationships in an attempt to demystify and demythify it as a special form of prejudice, distinct in nature from other types of prejudice. Langmuir himself acknowledges that such an effort may not necessarily prove effective, given the particular historical development of anti-Semitism. Nonetheless, the set of definitions he develops to describe group prejudices are useful in our present context. "Realistic assertions," Langmuir writes, are propositions that treat an outgroup (such as the Jews)—the collectivity as well as the individuals therein—in ways that are indistinguishable from the treatment accorded the in-group; "xenophobic assertions" are propositions that attribute a socially menacing conduct to the outgroup that are empirically based on the conduct of a small minority of the outgroup; "chimerical assertions" are propositions that attribute characteristics to an outgroup and its individual members that have no empirical basis" (1990, 327–28). Langmuir further notes that "xenophobic assertions" seem to be reactions to "ill-understood menaces to social organization," whereas "chimerical assertions" seem to be a reaction to "ill-understood menaces to individual psychic integration" (338). The anti-Semitism in *Bagatelles* is based for the most part on a systematic slippage from xenophobic to chimerical assertions. For example, it is xenophobic to complain that because Jews occupy important positions in society in numbers that are disproportionate to their percentage of the population, they will tend to favor other Jews. It is chimerical to assert that such positions of power are a manifestation of a world-wide conspiracy to transform the non-Jewish population into mindless slaves. Chimerical assertions may contradict xenophobic ones. If the Jews are subhuman, as Céline asserts, how could they possibly attain the influence they are purported to have?

In his review of the film, Céline necessarily has recourse to chimerical assertions to refute the perception that the Jew can be a "man like any other" by denying that the Jew is as human as the Aryan. Earlier in *Bagatelles*, he had raised the question of the Jew's humanness in similar terms. He notes that "for the [common] people a Jew is a man like any other" (127). Céline then proceeds to negate such a possibility with respect to the moral qualities that he maintains are inherent to his subject. The "treachery," "racism," "mendacity," and "rapacity" Céline ascribes to the Jews transcend in degree what non-Jews are capable of attaining—they are "infinite," "prodigious," "implacable" (127). In this respect, one might say that the Jews are, according to Céline, superhuman. But it is ultimately biology, based on a chimerical geographical determination, that separates the Jew as a subhuman from the rest of Aryan humanity. Although Céline does not reiterate his pseudoscientific ethnology as such in the review, it is one of its premises, based on earlier elaborations. However, the conclusion of the review in which he refers to the "Mongolo-kikes" (274) forcing France into a war with Germany by 1940 recalls previous statements regarding the origins of the Jews and thus their irredeemable defects.

In *Bagatelles* we find the north-versus-south polarity that is a familiar theme in Céline's fiction. The warmer, more primitive south is associated with an intellectual, perceptual, and cultural inferiority as opposed to the cooler, more intelligent, sensitive, and cultivated north. The zero point on the southern axis is Africa. Céline does not situate the origin of the Jews in the Middle East; he places it in sub-Saharan Africa, thus equating the Jews not with Caucasian Semitic peoples but with negroes. Given Céline's assumption that the latter are primitive, uncultured, and subhuman savages, Céline can "confuse" them with the Jews: "The Jew is a negro, the Semitic race does not exist, it's an invention of the Freemasons" (191–92). He reinforces this racism by adding an Asian component to his geographical determinism, associating the Jews with the Asiatic hordes that have historically ravaged parts of Europe: "The Jew is but the product of a crossing of negroes and barbaric Asians" (192). Given such origins, Jews have "nerves of zinc" (192) and are thus incapable of having the "spontaneous emotional sense" (194) that would permit them to respond to Céline's writings, his "emotional subway." Hence, the rejection of Céline's ballets by the Jews could have no valid aesthetic basis and, by extension, no work that would appeal to Jews, such as *La Grande Illusion*, could be authentic.

Céline's second argument that Rosenthal, as Jew, cannot be a "man like any other" is founded upon racio-political premises. The only basis for a relationship between a wealthy Jew and a proletarian would have to be predicated, according to Céline, upon an illusion on the part of the proletarian and a deception on the part of the Jew. For Céline, this sort of "friendship" has a dangerous historical precedent—the Russian revolution.

Céline begins his analysis of the film by posing what he perceives as a fundamental contradiction in *La Grande Illusion*. How can Rosenthal be at once a "perfect millionaire" and a "perfect man of the people" (269)? He compares Rosenthal to the swindler Stavisky and notes that *L'Humanité* would consider someone like Rosenthal "the enemy incarnate of the people" and an odious example of "vampiristic capitalism" (269). He then wonders how, given Rosenthal's attributes, *La Grande Illusion* could resolve such "incompatibilities" (270). He inflates Rosenthal's virtues as he ironically extols him, portraying him as a kind of "Messiah" (an epithet that may reflect Rosenthal's remark in the film about Jesus having been a Jew), committed to ushering in a new world "without inequalities, without wars, without privileges on the basis of race or birth" (271). All these qualities would thus unite Jewish millionaire and proletarian—"systole of the worker, diastole of the Jew... ventricle against ventricle" (271).

Céline's irony is meant, of course, to convey the notion that no reconciliation between a wealthy Jew, and by extension any Jew, and a proletarian is possible; their hearts cannot beat as one. He also associates Rosenthal with a group of "terrific proletarians like Mssrs. Warburg, Loeb, Jacob Schiff, Kerensky, Trotsky, Zaharoff and Blum" (271). The first three are Jewish-American bankers whom Céline accuses of financing the Russian revolution. The second group of three were principal figures in the revolution, all of whom had Jewish origins. Placing Blum in their company ties him as a Jew and as the leader of the Popular Front government—the so-called creator of *La Grande Illusion*—to the Russian revolution.

Throughout *Bagatelles* Céline maintains that the Russian revolution was funded and orchestrated by the Jews for the benefit of Jewish interests, a chimerical assertion advanced by conservatives in Russia and elsewhere at the time of the revolution and that had become a staple of anti-Semitic literature. "The triumph of the Bolshevik revolution can only be conceived in the long run," Céline proclaims, "with the Jews, for the Jews, and by the Jews" (50). For Céline, the Russian revolution is not merely a local phenomenon but is part of a larger "world conspiracy" (50), and in postulating the friendship between a Jew and a proletarian, *La Grande Illusion* is furthering that conspiracy.

Céline also addresses the film's treatment of the aristocracy. As noted, one of the film's major themes is the demise of the old aristocracy in the face of the reordering of society that will emerge from the war. For Céline, the "enthusiasm" with which the two aristocrats "justify" the "decree of death that condemns them" is one of the "hits" of the film (272). If indeed, as Céline seems to believe, the aristocracy favored war, then its demise is significant. But his interpretation of history differs radically from the progressive view that Renoir espouses. Céline's conception of history, at least in *Bagatelles*, is scientific, in that history, as he tirelessly reiterates, has been shaped by the struggle for dominance between Jew and Aryan, and by an ongoing conspiracy on the part of the Jew to seize power. In that struggle, the aristocracy has been used as an instrument of Jewish imperialism: "The aforementioned aristocracy, abundantly married to and allied with Jewish banks, is but, in truth, one of Jewry's tribes" (272). Céline implies that with their new power, as manifested by the Popular Front government, the Jews can replace the aristocracy by acting in their own name— Rosenthal replaces de Boeldieu. The end result is still the same: wars that are fomented by Jews to serve their own interests.

Céline's conception of history is one of the chief elements that shapes his review of *La Grande Illusion*. Just as his perception of the cinema as an instrument of Jewish propaganda introduces his review, the review itself is followed by two historical "analyses" that complete it, as it were. One of these analyses deals with Jewish involvement in the Russian revolution. The other concerns a "Jewish" document that serves to validate Céline's view of history as Jewish conspiracy: *The Protocols of the Elders of Zion*, the best-known anti-Semitic document of the period, which even today remains popular and widely available throughout the world.

Céline's introduction to reading the *Protocols* recalls his preamble to reading the "text" of *La Grande Illusion*. Whereas *La Grande Illusion* seems to be "textual" but is in effect "symbolic" when viewed as masking a Jewish plot for worldwide domination, the *Protocols* seem "symbolic" (too fanciful to be true, a fiction rather than an objective historical document) but are "textual" when examined in the light of historical events, notably the Russian revolution. He states: "It is the evolution of things which has come to impose itself, geometrically, miraculously, on such nightmares" (277). I have referred to Céline's reading of the film as a palimpsest. The *Protocols* would, analogously, constitute a kind of ur-text that the film seeks to overwrite and Céline wishes to uncover.

According to Norman Cohn, whose *Warrant for Genocide* (1967) is the definitive study of the *Protocols*, the document was concocted in

Paris by agents of the Russian Secret Police for the benefit of Russian anti-Semites at the turn of the century. It was first published in a St. Petersburg newspaper in 1903 (Céline gives 1902) and then appeared in book form in 1905. It became popular at the time of the Russian revolution when it was widely circulated in order to discredit the Bolsheviks as agents of a Jewish conspiracy. The *Protocols*, a series of twenty-four lectures (the number varies according to the edition), are presented as the minutes of a secret meeting held during the first World Zionist Conference in Basel in 1897. Roger Lambelin, a well-known anti-Semitic writer, authored the first French translation in 1920. A year later, the *Protocols* were shown to be a forgery, derived largely from an obscure novel by Maurice Joly, published in 1864 and entitled *The Dialogues in Hell between Machiavelli and Montesquieu*, in which the author denounces the autocratic policies of Napoléon III (Machiavelli). The anti-Semites who had greeted the publication of the document so enthusiastically simply ignored the evidence that condemned it as a fraud. In the *Protocols*, which Céline quotes extensively, an Elder of Zion, a member of the clandestine international Jewish government, reveals before a group of representatives to the Conference an elaborate, long-term plot to undermine Aryan societies through such strategies as political liberalism, the control of capital, subversion of Christian morality, and manipulation of the masses through the written word and systems of education. Ultimately, out of this turmoil there will emerge an all-encompassing Jewish tyranny. If what the *Protocols* say is true, and *Bagatelles* indicates that such is the case, then *La Grande Illusion* must be, as Céline would have it, more than just a "Grand Illusion" but "the most supremely magnificent Illusion" (274).

It would be appropriate to leave the last word on Céline's review of *La Grande Illusion* to Jean Renoir himself. He responded to Céline's criticism of the film on January 20, 1938, in one of the weekly articles he wrote for *Ce Soir*, documents that Claude Gauteur (1980) has compiled. Having been informed of what Céline had written about his film, Renoir states that he purchased a copy of *Bagatelles* but did not read the review, having found, after perusing the first few pages of the book, that Céline's "crude language" (147) had become too tedious for him to continue reading. A friend then volunteered to spend the night reading the whole volume and to inform Renoir (who was present for part of the session) of what Céline had said about the film. Renoir refutes Céline's claim that *La Grande Illusion* was a work of Jewish propaganda and insists that it was not made for the benefit of anyone in particular. He was able, he relates, to dissuade some angry friends from giving Céline a "spanking" (147). He concludes the article by recalling that if in *Bagatelles* Céline labels so many artists Jewish, including Cézanne and Racine, then he can take consolation in having found himself in such "good company" (148).

▼

Céline's
Masquerade

▼

THE ASPECT OF Céline's writing that has generated the most controversy—his anti-Semitism—is, in the final analysis, its most commonplace. His century and his generation were as spontaneously anti-Semitic as they were misogynist. In my French thesis on Céline's ideology (1987), I availed myself of a plentiful supply of references to Jewishness made by his contemporaries; from Apollinaire to Siménon by way of Clément Vautel (a writer now long forgotten but who was more popular and widely read in his day than all the others combined). They spoke of Jews as they spoke of blacks, with condescension and scorn, but without any of the paternalism shown the latter; much as earlier generations denigrated peasants, whose designation *villain* (derived from *villanus* but confused with *vilis*) has become synonymous with "criminal" in English.

Although anti-Semitism was unquestionably widespread during the period in which the young Destouches was coming of age, it was not yet one of the touchstones of the divide between Right and Left. For instance, Jules Renard, a republican, secularist, and Dreyfusard, condemned Claudel's anti-Semitism ("He relies on his abhorrence of the Jews, whom he can neither see nor stand"),[1] while elsewhere stating: "We are all anti-Semites. Some of us have the gallantry or coyness not to flaunt it."[2] It is important to recognize that the "neither see nor stand" Renard attributes to Claudel is not meant in any physical sense. Rather, it implies a moral aversion that Renard recognized in himself and claimed to share with his peers: Parisian writers and intellectuals who would not admit they were anti-Semites for anything in the world.

André Gide, the period's preeminent literary figure, displayed this type of anti-Semitism time and again. Having convinced himself that there was such a thing as "Jewish literature," he provided examples and underscored its flaws and excesses. Gide places these deficiencies on exhibition in the writing he has his character Bernstein practice in the *Journal*, a work published on the eve of World War II, when being Jewish (or anti-Jewish) had taken on new significance. For Gide, the term *Jew* always signified a difference in mentality to which he opposed his own values, those of the *N.R.F.* (the *Nouvelle Revue Française*) that entailed notions of rigor, balance, decorum, discretion, and precision of language.[3]

A recent study by Marc Crapez (1991) goes so far as to suggest that from the outset, European racism and socialism were closely affiliated. Crapez provides convincing evidence of anti-Semitic sentiments expressed in the writings of socialism's founding fathers, including Fourier, Proudhon, de Toussenel, Tridon, and Vacher de Lapouge (a writer to whom Céline had at one time thought of devoting an essay). Seen from this historical and cultural perspective, Céline, the inventor of "Labiche Communism" (BD, 137),[4] was not entirely off the mark in casting himself as the scapegoat of his society and his times. He had merely said and written what others had said and written. He had been read and actually acclaimed for his anti-Semitic writing. And yet, he alone was relegated to the wastelands of Denmark in the aftermath of World War II's catastrophic destruction.

The commonality, which is not to say complicity, between Céline and his contemporaries has been difficult for his younger generation of critics to fathom. It has required a feat of mental reframing to comprehend that the apparent contradiction between subject matter, popular style, and racist thought was not a burning issue in Céline's day, and that what was banal and widely agreed upon in the past is inconceivable today. In the period between 1932 and 1945, on both the political Left and Right, one simply did not balk at things that are so astonishing to readers who have been formed by postwar ideology and who are acutely aware of the events of the war. For instance, I believe I was the first to point out three words that more than a few readers of Céline's first novel, *Voyage au bout de la nuit*, have consistently overlooked. The passage is located near the beginning of the novel:

While the war was still on, the seeds of our hateful peace were being sown.
  A hysterical bitch, you could see what she'd be like just by watching her cavorting in the dance hall of the Olympia. In that long cellar room, you could see her squinting out of a hundred mirrors, stamping her feet in the dust and despair to the music of a Negro-Judeo-Saxon band. (J, 59)

The phrase "Negro-Judeo-Saxon" that insinuates itself so breezily into the narrative is nonetheless disconcerting. That Céline would invoke black music is quite understandable, as at the time "Black ballet" (le Ballet nègre) was very much in vogue. But Jewish music? This is as puzzling as his earlier reference to "orientalo-Fragonard" eyes (J, 44). The adjective "Judeo" has a false ring to it, but no more so than the "Negro-Judeo-Saxon" composite that exceeds standard anti-Semitic discourse at both ends of the formula.

The "Saxon" reference is quite significant, because it points directly to the United States where from 1927 on, Céline the medical doctor, whom Ford was supposed to have employed for a time (factually inaccurate but symbolically meaningful), derived a good many of his pet racial ideas. The jazz reverberating in *Voyage*'s Olympia dance hall is indeed black and (Anglo-) Saxon; it is viewed as the product of cultural miscegenation. A coupling of despair and optimism, it is spasmodic and cheerless. The post–World War I period was indeed very much influenced by American jazz. In seeking to understand its transatlantic transmission and reception, however, it is important to keep in mind that in France, antiblack sentiment was and still is not prevalent. Although they were certainly perceived as inferior, blacks were also seen stereotypically as naive, in need of protection, and forever exploited—never exploiters. Believed to be close to the human being's animal origins, those of African descent aroused curiosity and, on occasion, a possessive attachment as the white man's "inferior brothers."

And what is to be made of the "Judeo" portion of this hyphenation? Nothing at all as far as the casual reader was concerned. Whether or not one was an intellectual, on the Left or the Right, for the typical French reader of Céline's day this was merely a fluke, a deviation from the norm at which the author of *Voyage* was known to excel—an example of one of those dissonant formulas that Sartre and de Beauvoir found so enchanting. Under scrutiny, the descriptor "Negro-Judeo-Saxon" instantly reveals the differences between Céline's anti-Semitism and that of his predecessors. Céline's prejudice can be traced to Henry Ford, the American automobile manufacturer, who launched anti-Semitic campaigns through the *Dearborn Independent,* a publication that tirelessly denounced jazz as "Nigger" music managed by New York Jews that was bent on destroying the natural rhythms of "authentic" whites; this was the same Ford, who, according to his biographers, cancelled board meetings so he could drag his colleagues off to square dances. Years of association with Ford would see to it that the specifically French anti-Semitism to which writers such as Renard and Gide subscribed gave way in Céline to his racist vision of a world inhabited by victimized whites, degenerate blacks, and insidiously corrupting Jews. Like Ford, he imagined a Nordic purity tainted by alcohol and jazz. He also saw struggles among species being waged across nations as heterogeneous as France and the United States. In his mind, it was not power and wealth that triumphed but, rather, sheer cunning. That a Jewish-American community that had resolutely boycotted his automobiles succeeded in bringing Henry Ford to his commercial knees was ample proof of this.

Many of *Voyage au bout de la nuit*'s readers are unaware of Céline's earlier work relating to these themes, most particularly his two plays *Progrès* and *L'Eglise*, both of which served as sketches for his subsequent novels. *L'Eglise*, especially its third act, outlines *Voyage*'s itinerary. The setting is Geneva and the central protagonist is Yudenzweck, whose German name signifies "the Jewish mission." Although the manuscript for *L'Eglise* has not been recovered, critics have hypothesized that the third act was actually inserted into the manuscript, composed in 1927, at the time of publication in 1933. This suggests that after the heady success *Voyage au bout de la nuit* enjoyed a year earlier, Céline felt confident enough to attack openly Ludwig Rajchman, his former superior at the League of Nations and model for the Yudenzweck character. In this section of *L'Eglise*, Yudenzweck and his accomplice Yubelblatt are seen orchestrating the operations of the international agency, exerting influence in the conflicts they were charged with mediating. If one accepts the hypothesis that the third act was added to the play well after its initial composition, then *L'Eglise* might be considered the preface to *Bagatelles pour un massacre*, which it preceded by only four years.[5] This assumes, however, that the author reworked a discarded manuscript that, except for additions made for a special edition containing the editorially censored passages of *Mort à crédit*, would be a first for Céline. Moreover, this addendum can hardly be seen as comparable to inserting an entire act into a text that had already been abandoned for some time and that Céline repeatedly characterized as a failure.

The more plausible explanation for why the Geneva episode of *L'Eglise* does not figure in *Voyage* is that when Céline changed genres, shifting from theatre to the novel, this bureaucratic interlude was dropped from the novel for reasons of internal coherence. *Voyage*'s Bardamu is a mere drifter whose adventures are surpassed in their calamity only by those of his ill-fated alter ego, Léon Robinson.

Bardamu's fellow traveller perishes before dawn while Bardamu carries on his journey to the end of night. Altering the tone as well as the genre, Céline deleted the portion of the *Eglise* scenario that amused Dr. Rajchman about as much as it seduced Gallimard's editorial board. Bardamu-*Voyage*, in contrast to Bardamu-*Eglise*, is not presented as an example to be followed. He does not stand out among his peers and possesses no secrets, power, or inscrutable truths. He is an entirely unremarkable character—a figure known in Italian as the *uomo qualunque* and in English as the *little man*—who expresses himself in everyday speech. Bardamu becomes a paradigm of ordinariness; any trait that might lend him prestige or authority is effaced. *L'Eglise*'s Geneva episode, which was appropriate to the bureaucratic setting of the play, no longer conformed to the tone and substance of the novel and was therefore removed.

Dr. Destouches continued to denounce the world in which he found himself obliged to live, and he did so by identifying with it in his fiction. The acclaim his writing won was sudden and brought him a considerable following. Some critics, most notably Claude Lévi-Strauss, read *Voyage* as the harbinger of great social change. Georges Bernanos hailed it as the advent of spirituality, whereas other, perhaps more discerning, readers, such as Léon Daudet, saw it as pure provocation. The various reactions *Voyage au bout de la nuit* elicited were thought to be fundamentally beneficial, in much the same way that revolutions are deemed liberating.

Yet, most observers overlooked one of the novel's most important messages, which the author himself had muttered to a journalist: "[The subject of the book] is ill-fated love in our time" (CC1, 31). Céline is referring here neither to Stendhal's rapture nor to Breton's crazed love (*amour fou*) but to sheer erotic pleasure liberated from all moral strictures, to unadulterated carnal desire inspired by physical perfection. It is here that Bardamu finds the ecstasy that frees him from the contingency and calamities of his bleak surroundings, that allows him to fathom a new world "right next to Lola's [American] rear end" (J, 44) and, thanks to Sophie, that sustains him through his ordeal at Dr. Baryton's clinic. Lola, Sophie, and the other feminine figures Bardamu desires are not of the "orientalo-Fragonard" type. The women who most beguile him are foreigners who act on their animal instincts without moral reservations and without the flirtatiousness, game-playing, and ulterior motives of French women such as Mme Herote. Given his obsession with biology and anatomical perfection, it is not in the least surprising that Dr. Destouches, who devoted himself in his professional life to caring for the human body, was so enamored of athletes and frequented dance studios; it provided respite from his daily palpitation of invalids, alcoholics, and the diseased, as well as from the routine business of selecting tomorrow's dead.

The controversy surrounding the Prix Goncourt for 1932, initially promised to Céline and then awarded—to the great consternation of *Voyage*'s partisans—to Guy Mazeline, did more to promote *Voyage au bout de la nuit* than twenty laudatory reviews. Journalists scrambling for information on Céline, the newcomer, discovered Dr. Destouches, a physician working in a community health clinic in the working-class suburbs of Paris. He chatted with them, and they got him to speak his mind. He expressed himself much like Bardamu, or rather, like journalists had heard Bardamu speaking. What follows is a sampling of statements about himself that Céline made to reporters following the publication of *Voyage au bout de la nuit* in:

Je suis partout:
I went and put on a nice clean shirt and worse yet, a white tie... So s[hit] gentlemen, that goes to show you what a stupid a[ss] I am. And yet I'm still one with the people, you see.[6]

Paris Soir:
I'm [a man] of the people, the real people. I worked delivering groceries all though my high school years and my first two years of college. (CC1, 22)

L'Intransigeant:
During the day I work for a living, to support my mother and two kids. . . . I am forty years old and ailing. I'm washed up. . . . The dead? I've devoured their books, milked the sacred cows [we call] the classics, by working, first with my hands, then as a soldier, to get my high school diploma. I kept this up until I got my degree in medicine. (CC1, 30–32)

Les Annales politiques et littéraires:
I was born in Asnières in 1894. My father, at first a teacher but then later dismissed, [ended up] working for the railroad; my mother was a seamstress. At age twelve, I went to work in a ribbon factory. That lasted until the war. Wounded in 1914, trepanation, medical discharge, medal of honor. During my convalescence, I studied medicine. I couldn't continue; I had to make a living. I left for Africa. (CC1, 33)

Monde:
My life interests you, right? Well, let's get to it. It's complicated by pretty much the same story when you get right down to it. My mother worked with lace; my father was the intellectual of the family. We had a small business and traveled from town to town. Things never worked out. Broke! Broke! Broke! (CC1, 35)

Judging from these quotations—presented here in the order in which they appeared in print—it would seem that Céline's fabrications accrued over time to yield the following profile: Louis Destouches was born in Asnières (false) in 1894 (true); his father, who was dismissed from his teaching position (false), worked for the railroad (false); his mother, a seamstress (false), had an itinerant small business (false) that went bankrupt several times (false). At age twelve he began working in a ribbon factory (false). He delivered groceries during high school and his first two years of college (false). He fought in the war (true), was trepanned (false), and pursued the study of medicine during his convalescence (false). He then left for Africa (true). Currently age forty (false), he was ill (false) and was working to support his mother and two children (false).

These distortions no doubt sprang from a desire on Céline's part to identify *Voyage au bout de la nuit*'s Dr. Bardamu with his creator, Dr. Destouches. Not one of the journalists covering the story bothered to verify his statements. In defense of the profession, however, it should be noted that very often Céline deliberately sought to muddy the waters. The press did not, indeed could not, have invented the trepanation, the lace-making mother, nor the ribbon factory where the young boy was fettered to his machine. Not only did the neophyte make no attempt to clear up the inaccuracies, but he compounded them. Céline accepted whatever guise he was handed, whether this meant being portrayed as a lucky devil or hapless soul living in a palace or a thatched-roof hut. And yet if one of these journalists were to have shown up at the Clichy medical clinic for an appointment, he would have encountered a very different man, one whose speech was quite refined and who had thoroughly conventional advice to offer his patients on moderation, diet, and other health concerns. Here, Dr. Destouches would have been caught off guard, his mask lifted.

If the public had great difficulty getting his life story straight, *Voyage au bout de la nuit*'s crudeness threw it into even more of a tizzy. The monarchist Léon Daudet expressed his admiration for the novel and lobbied for the Prix Goncourt alongside Lucien Descaves, a veteran pacifist and Dreyfusard closely identified with the Left. The literary Right as a whole prissily scoffed at the work's plebeian style. As noted, the great Georges Bernanos praised *Voyage* and responded in *Le Figaro* to its hostile reviewers. Everyone read the novel in his own way, came to his own conclusions, and discussed the work with others. It was a formula for success, and sales skyrocketed. No wonder the author had so little interest in revealing a countenance so greatly at odds with the one he had been given. Only recently have we had the opportunity to see a different Céline by reading the testimony of people he had not betrayed and in whom he had confided—such as Elisabeth Porquerol, Robert de Saint-Jean, or even Joseph Garcin.[7]

There were, however, several instances in which Céline found himself cornered. He seemed ill at ease carrying out Lucien Descaves's request in 1933 that he deliver a speech commemorating Emile Zola in front of the latter's former residence in Médan. Asked to fondle the relics of both naturalism and the Dreyfus Affair, Céline winced at the prospect but managed to accommodate the request by making a murky speech that focused on the limits of naturalism, the "direction of Man" and the death instinct, a notion recently pilfered from Sigmund Freud. The numerous spectators in attendance were no doubt surprised by the appearance of the poor former ribbon maker they had come to know as a sickly, wounded war veteran who was, nonetheless, an exemplary father. They found a robust and jocular Céline clad in fine wool. Photographs of the event show him leaning against Zola's house, notes in hand and a twinkle in his eyes. His restraint here was not merely an expression of common courtesy. At the time, he was still employed at the Clichy clinic by a leftist municipal government and was working under a Russian-born Jewish doctor by the name of Dr. Ichok, an individual Céline would remember when the time was right.

Whether its third act was part of the original or was tacked on later, with the 1933 publication of L'Eglise, Céline clearly ran the risk of divulging his anti-Semitism. But this is precisely where the period's prevailing anti-Jewish sentiment to which I referred comes into play. Neither Yudenzweck nor the role Céline has him play were the least bit shocking to his audience. We know that L'Eglise had at least two readers. One of them was Jean-Paul Sartre, who paid homage to Céline on the eve of World War II by opening his novel La Nausée (1938) with a quotation from the play. The epigraph was in fact drawn from the same third act in which Yudenzweck is seen manipulating world affairs at the helm of the League of Nations. Sartre took a cynical remark made by Yudenzweck in reference to Bardamu that apparently struck his fancy—"He is a guy without any collective importance, just an individual"—and gave it an emblematic status.[8] The other reader was a writer on the staff of Le Canard Enchaîné, a solidly leftist satirical newspaper.[9] The journalist in question was among those who thought the play was excellent—particularly this same Act III, which he found hilarious. To ridicule Jews by presenting a half-blind Yudenzweck sporting a Polish rabbi's mantle was not judged harshly by the Left in

1933, even after Hitler's accession to power in Germany earlier that year. Céline's caricature simply did not merit the Left's notice, much less its censure.

It took Louis Aragon (spouse of Elsa Triolet, Mayakovsky's sister-in-law and translator, who had translated *Voyage au bout de la nuit* into Russian) and his eagle eye to spot the play's rather "petty ideas about Jews."[10] But, he surmised, those ideas were not necessarily an obstacle preventing Céline from taking the right side and signing on with the anti-fascist camp. At the time, Aragon was frantically attempting to organize French intellectuals and to lead them in an "anti-fascist struggle" for the defense of the Soviet Union, sanctuary of the proletariat and promise of a new world. Doctor Elie Faure was also approached and quickly acceded. The economic crisis that struck France somewhat belatedly generally revived a social awareness that had atrophied during the prosperous years following World War I. Attempting to recruit his colleague Destouches, Faure, who had commended his achievement in *Voyage*, informed him that he, too, had an obligation to take "the side of the people." Livid, Céline-Destouches retorted that in his mind, the people didn't even exist, that they were but a "hateful, petty, factionalized horde" (HER, 73). At any rate, he wrote Faure that he had no intention of "tooting the horn of that supreme asshole, Aragon" (HER, 74). While Faure babbles on like a "woman or Southerner" (femme et Midi), Céline invokes the lessons of the Paris Commune, which had demonstrated to him that collective ventures were the wrong course of action to take.

The first editor of the correspondence with Faure in the *Cahiers de l'Herne* (1963/1965; reprt. 1972) mistakenly quotes Céline as saying that "the February wall [le mur de février] is not an example of what should be done." Although the statement is actually meaningless in this context, it appeared to allude to current events that helped to date the Céline-Faure letters, placing them after February 6, 1934, that is, after the bloody riots provoked by the Stavisky affair—the Third Republic's umpteenth scandal in which a number of political figures on the Left were implicated. The correct reading is that in this passage Céline is actually referring to the *Mur des Fédérés*, the site of wholesale executions that brought an end to a week of bloodshed and to the popular uprising in 1871 known as the Paris Commune.[11] In Céline's eyes, this wall symbolized the failure of anarcho-patriotism, and he violently objected to the ritual celebration of defeat that revived memories of the event each year in the ceremony held at this historic site.

At first just a hunch, this corrected reading has been decisive for me in my understanding of Céline. Once I had confirmed the dates and the history "lesson" he was actually offering, I realized that where Céline is concerned, one must abandon all preconceived notions and start with a clean slate. Suppose, for example, that when Céline chided Faure for his "femme et Midi" proclivities, he knew perfectly well what he was saying; the writer, as Marcel Proust suggests, forges a pact between intelligence and expression. Céline claims that Faure is reasoning like a woman (i.e., with his nerves) or like a Mediterranean man (as opposed to a Nordic man). This would indicate that the sexist and racist foundations of his belief system were already well established. As a number of allusions in other letters situate this exchange temporally just prior to the publication of *Voyage au bout de la nuit*, it can be concluded that the author was thinking along these lines both before and after he produced a literary work that has been dubbed socialist, communist, populist, anarchist, and even spiritualist.

The system of values adopted by Destouches, the writer-physician, privileged the north to the detriment of the south just as it marginalized women, whose sole function was to be as shapely and beautiful as possible in order to inspire the poet. Personal hygiene and physical fitness were of the utmost importance. If the woman were a dancer, this meant rigorously working the bars. The man's task was to remain vigilant, resisting "romanticism" and maudlin sentimentality of the type exhibited by Robinson and Madelon in *Voyage au bout de la nuit*. With respect to things southern, that is, to the Mediterranean, its warm climate and its culture, Céline was equally categorical. Rereading *Voyage* from this vantage point, one can see that the situation rapidly begins to deteriorate just as the Amiral Bragueton moves beyond the Portuguese coast. African heat ravages the white man. In 1934, he told Eugène Dabit, who was intent on luring him to Morocco, that although he was tempted "by the comforts that were so dear to [him]" (HER, 58), his body simply could not take the scorching heat. This is a minor detail, but it is one that goes very much against the grain of his times when many of Céline's contemporaries, Colette, for instance, were roasting away in southern vineyards. But for Destouches, truth resided elsewhere. It might also be considered significant that Elie Faure, the author of *Trois Gouttes de sang*, was so readily able to decipher the cryptic coupling of "woman and the Southerner." Yet, Faure understood instantly what I am only getting at here in an incomplete manner. He and Destouches had the same artistico-biological interests and had undoubtedly read many of the same works, such as Gobineau's *Essay on the Inequality of the Races* (1853–55). Faure had taken up describing the mentality of various human groups—blacks, Semites, Asians—and was very much in favor of racial mixing. As we shall see, this is what set him apart from his cohort Céline.

Unlike Faure, who in his last letter to Céline complained he was lacking subject matter (HER, 77), Céline had no shortage of ideas. An example of this was the second, eagerly awaited novel, *Mort à crédit*, in which Céline drew on his own childhood experiences. After toiling away at his task, he came to the conclusion that only descriptions of delirium could set the right tone. When the book was released in 1936, less than four years after *Voyage*, the tenor of the times had dramatically changed. Pacifism had lost its luster and war was on the horizon. The antifascist struggles he so adamantly refused to join had united communists, socialists, and radicals on the Left. The Popular Front had raised expectations but in the meantime had triggered mass strikes, factory occupations, declining productivity, and the collapse of the French franc.

Mort à crédit both stunned and disappointed its readers. People were no longer taken aback by Céline's language but were shocked by the graphic physiological details his publisher Denoël had tried to keep to a minimum. A review of the press coverage shows that the reaction was by and large negative; initially brisk sales quickly fell off. Céline had not yet seen any royalties when he was already watching them vanish right before his eyes (Robert, 1991, 175). Just as he had done after the publication of *Voyage*; he went into reclusion. After considering trips to New York, Brittany, and Norway, Céline finally decided to board the steamship *Polaris* for St. Petersburg, in summer 1936, where he was able to draw on the royalties from Elsa Triolet's Russian translation of *Voyage au bout de la nuit*. While he very much appreciated his muscular and emancipated guide Natasha, he despised what he saw of the Soviet Union. Several months after his return to France, he published *Mea Culpa* (December 1936), a brief essay—supplemented by his medical thesis—that is proffered as an act of contrition but that contains not the slightest bit of repentance. In essence, he bellows that Soviet communism was an immense fraud and that the future it heralded would be even worse than the present: "They'll do anything to give the impression that they're not in charge. They'll get rid of every escape hatch. They'll become 'totalitarian'! With or without the Jews" (CC7, 44).

And so we come back, once again, to the Jews. As I noted, they figured as much in Destouches-Céline's everyday life as they did in that of his contemporaries. But by 1936, Jews were cast in a new role relative to "totalitarianism" and to the presence or absence of their ties to communism. When he sent a copy of *Mea Culpa* to his friend and ally Joseph Garcin, Céline wrote: "the important thing is to feel liberated. . . . We'd better hurry up and settle all scores before the catastrophe strikes" (LJG, 86). Fully convinced (in this he was quite prescient) that a disaster was about to strike and in an effort to "liberate" himself, Céline drafted the book that would be his downfall. The meaning of his title, *Bagatelles pour un massacre*, is quite clear: here is a little melody that is of only minor significance (*bagatelles*) to its composer. In the face of the impending massacre, let's remain upbeat, keep on frolicking, right up to the bitter end. Yet, understood in a musical sense, this title—alluding perhaps to Maurice Ravel's opus *Pavane pour une Infante défunte*—also conveys a more ominous meaning. It signals intentionality and direction; those who thought they were being attacked in the work had good reason to feel that way.

The pamphlet was presented as an aesthetic statement, an *Art poétique*. Critics had focused on *Mort à Crédit*'s vulgarity; the commissioners of the 1937 World Exposition had refused his ballet sketches. The public at large was called upon to be the judge of what constituted cultural refinement. This was not merely a matter of style, for it turns out that, thanks to his roots and a few biographical quirks, *Bagatelles'* protagonist Ferdinand was the only French Aryan who had escaped Latino-oriental indoctrination into the classical Greek and Judeo-Christian traditions. Fortunate enough not to have had a single hour of secondary education, his style was free of *N.R.F.* pedantry, his blood was unsullied, and he was the Celto-germanic world's last poet: an authentic specimen of true refinement.

Bagatelles was composed, much like *Voyage*, as a series of fragments placed end to end, spurts of lyricism in tones ranging from the violent to the humorous. Its grotesque exaggeration is all too apparent. Ferdinand is a burlesque character the author uses to enunciate his doctrine of "biological racism"—in other words, life returned to its original, most basic drives. André Gide believed that *Bagatelles* was a huge joke, one whose zest he rather admired.[12] He himself had not jumped into the fray when critics were besmirching *Mort à crédit*. He claimed to have seen piles of the novel stacked up in remote provincial bookstores. In *Bagatelles pour un massacre*, Gide believed Céline was not depicting reality but, rather, the effect it had had on him. It is all a matter of perspective: Gide was used to waiting ten years to see the first edition of one of his books sell out, while Céline, spoiled by the *Voyage* "jackpot," howled persecution when he sold anything less than 30,000 copies. *Bagatelles* was to enjoy the success that had eluded *Mort à crédit*. By Céline's calculations, *Bagatelles* earned 60,000 to 80,000 francs (160,000 to 210,000 new francs) in royalties. This revenue gave him financial independence, allowing him to resign his position at the Clichy clinic. Not long after *Bagatelles* appeared in print, he was relieved of his functions at the Biotherapy Laboratory where he had been moonlighting. The pamphlet's royalties represented a small fortune, but Céline still had to prod Denoël, his publisher, into paying him. Because the value of the franc was rapidly falling, he decided to convert his earnings to hard currency or gold as quickly as possible.

Bagatelles' success encouraged him to produce a sequel in December 1938. *L'Ecole des cadavres* allowed him to apply his theories of the past to the circumstances of the present. A running account of 1938's headlines—the year of the Munich crisis and Hitler's invasion of the Sudetenland—*L'Ecole des cadavres* is Céline's most straightforwardly "political" pamphlet, and the one that is most marked by current events. Given his international experience, Céline felt competent to offer his own solution to the problems of war and peace: he advocated nothing short of a shifting of France's diplomatic alliances and the formation of a Franco-German army. The book's composition and publication coincided roughly with Hitler's annexation (Anschluss) of Austria, March 15, 1938, and Kristallnacht, November 11–12, 1938, the anti-Jewish riots following the assassination in Paris by a Jew, of a member of the German diplomatic corps. Although the Parisian profascist newspaper *Je suis partout* reserved judgment on Céline's new work, its own political discourse had a troubling ideological consonance with these events.

Nineteen forty-one would bring a sort of Célinian postscript to France's June 1940 military fiasco that, although devastating, fell short of the author's much-anticipated massacre.[13] The author titled his final pamphlet *Les Beaux Draps* (a colloquial expression in French signifying "a fine mess"; literally "a fine set of bedsheets"), thereby carping that France had made her own bed and that she would now have to lie in it. No less anti-Semitic·than many of his compatriots, Céline argued strenuously in this third and final pamphlet for a revitalization of the country through educational reforms and a "purification" of its population; nothing destroys, he argues, a Nation like racial pollution.

Céline is finally unmasked, exposed, and openly engaged in disseminating an all-too-familiar belief system. From 1943 on, he was also in danger, unable to hide from his adversaries, the soon-to-be-victors craving revenge. He escaped their wrath by accepting an invitation tendered by the German minister of foreign affairs who graciously welcomed Céline and other compromised French dignitaries to Germany, first in a swank Baden-Baden hotel and later in a castle near Berlin. Managing to reunite with the clan of French collaborationists in exile at Sigmaringen, a medieval fortress near the Swiss border, Céline was the only one of the condemned men who was able to obtain a visa for Denmark, where he had already squirreled away financial resources. There, he went into hiding, was discovered, imprisoned, and subsequently released on parole to the custody of his lawyer Thorvald Mikkelsen, who agreed to lodge him and his spouse Lucette on his estate at Korsör. During his stay at this Baltic outpost, Céline launched an extraordinary epistolary campaign designed to bring about his rehabilitation. Employing the same techniques that had been his undoing—his literary and rhetorical genius—he resolved to get himself out of his terrible predicament.

Bagatelles pour un massacre, L'Ecole des cadavres, and, to a far lesser degree, *Les Beaux Draps* are laced with morsels of high comedy. During his postwar trial, where these texts took center stage, the author did not bother resorting to the lame excuses made by other literary anarchists and surrealists when they found themselves hauled into court for their outrageous affronts to the army or for inciting murder; he did not, for example, invoke poetic license as a diversionary tactic. Céline settled for sticking to his original story, now stretched to the limits of credibility, in which he pleaded diminished mental capacity (delirium) as a result of his (fictitious) trepanation. Just as his earlier works had amused his readers, his epistolary antics now cajoled the judges trying his case. In the course of these proceedings, Céline capitalized on his prewar reputation as a pacifist, one who had advocated the creation of a French-German army solely as a means of heading off a second disastrous war. He also exploited the admiration of a naïve Jewish-American academic named Milton Hindus. Céline made ample use of the admiring letters Hindus had sent the novelist prior to his visit to Korsör in the summer of 1948, an encounter that quickly turned sour. Yet, the American scholar's unflattering account of that contentious meeting would only become known in France after the outcome of Céline's trial had been decided. Céline had now redonned his mask and was anxious to hasten the process of forgetting. His own interdiction of the republication of his "pamphlets" served this end quite well. Yet, the grand finale had yet to be staged. This formidable undertaking would involve finding a way to get the great imprecator back into the literary limelight.

Initially, things went off without a hitch. Convicted in 1951 of charges relating to the pamphlets, thanks to his status as a veteran of World War I, Céline was granted amnesty soon thereafter and allowed to return to France with impunity. He had been without an editor since Robert Denoël's assassination in 1944. Apprised by André Malraux of Céline's availability, Gaston Gallimard rushed to place him under contract, a transaction that covered the author's entire past and future literary output. Céline returned to France with a new manuscript in hand, a "novel" provisionally titled "The Bombing of Montmartre," on which he had worked during his years of exile. A resident of the Butte Montmartre both before and during the war, he had witnessed the Allied bombardment of Paris. In his literary account of the air raids, few bombs are actually dropped, and in this particular context, the attack is not nearly as deadly as the actual events. Yet, these historical circumstances prompted Céline to write a new novel, full of havoc and onomatopoeia, which quickly expanded into the two volumes of *Féerie pour une autre fois*. For many, the bombing of Montmartre represented an English attack on one of the most enduring symbols of the Parisian working classes' cultural heritage. This may seem trivial, but it does raise a number of issues that are worth exploring. For instance, the small town in Normandy in which I work, Lisieux, was decimated by the Allied bombings. Although the community commemorates numerous other historical losses, there is not a single monument to the 1,100 civilians who perished in those air strikes. To my knowledge, Céline's *Féerie pour une autre fois (II)* is the only work, besides Marcel Aymé's *Uranus*, that bears witness to this aspect of the war.

By the time Céline got down to writing *Féerie*, much had changed; he had spent time in prison and, contrary to prevailing notions regarding Scandinavian jails, the experience had ravaged him both physically and morally. During his prison stint in *Féerie (I)*, Céline's protagonist Ferdinand is exposed to lewd propositions from a black person named Hortensia who is eager to see him dead. This Black Hortensia represents the Fourth Republic's presence in Copenhagen. The French government official overseeing Céline's extradition proceedings was Guy Girard de Charbonnière (*charbon*, "coal," i.e., "black"), originally from the French Caribbean. Céline's character Hortensia represents not only the vengeful postwar regime's diplomatic maneuvering but its questionable morals as well.

Yet, in *Féerie*'s introductory segments, Céline's calling into question of the Fourth Republic's moral legitimacy is so oblique that it is hardly intelligible. The general public, which Céline had always seen as his audience, did not pick up on the reference. Nor was it interested in the misfortunes of a writer whose peers—Ciboire (Claudel), André (Malraux), François (Mauriac), Larengon (Aragon), and Narte (Sartre)—were energetically seeking to catapult on to the manure pile of literature. The "Palestine" writers Dondurand, Dumaine, and Farigoux (perhaps a reference to Jules Romain) were also ready to cart him off to Achères.[14] They all had an ax to grind with Céline's texts and were just waiting for him to die so they could tamper with them. The proper names and places Céline evokes in *Féerie (I)* are only vaguely recognizable. Perhaps Sigmaringen is lurking behind "Blaringhem," Dachau behind "Claunau," Buchenwald behind "Lüneburg" ("at Lüneburg there were foot stools too, not just slaughterhouses" [F1, 108]).[15] There is no way to be sure. It can, however, be said that Céline sought here both to reopen the great debate he had initiated with *Bagatelles* and, in the process, to settle a few scores for his eight years of suffering. Although the stakes in *Bagatelles* were clear and its attacks frontal, in *Féerie* the references are veiled. Meaning must be decoded step by step and charted out according to the change of venue, depending on whether the narrative moves from Montmartre to the Danish prison, from the prison to St. Malo, or touches down in London, Africa, or Germany. A little of everything finds its way into this potpourri of self-exoneration in which Céline is clearly making up for lost time. And ultimately, only Céline cowered before his own text. He felt so vulnerable and imagined his enemies to be so mighty and vindictive that he prevented his editor from promoting the novel commercially.

The body of the work itself—the end of *Féerie (I)* and the whole of *Féerie II (Normance)*—was no more appealing than the opening. The apocalyptic rumblings of the Montmartre apartment building by which Céline had hoped to recapture the chaos of the war left readers nonplussed. People began to speak of a "befuddled Céline." He was eventually able to make a literary comeback thanks only to Roger Nimier's journalistic coup, an interview with Céline in a 1957 issue of *L'Express*—at the time, France's most trendy and widely read weekly magazine—where *D'un Château l'autre* was presented as a "Voyage to the End of Hatred." According to Nimier, Céline walked a very fine line when he responded to questioning about his political "ideas" during the interview.

Strangely enough, those most incensed by *D'un Château l'autre*, the first installment of Céline's German trilogy, were the vanquished of

1944: collaborators of all stripes, and die-hard supporters of Vichy-era notables such as Pétain, Laval, Doriot, Déat, and Darnand, whose misfortunes became the object of Céline's ridicule. In Céline's narrative, we find them rounded up by order-obsessed Germans in a small, regal village, Marshal Pétain, head of the Vichy government, tucked away on one floor of the castle and Pierre Laval, his prime minister, on another. The lesser personalities find shelter where they can and scurry about in search of medical care, food, and an escape route. When the novel appeared, unrepentant collaborators accused Céline of exploiting their adversity in order to further his own literary career; his novel handed them over as fodder to be fed to peacetime France. They did not comprehend the proud aloofness of the prophet of biological racism: he had not supported the policies of, nor felt any solidarity with, the apologists of the Collaboration, just as he had refused to pledge allegiance to Philippe Pétain. *D'un Château l'autre* gave Céline a new audience that would allow him to get up on his soapbox once again. But this time, he changed his approach: the racist "prophet" was now a "chronicler." He planned to use his own recollections to document what his contemporaries, whether implicated in the subject matter or indifferent to it, were conveniently erasing from memory.

If the neo-rhetoricians analyzing Céline's narrative techniques have failed to consider the "signified" content of his postwar writing, his reading public has not, focusing as much on its substance as on its form, savoring the twists and turns of Céline's language while recognizing fully what he was up to. Céline is rarely gratuitous. For instance, in *D'un Château l'autre* Céline painstakingly reminds his public of the circumstances surrounding the sordid death of Louis Renault, founder of the automobile manufacturing company bearing his name. Accused of having aided the Nazis by turning his production facilities over to the German war effort, Renault was imprisoned at the Liberation and apparently suffered an unfortunate skull fracture during his incarceration. His untimely death in a prison into which he had entered in good health presented something of a nuisance to the postwar regime in that it brought to a premature closure the judicial proceedings undertaken against him. A decree signed by Charles de Gaulle himself posthumously nationalized Renault's property.

Literary scholars have tended to gloss over Céline's statements regarding the excesses of the period. Henri Godard, for example, limits his commentary to descriptive remarks such as "Renault described his ill treatment in vague terms to his wife" (R2, 1067) or "Laval indeed tried to kill himself with cyanide several hours prior to facing a firing squad" (R2, 1071), thereby sparing us any Célinian emotion or historical pathos. Yet, Laval's stomach had to be pumped several times in order to render him conscious enough both to understand the death sentence and so he could be dragged before the firing squad. The state prosecutor actually proposed carrying him there strapped in a chair. In a very real sense, Laval was made to die twice. It would appear that in its understatement, Gallimard's Pléiade series, often said to preserve great literary works in a padded coffin, can also have the chilling effect of an ice box.

If others had resolved to entomb the past, Céline (not one to let bygones be bygones) took full advantage of his newfound public renown to update his prewar doctrines. In an early version of D'un Château l'autre (R2, 1022–1060), he seems to be preparing for an all-out attack. Sartre is described as a mongrel cross between François Mauriac and parasitic crabs (morbacs)[16] He also places Mauriac in the same species as Pierre Laval, who in his mind was "as much of a Kike as Mauriac or Sartre" (1036) and as "oriental as Bonaparte" (1037). Apparently, Laval and Céline instinctively mistrusted and had a mutual dislike for each other. Or, as Céline puts it, Laval with his "black hair, black as a raven, [and] real wog face" resented "me, a blonde man on horseback" (1045). The racial stereotyping that is introduced subliminally in Voyage and made explicit in Bagatelles surfaces once again in ideology that goes something like: "me - Celto-germanic, big blonde man on horse; them - Orientals, little dark crab-lice." Yet this racist typology is swiftly driven underground again because it is apparently still too risky to be trotted out into the open. In the published version of D'un Château l'autre, Laval certainly has the same swarthy look to him, but the narrator refrains from parading his blondeness. The mask is judiciously put back in place.

It lifts a bit in Nord, a text whose early versions are not available. After perusing the published novel, however, one can well imagine what they contained: "My racial brothers are domestic servants . . . Ester [Loyola][17] is one of those who gives orders... Here's what they should have told me when I was in the cradle: 'Kid, you belong to a race of flunkeys, so always be meek and grovelling, and above all, never concern yourself with what's going on at the masters' table.' [Had I known], I would have been a real slacker in '14, I wouldn't have opened my trap... except to say 'yes'um! yes'um! yes'um!'" (R2, 502). And when Nord's narrator engages in a mock dialogue with Roger Nimier in which he is asked: "Are you going to say you're sorry?" he coyly replies: "Why Roger[!] Me? Never!" (507). Unrepentant, the author of Nord had counted on the passage of time to dissolve the political tensions the war had generated, so much so that he included the real name of his hosts at Schloss Scherz, his second German stopover near Baden Baden. This reckless act drew him into yet another judicial escapade. The novel had to be reprinted employing pseudonyms and the Scherzes, who had not been engulfed by the conflagration described in the novel, demanded reparations. Nor did Robert Le Vigan, who had vanished into the backwoods of Argentina, appreciate the way he was characterized in the Schloss Scherz episode or the transparent name (La Vigue) his friend and traveling companion had given him. The novel's publication brought a precipitous end to their friendship.

Céline opened his final novel, *Rigodon*, with an attack on yet another friend, Robert Poulet. Apparently seeing the novel as an opportunity to set the record straight, he remained not only impenitent but also became a firm nonbeliever: "absolutely antireligious" (R2, 711). Published posthumously, *Rigodon* did not go through extensive revisions by the author and his assistant Marie Canavaggia; it can thus be considered the original draft. This would account for its remarkable candor. Henceforth, organized religion is to bear the brunt of Céline's verbal attacks and this, the author himself explains, for reasons of race. In his mind, Judaism, Protestantism, and Catholicism had but a single common objective: the destruction of the white race. Even during the war he had denounced the Catholic church, "the great half-breeder of the noble races" (la grande métisseuse des races nobles [BD, 81]), for seeking to mollify Vichy's October 1940 racial decrees. Perhaps the inclusion of the Jewish and Protestant religions in his final antireligious diatribe is a concession to the sensibilities of his times, a way of slyly conveying his separatist ideas; Protestantism, after all, has been known to favor racial segregation just as Judaism encourages endogamy.

In Céline's postwar novels, knowing precisely what he could and could not say as well as how to get a core message across while prudently playing the clown was central to his art. Ostensibly, the sequel to the German saga recounted in his two previous novels, *Rigodon* vacillates constantly between the time of the composition (1960–61) and that of the narration (1944–45), thereby offering ample opportunity for backsliding into the old material. Presenting himself as the target of persecution by adversaries of all persuasions, he reiterates his diagnosis: the white race is courting its own destruction through alcoholism, gluttony, and crossbreeding, a leitmotif in *Rigodon* (R2, 721, 729, 730). In the background of the German conflagration that constitutes the corpus of this narrative, Céline is already sketching a Chinese onslaught. In the closing passage of *Rigodon*, Céline's narrator declares to his interlocutor that it is "only blood that matters," "only biology is real, the rest is blabla" (R2, 926). The trivializing "blabla" to which the narrator is referring here is Gallimard's élite Pléiade series, a literary hall of fame of sorts into which the author himself was ultimately inducted. But in the closing passages of his last novel where he stages himself in dialogue with Jean Ducourneau, one of Céline's subsequent editors, his narrator is still far more preoccupied with the impending annihilation of the Aryan race than with his own literary glory, portentously reminding his racial brethren that the Byzantines had foolishly spent their time "debating the sex of the angels" while "the Turks were already shaking the ramparts" (926).

After the war Céline's fragmentary style, abounding with exclamation points and his characteristic "three dots," allowed him to get by with making statements that might have presented legal risks had they been pronounced in "normal" discourse. From the beginning to the end of his career, Céline viewed literature not as an avocation or as an end in itself but, rather, as an instrument. In the literary scenario he configured for himself, he took on the role of the jokester but was always careful to distinguish between the part he was playing and his authentic self. It was a pose he found he had to strike in order to retain the attention of the "factionalized horde" that made up his readership, a posture requiring that he make a constant, painstaking, and tormented effort to appear outrageously brazen without actually overstepping the bounds of tolerated public discourse. In present-day France, the best analogy for Céline's situation might be found in that of a reviled but popular political figure who draws throngs of supporters eager to hear the slogans and sound bites he feels compelled to vocalize and that carry some risk of legal or public sanction. The leader walks a tightrope, placing himself in jeopardy by "saying out loud what others think to themselves," only to find himself later consigned to the trash bin of history when he has outlived his usefulness.

Translated by Jean Fallow and Rosemarie Scullion

▼

L.-F. Céline:
"Just an
individual"?

▼

The scientist generalizes, the artist individualizes.
— JULES RENARD, *Journal*

Before the war, I considered myself simply as an individual
— JEAN-PAUL SARTRE, *L'Autoportrait à 70 ans*

WHEN JEAN-PAUL Sartre's first novel, *La Nausée (Nausea)*, was
published by Gallimard in April 1938, its author was an aspiring
philosopher and writer, thirty-three years of age, and virtually unknown. The genesis of the text went through several stages, the earliest
of which was written in 1931 while Sartre was concluding his military
service. Titled "La Légende de la vérité" ("The Legend of Truth"), and
described by Michel Contat and Michel Rybalka (Sartre, 1981, 1659)[1] as
the scurrilously narrated adventure of a solitary man at odds with his
adversary (the bourgeois social order), this was to be one of Sartre's
several failed attempts in 1931 to break through the literary front. It was
while he was a fellow at the French Institute of Berlin in 1933–34 that
he worked on a second draft that, after several revisions, he ultimately
completed in early 1936 under the title "Melancholia."

Two events, one literary, one political, marked the period just before
his arrival in Berlin: the publication of Louis-Ferdinand Céline's *Voyage
au bout de la nuit* in October 1932, and Hitler's consolidation of power
in January 1933. In the meantime, while Sartre was in Berlin, Paris was
undergoing a series of major upheavals that, unleashed by the disclo-
sures and coverups surrounding the Stavisky affair, gave vent to a
number of extreme right-wing protofascist groups.

After an initial refusal by Gallimard in the spring of 1936, Sartre made further revisions on his manuscript, which now bore the signs of a discernible Célinian influence, namely, a vocabulary that was suddenly and violently liberated from the literary proprieties that for nearly four centuries had dominated literary production in France (OR, 1666). A year later, in April 1937, Sartre's first novel (still titled "Melancholia") was accepted by Gaston Gallimard himself, who nevertheless exacted yet more revisions prior to publication and who even coerced its author into accepting the editor's choice of title, *La Nausée*.

By the time it was published in April 1938, several other important events converged to color the atmosphere of the moment. The Spanish Civil War (referred to by Simone de Beauvoir as "a drama which dominated our entire life for two and a half years" [cited in OR, lii]) had been raging for over a year and a half. Furthermore, Hitler had just accomplished his Anschluss in Austria a month earlier, while in France, Prime Minister Léon Blum's Popular Front government was crumbling, resulting in his ouster on April 8. In addition, Céline's *Bagatelles pour un massacre*—the first of three desperately antiwar, violently anti-Semitic, and openly racist pamphlets first published in December 1937—was enjoying its fourth month of continuing success. Beyond its largely favorable reception by the "literary, libertarian and even political press (right and left wing alike)" (Dauphin and Fouché, 1985, main entry for 1938) in January 1938, *Bagatelles* was the subject of a controversial public debate held on March 16 (published on March 24 in the newspaper *Le Rouge et le Noir*); between April and August, it was reviewed on numerous occasions in the German press and then translated into German in an expurgated version in November. Even *Time* magazine commented on *Bagatelles* in a May 30, 1938, article entitled "Anti-Semitic Exercise." Its widespread dissemination and critical notoriety could not have gone unnoticed, not even by the emerging philosopher-novelist Jean-Paul Sartre, who, according to Contat and Rybalka (OR, 1669), later acknowledged having been politically blind in the 1930s. During the same period, he was waxing enthusiastic over the early victories of the Popular Front—to the point of submitting an article of support in 1936 (again, rejected) to the liberal weekly *Vendredi*.[2] However, fascism, for Sartre and his fellow cohorts at the French Institute in Berlin, seemed to be little more than a rallying point for antifascist leftist intellectuals who viewed the rise of Hitler as a temporary obstacle to the advent of a new, just order (OR, xlix).

Contat and Rybalka call attention to the complex historical conjuncture and political circumstances that frame the time period during which Sartre was articulating his first novel. Pointing to the "aesthetic of opposition" that united Sartre and Simone de Beauvoir in their "temptation of political commitment," and referring to Sartre's own characterization of *La Nausée* as anarchistic, they nonetheless conclude that, despite its protagonist's claims of solitariness, Roquentin reveals a fundamentally leftist sensibility.[3] Although one would be hard-pressed to dispute their claim that, by comparison, the only temptation to which Roquentin does not succumb is the fascist seduction, it is difficult to accept their synthesis that by concluding his novel with the examples of the Jew and the Negress in the process of composing/ executing the blues ballad "Some of These Days," Sartre's Roquentin articulates his evolution toward a greater recognition of otherness.[4] In any case, what "saves" Sartre's Jew and Negress from the contingencies of existence is their ultimate deindividualization, along with the kind of crystallization they undergo in becoming fetishized objects of Roquentin's meditation. Although *La Nausée* may indeed have heralded the end of Sartre's existential posture as the "solitary man" (l'homme seul [OR, 1673]), its protagonist's characterizations of otherness are rife with an antisocial pathology that, by novel's end, betrays a deeper rift. For, in order to satisfy his impossible nostalgia of an idealized reunion and reconciliation of his sense of identity in the wake of the dissolution to which the nausea of contingency has subjected him, Roquentin saw no alternative but to displace the other.

Sartre seems to have been blind in the 1930s to more than just the machinations of world politics, or even to the political realities of his immediate surroundings. Indeed, his choice of epigraph for *La Nausée*— "He's a fellow with no collective importance, just barely an individual" (C'est un garçon sans importance collective, c'est tout juste un individu) taken from Céline's 1933 play *L'Eglise*—together with his later claim that because he had not read the work he was unaware of the third act's anti-Semitic tenor (OR, 1719), bespeaks a diffidence bordering on the disingenuous.[5] Sartre's casual attitude regarding his ignorance of what he was actually quoting in his epigraph is rather odd. For one thing, he might just as well have found an equally suitable quotation in Céline's *Voyage au bout de la nuit*, the novel from whose liberating style he derived, he himself acknowledges, much of his inspiration. Céline's impact on Sartre—despite the latter's relative disappointment with Céline's second novel, *Mort à crédit*—makes

Sartre's insouciance, if not his lack of curiosity, especially problematic; for by the time *La Nausée* went into publication, Céline was no longer recognized solely as a revolutionary stylist with two novels and one dramatic text to his credit. He had also become a vituperative pamphleteer. His first tract, *Mea Culpa* (1936)—with its ambiguously and prophetically hateful epigraph, "I am still lacking a few hatreds. I am certain that they exist"—enjoyed a press run of 25,000 copies, whereas, as noted, his unequivocally anti-Semitic and widely read *Bagatelles pour un massacre* (1937) had a press run for its first edition of 44,600 copies (Dauphin and Fouché, 1985 item 37A1). By comparison, *"La Nausée,"* Contat and Rybalka write, "is a book which went far from unnoticed . . . with its initial run of 7000 copies" (OR, 1701). It is difficult, indeed, to accept the notion that Sartre was entirely oblivious to what Céline had been up to since 1936. It is entirely possible that Sartre culled his epigraph from Céline in order to strengthen the presentation of his first novel (which, as we have seen, had not been accepted without several nagging delays and numerous revisions). In quoting Céline, he was, after all, invoking a (notoriously) recognizable contemporary literary figure. However plausible such a maneuver might seem, it does little to dispel the lingering doubts regarding Sartre's intentions.

At the very least, then, Sartre's choice of an epigraph for *La Nausée* constitutes a supreme ideological irony, if not an act of outright bad faith. For by 1938, Céline's own star had ascended well beyond the limits of the "individual with no collective significance," terms in which the Jewish character, Yudenzweck, describes Bardamu in the third act of *L'Eglise* (161). The epigraph, of course, was not intended to reflect on its author Céline but, rather, to deflect meaning toward the protagonist of Sartre's novel. By thus imbuing his own fictional persona with a pathos derived from a racially motivated exclusionary discourse, Sartre (unknowingly? unwittingly?) contributed to the conjunction of several forms of antisocial literary anarchism and ideological antiegalitarianism that the crisis of European modernity generated in the late 1930s.

Yet, it was not Sartre alone who was subject to this political blind spot. As part of Denoël and Steele's series *Loin des foules* ("Far from the Crowds"), the publication of *L'Eglise* in September 1933 was enthusiastically hailed, largely by the liberal Left, whose praise focused on Act Three's biting satire of backstage machinations at the League of Nations[6] (from which Germany withdrew just one month later). Little was made of the fact that in his satire, Céline singled out, by way of caricature, the figure of the Jew as the manipulator of global, political destiny, making the League of Nations a temple of the "international religion of the rapprochement of peoples" (CC1, 68).

Céline's *L'Eglise* was a fictionalized transposition of his experiences as member of the Hygiene Section of the League of Nations. The agency was headed by Dr. Ludwig Rajchman, a forty-three-year-old Polish Jew (thirteen years Céline's senior) from a solidly implanted and assimilated family of the Warsaw "intelligentsia." Céline's caricature of Rajchman as "Yudenzweck" (signifying "the way, or goal, of the Jew") in *L'Eglise* and as "Yubelblat" ("The Jewbilator") in *Bagatelles pour un massacre* (98–103), both of which were first published during the period in which Sartre was composing his novel, vividly illustrate the political tensions pervading the troubled interwar period in France. Although it may be more accurate to describe Sartre's personal attitude at the time as one of *indifference*, the avowedly antisocial ethos of *La Nausée* was, given the date of the novel's publication, necessarily contaminated by the anti-Semitic pathos of Céline's polemical writings.

From this historical juncture, there emerges what can be seen as a kind of solidarity of solitariness. Céline's Bardamu and Sartre's Roquentin both partake of the same antiegalitarian spirit, the latter's having been, as it were, infected by the former—notwithstanding the fact that by December 1945, with his "Portrait de l'antisémite," Sartre would effectively distance himself from any further association with Céline, claiming that "if Céline supported the Socialist theses of the Nazis, it was because he was paid to do so" (Sartre, 1948, 4).[7] This would be the only other noteworthy mention of Céline to appear in Sartre's writings over a period of forty years, that is, since the 1938 epigraph.[8]

Bardamu's nascent individualism in *L'Eglise* is exemplified primarily by his refusal to adapt to the League of Nations' politics. In his presentation of *L'Eglise*, Jean Ducourneau writes that "Bardamu's notion of human dignity makes him repel the laws of a League which he judges to be governed by buffoonery, corruption, and individual persecution" (O, 1, 760). Thus, Céline becomes the defender of individual nobility in the face of collective backroom machinations, scheming that is caricatured in the representation of a conniving trio of rapacious money-handling conspirators, led by "Alexandre Yudenzweck, a stunted, very little, very thin man, wearing the garb of a Polish Jew, with a long black duster, small cap, thick glasses, an extremely hooked nose, brandishing an umbrella, wearing spats, [making his entrance from the orchestra by] slithering carefully, very carefully, towards the stage, which he then mounts, furtively and stealthily, as the half-darkened stage gradually empties of various personnel, and Yudenzweck begins to speak in his fragile, agile little voice" (E, 144–45). Yudenzweck is identified as the "Director of Compromise Services at the League of Nations, Jew, 45 years old," and is backed by a "Mr. Mosaïc, Director of Transitory Affairs, Jew, same age," and by Mr. Moïse [Moses], Director of the Service of Indiscretions, Jew, same age" (124). Together, the members of this sinister trio single out Bardamu as the unadaptable cog in their wheelings and dealings, thereby precipitating his forced departure from the inner sanctum of the League. "C'est un garçon sans importance collective, c'est tout juste un individu," explains Yudenzweck (161), noting that individuals such as Bardamu, who "speak the language of the individual" are anathema to him, someone who "speaks only a collectivist language" (163). With Bardamu's dismissal, Act Three comes to an end, and Yudenzweck exits the stage with the same furtiveness with which he entered, "smiling softly and round-shouldered" (176).

Caricature, or representation by stereotype, is an elevation of the singular to the universal by way of paradoxical juxtaposition. Yudenzweck's carefully detailed appearance makes him uniquely identifiable, underscoring his "otherness" vis-à-vis the "norm," as it is represented by Bardamu, a character whose description is limited to his age and nationality ("French, and 35 years old" [13]). Bardamu is the spokesman for individuality, whereas Yudenzweck, in all his particularity, incarnates the universal(ist) Jew. Concomitantly, it is the indistinguishable individual who is represented as the object of persecution by the particularized universalist. Céline's politics of difference could hardly be more clearly represented than in the third act of L'Eglise.

It is a curious coincidence that Yudenzweck should bear the name "Alexandre": for it was also in 1933, just two months after L'Eglise was published, that Parisian newspapers announced that a warrant had been issued for the arrest of the Serge Alexandre, alias Sacha Stavisky, a "financial consultant" born in Kiev in 1886 to Russian Jewish parents who had immigrated to France at the turn of the century. As mentioned, the Stavisky affair had the effect of rallying the many right-wing and anti-Semitic "leagues," as they were known, spawning the violence that erupted in the bloody Parisian riots of February 6–9, 1934, a civil

disorder that threatened to overthrow a government seen as complicitous in the scandal. At the time of the public announcement of
Stavisky's arrest warrant (December 1933), Céline was on a three-week
research tour investigating social medicine in Nazi Germany, the last of
several such excursions sponsored by the League of Nations. After his
return to Paris in mid-January 1934, he learned that Stavisky had earlier
proposed establishing a literary prize to promote "decent literature" and
that this decision came as a reaction to his apparent shock when he had
read *Voyage*. In an interview with the *Chicago Daily News* on July 18,
1934, Céline claimed to have been victimized by the self-proclaimed
"guardian of French morality," Serge Alexandre Stavisky (Alméras,
1987, 108).

Bardamu/Céline the individualist Frenchman persecuted by Yudenz-
weck/Rajchman the collectivist-internationalist Jew (with the scandal-
ous Jew, Stavisky, in the wings): such was the scenario already well
configured by the time Céline authored his highly successful mini-
pamphlet *Mea Culpa*, a scenario animating notions of cultural and
political difference that were echoed in numerous right-wing newspapers of the day that linked the Jewish presence with the economic woes
and the increasing political corruption plaguing France (Alméras, 1987,
124). By a kind of inverted logic, the Frenchman, in Céline's eyes,
acquires his individuality by virtue of what he is not: a Jew, hell-bent on
erasing all forms of national identity.

However, the discursive opposition between self and other is not
always so stable in its categorical binarism. We recall in the opening
chapter of *Voyage* Bardamu's first spoken words, the gist of which
constitutes an ironic dismissal of French identity on the implicit
grounds of its racial impurity. " 'The French race can do with some
defending, seeing it doesn't exist. . . . [It's] nothing but a collection of
riffraff like me, bleary-eyed, flea-bitten. . . . [Co]me from the four
corners of the earth. . . . That's France. That's the French people' "
(J, 3–4). By an insidious twist, Bardamu's self-portrayal as representative of the "non-existent" French race amounts to an internalization of
the commonplace representation of the influx of the Jews of Mitteleuropa
in the interwar period, "driven by hunger, plague, tumors, . . . [unable to]
go any further because of the ocean" (J, 4). Having thus absorbed the other
to the point of near-fusion ("a collection . . . *like me*"), Bardamu views
his very identity and individuality as having been subsumed by the
collective invasion of a migrant population driven westward from the
bowels of a racially degenerate (Central and Eastern) Europe. In these

circumstances, his sense of individual identity can only be salvaged by way of rebelling against the very presence of the other within him. In the process of this inner rebellion, Bardamu's sense of individual identity (via the internalized other) turns in on itself; he thus becomes the object of his own persecution: "That's right . . . I'm an anarchist. And to prove it, I've written a kind of prayer of social vengeance...: 'A God who counts minutes and pennies, a desperate sensual God, who grunts like a pig. A pig with golden wings, who falls and falls, always belly side up, ready for caresses, that's him, our master. Come, kiss me'" (J, 4). Akin to a popular anti-Semitic cartoon of the Middle Ages that depicts a gigantic pig tended to by Jews in pointed hats, some of whom sit under the pig, sucking its milk,[9] the "prayer of social vengeance" that *Voyage*'s Bardamu conjures up in his openly anarchistic rebellion resonates with the same kind of implicit internalization of the other—within the discursive folds of an ironic and antiegalitarian diatribe—that one readily finds in the canon of polemical works even before the opening of the Dreyfus Affair in 1894.[10] Eugen Weber notes a similar phenomenon during the fin-de-siècle period: "Countless voices rose to warn that the country was in danger of disappearing. And, as its numbers shrank, those who were left rotted *from the inside*." Quoting a letter (undated) from the fauvist André Derain to his like-minded cohort Maurice Vlaminck (also a friend of Céline), Weber illustrates this preoccupation with: "'The degeneration of the race *pour-[ing] out of every pore*. . . . We are the mushrooms of ancient dunghills'" (1986, 13; my emphasis).

Following a similar dynamic, Bardamu's minimal and marginalized individualism, both in *L'Eglise* and in *Voyage au bout de la nuit*, serves to engender a collective importance. One might even imagine Céline's reaction to Sartre's epigraph in *La Nausée* along such lines: as if Céline, rising to the challenge that came on the heels of his *Bagatelles pour un massacre*, had been spurred on by the denial, implicit in Sartre's choice of epigraph, of any collective significance whatsoever of Céline's most explicitly political and "other"-directed writings to date. Emboldened for his subsequent thrust, Céline then sets out to write *L'Ecole des cadavres* (in May 1938, just one month after the publication of *La Nausée*), an even more pointedly political and "collectively" (indeed, universally) anti-Semitic diatribe than its predecessors,[11] which was published just six months later (November 1938). Already committed in 1933 to the subterfuge of "substituting his voice for that of others" (Alméras, 1987, 12), Céline forged ahead in this troubled and troubling period of the mid- to late 1930s with its increasingly subversive (con)fusion of individual impulses and collective anxieties.

Just as the years that preceded World War I witnessed a revival of nationalism, so did those preceding World War II. The Jew, as Céline saw him in *L'Eglise*, was working away in the inner sanctum of the League of Nations seeking to harness and collectivize the energies that were rotting away in bourgeois Europe. In Bardamu's view, the Jew was, for all intents and purposes, behind the rise of nationalism as well; for, according to Céline's understanding of the geopolitical situation in the interwar years, nationalism provided a convenient means of dividing and thus further weakening the bonds between individual (read Aryan) nations prior to their collectivization under the dictatorship of international Jewry (Alméras, 1987, 82). A particularly curious, yet symptomatic, ideological conflation lies at the heart of Céline's opposition of individualism and collectivism. That opposition is articulated by means of the following ironic transposition: On the one hand, nationalism (i.e., the sense of national "selfhood," whether felt on an individual or national scale) plays into the hand of the internationalist, hence collective, conspiracy. Conversely, racism, although "analytically" categorizing humanity and its individuating differences in terms of collective bodies of "otherness," serves to focus on individual (and individualizing) traits. The solution to the quandary is obvious: by applying rigorously racist and exclusionary policies, one can at the same time strengthen one's "individual" race and thus save the "nation," thereby eradicating the threat to nationhood through the expulsion of readily identifiable agents (those "other" individuals) of internationalism.

"Racism! Racism! Racism! All the rest is idiotic—I'm speaking as a physician—Equity? Justice? What sick and disastrous casuistry—It will always work against us!... I don't mean to quote myself, but read *L'Eglise*—my first book—Read also Webster's *Secret Societies*[12]—a capital work," writes Céline in an undated letter (but in all probability written in the late 1930s) to Lucien Combelle, then the editor-in-chief and director of *Révolution Nationale*, a publication that became the leading collaborationist weekly during the war (cited in Gibault, 1985, 156). "One must resign oneself to the fact that Céline harbors two points of view that are *a priori* incompatible: a rather unique lucidity when it comes to removing the veil from the military-industrial complex that constitutes the core of the totalitarian politics of our century, and a rather banal and conformist compromising, alas, when it comes to holding all the persecuted minorities of this same century up to public obloquy" (Pagès, 1991, 211–12). It is, however, this implicit incompatibility between Céline, the individual, anarchistic observer-diagnostician and Céline, the racially motivated ideologue, that Sartre's 1938 epigraph from Céline's *L'Eglise* raises. By the time *La Nausée* was published, Céline's *Bagatelles pour un massacre* had already struck a collective nerve; when, "substituting his voice for that of others," he had given an even wider voice to those deeply implanted collective forces and energies, that, together with their attendant individual anxieties and phobias, were to lead France by the turn of the decade, down the path of the infamous Collaboration.

As Henri Godard observes (1985, 293), Céline's pamphlets are pivotal in the evolution of his writing in that they give rise to Céline's authorial identity. This occurs largely by virtue of the fact that it is with *Bagatelles* that the narrative voice began to speak in the name of "Ferdinand" and of "Céline" himself. In contrast, the previously "fictional" Ferdinand Bardamu spoke in a voice not entirely his own (Alméras, 1987, 323–24); paradoxically, the "authenticity" of Bardamu's voice was the result of his having been stripped of his sense of autonomy by a forced immersion in the world of others, as was made so poignantly clear in the opening section of *Voyage*. Bardamu's entire journey, from *L'Eglise* through *Voyage* and *Mort à crédit*, is indeed one of "total immersion" whereby his sense of selfhood is reduced to a powerless expression of disappointment, disillusionment, and distrust. From within this collective miasma of oppressive otherness, then, only the voice of his own victimization can ring true to him. Bardamu, whose name could mean "mute bard," is the solitary mouthpiece of voiceless impotence in the face of the onslaught of the collective.

By inserting his own names ("Céline" and "Destouches") within the very fabric of *Bagatelles*, Céline brings into relief the singular, individual significance of his voice as one of violent protest. His authorial identity thus put on the line, this subjectivity becomes one with the referential backdrop of *Bagatelles'* diatribe. Hence, the renewed charge and vigor in his voice—as he can now rail on his own, and in his own name—in his revitalized efforts to resist what he perceives to be the negative pull of the collectivity. However, as if to achieve a kind of metaphysical symmetry, just as his own individual identity now begins to be brought into sharper focus, so too does the identity of the collectivity against which he defines himself. Enter the grimacing, pernicious figure of the Jew, that other of all others.

Therein lies the dilemma: How, as a vulnerable individual who emerges from the collective miasma, can Céline launch his assault on the other without undermining his own sense of vulnerability, which is the very guarantee of his individuality? The persecution of the other can only be rationalized in terms of one's own sense of being persecuted. This might at least partially explain Céline's vested interest in constructing himself as the scapegoat par excellence.[13]

Written during the waning of the Popular Front (under Camille Chautemps's presidency) when European peace and future economic prosperity were increasingly threatened, *Bagatelles pour un massacre* is a direct assault on individual, collective, and national frailty stemming from what is perceived to be a racially and ideologically driven process of national disintegration, cultural decay, and biological degeneration. Ferdinand/Céline makes a spectacle of his own vulnerability, setting himself up as the singular, narrative foil, against the backdrop of the silencing forces of collective annihilation. As tragicomic foil, however, he thrives on his own sense of disempowerment; the numerous affronts to his presumably threatened identity provoke his repeated assaults against those whom he identifies as the perpetrators of his (and his nation's) victimization. Presenting himself in *Bagatelles* as a writer whose ballet scenarios are contemptuously rejected by the 1937 Exposition and the Leningrad ballet, both supposedly controlled by the Jews, Céline explicitly internalizes the pathos of the persecuted author. *Bagatelles*'s Ferdinand/Céline is the Bardamu of *L'Eglise*, *Voyage*, and *Mort* turned inside out. He wears his vulnerability on his sleeve, sparing no one in his frantic efforts to shake it off, while in the process giving full voice to his inexhaustible spleen: "Emerging from the blistering experience of the Popular Front, Ferdinand spits out his truth: beyond mystifying and deadly ideologies, there is but *one* reality: Jewish will, Jewish ambition, Jewish interest" (Alméras, 1987, 343). Ferdinand's venomous vituperations are a repeat performance, on an incomparably larger and richer scale, of the diatribe embedded in Act Three of *L'Eglise*, whose "violence and frankness [in the name of] Belles-Lettres Françaises" cost Céline the disaffection of his immediate superior, Dr. Rajchman—alias "Yudenzweck"/"Yubelblat" (B, 111). The pattern is now fixed for the remainder of Céline's career. As the solitary voice in the night of collective hysteria and the vocal incarnation of all that is worth preserving in the native Frenchman, in the native French language, and in the native French literature, Céline's narrating persona will repeatedly play the role of sacrificial victim in his mock-heroic struggle to counteract those democratic and egalitarian forces and agents of collective otherness (i.e., international Jewry) that have run amok: "After so many years, when I think about it, my leaving the League of Nations was a heroic stroke. I sacrificed myself, when you come right down to it; I'm a martyr, in my individual way. . . . They owe me some kind of compensation... I feel it coming" (B, 111).

According to Marie-Christine Bellosta, Céline's anti-Semitic verbal attacks are expressions of a "nostalgic individualism" in which the "individual" can assert his identity only through the scorn of others while he seeks to undo his singularity in an effort to prepare for his eventual reabsorption into a new social order. Bellosta further invokes Sartre, who views the "right-wing anarchists" who actively contributed to the Collaboration as "lacking the courage to draw conclusions from their rigorously individualistic attitude" (1990, 283). Although the facts surrounding Céline's individual contribution to the Collaboration are no longer in question, the degree to which his obsessively racist pathos was instrumental in the forging of a collective, genocidal ethos is impossible to measure. "Céline committed himself, but he did so under his own banner," observes Alméras, adding that the "gratuitousness" of his act, as Céline himself viewed it (based on the fact that he never received payment of any kind for his "letters to the editor" submitted to and published in numerous collaborationist and anti-Semitic publications), was the guarantee of his independence (1987, 131). However, as Céline also noted in the 1936 preface to his fictionalized biography of P. I. Semmelweis (his medical dissertation): "Nothing is free in this base world. Everything must be paid for, the good no less than the evil must be paid for sooner or later" (Mea, 40).

In order for his "independence," or individuality, to be preserved, Céline was thus obliged to stack the deck in his favor by internalizing within his own histrionic rhetoric the same/other duality of persecuted/persecutor. Only by thus rendering his emotive attacks unredeemable within a collective ethos could his individuality be sustained. And paradoxically, only in generating this unredeemability with renewed commitment, from one verbal assault to the next, could Bardamu/Ferdinand/Céline reclaim the authorial identity of his voice and stave off the constant threat of assimilation by the (institutionalized) world of the other. In 1948, during his exile in Denmark, he wrote to Jean Paulhan, the editor of the *Nouvelle Revue Française*: "It's the others, all the others, who are galloping, howling, to the flag, letting themselves get buggered by the highest bidder! And to do me in, of course, that's imperative! . . . Oh the difference [le différend] runs deep. *It's irreparable!* So as you see, my situation is inexpiable" (L, 47).

Céline: just an individual? He wrote *L'Eglise* during the last year of his three-and-a-half year tenure at the League of Nations; he wrote *Bagatelles* when the Popular Front was on the decline. In both cases (as with the works that follow), what emerges is the voice of the "last bard" (Alméras, 1987, 363), the French nationalist defender of racial purity, of the white Aryan (French)man's peace, in sum, the "heroic" agitpropagandist of a Europe rid of its Jews. The histrionics of Céline's rhetoric throughout his writings, beginning with *Bagatelles*, are symptomatic of his self-perception as a victimized and ostracized individual. Caught up in the maelstrom of history, Céline's personas have no one but the ubiquitous other to lash out against—that other who is both within and without, both individual *and* collective.

What, in the end, was Sartre's stake in claiming, a full seven years after the publication of *La Nausée*, that: "If Céline supported the Socialist theories of the Nazis, it was because he was paid to do so. At the bottom of his heart he did not believe them. For him there is no solution except collective suicide, nonreproduction, death" (Sartre, 1948, 4)? By dismissing the significance of Céline's polemical tracts with this more or less gratuitous apologia, was Sartre covering over his own political blindness of the recent past? In stressing the nihilistic impulses in Céline's reflections on the human condition, which he no doubt gleaned from his reading of *Voyage au bout de la nuit*, Sartre minimizes the specific, collective impact Céline's explicitly anti-Semitic writings had on the historical moment during which they were written, published, disseminated, and discussed. The fact that Céline is so casually rejected by Sartre in his 1945 essay on anti-Semitism—a text in which he makes a passing, ahistorical reference to Céline's neo-Manicheanism (CC7, 382–38)—is still quite puzzling. For Sartre, the post-*Voyage* Céline was obviously not a writer to be taken very seriously. Céline was, in his mind, but a nihilistic opportunist of little significance to the collectivity. However, Sartre's choice of epigraph for *La Nausée* reflects rather ironically his own persistent blindness in discounting Céline, in 1945 as in 1938, as a collectively inconsequential individual doing the bidding of the powers that be.

In light of these considerations, I return by way of conclusion to Céline's 1948 letter to Paulhan, in which, as a writer who participated in the collective persecution of others in the name of national and racial self-interest, Céline felt himself to be the object of persecution by an equally ostracizing collectivity: "I'm weary to the point of nausea of having to defend myself... The four years of this imbecilic persecution have exhausted me, I'm tired of it all... They bother me... The whole lot of them, rehashing their hateful drivel at my heels... Sartre and the clique... I have nothing in common with those dogs, my mistake was in not having disposed of them. When the next butchery gets going I promise that you'll be able to find me in the butchers' camp... never again on the side of the calves... never again" (L, 47).

Thomas C. Spear

▼

Virility and
the Jewish
"Invasion"
in
Céline's
Pamphlets

▼

A MAN OF verbal expulsion and anal retention, Céline publicly
unmasks himself as the authoritative Doctor Destouches in his political "pamphlets," the first major works in which he forthrightly transgresses the margins of fiction.[1] Much more than a visceral hate of
war—which the author speciously characterized as his purely "pacifist" stance—prompted these lengthy diatribes: the "people's" doctor
cum author had found a public and was bent on transforming the world.
The journalistic style of the intern hygienist Destouches, a social
reform and public health advocate in the 1920s and early 1930s, had
merged by the late 1930s with that of the brazen (but now established)
novelist to advance a program calling for the complete eradication of
society's "germ" elements (EC, 262ff.), the extermination of Jews (EC,
264) and the expulsion of all other racial and/or ideological waste, social
categories he terms "judeo-artistico-buggerying-commies" (B, 143).

Ironically, much as Céline seeks to purge Europe of all Jewish
domination, his various autofictional narrative personae suffer from
serious bouts of constipation. Although he sought figuratively to expel
his political and literary adversaries from the very entrails of his being,
one could also say that his will to expulsion more closely resembles the
Aryan impotence he despises than a manly verbal defense capable of
withstanding the enemy penetration he dreads. The Jewish "threat"

takes on various symbolic forms for this highly "virile" pamphleteer: "You'll see what I have to say... how I soak my dick in vitriol!... Bring me a good solid turd, right here!... Any old Kaminsky! so I can douse my pen" (EC, 15). Céline clearly illustrates the position he would take relative to his adversaries in this crudely formulated response to one of his critics, H. E. Kaminski.[2] Elsewhere, but most flagrantly in the pamphlets where he demonstrates the least restraint, Céline's verbal expulsion of "foreign" entities proves ultimately to be as unsuccessful as his defense of the primary victim, himself.

The virilized call to arms Céline issues in his pamphlets ("Erection day has finally arrived!"[3]) is truly pointless, for, in his mind, the home "front" was already foundering and in desperate need of a reinvigorated line of defense. For Céline, it is the Jew, portrayed as the (emasculated and emasculating) object of scorn for masses of pathetically devirilized Aryans, who is the representative (indeed source) of the corruption of humanity. The Jew is also the most frightful incarnation of power: a menacing (negroid) phallus capable of relegating the Aryan, the Jew's victim and prey, to a position of subservience. In Céline's mind, European Jewry, at the historical juncture from and against which he wrote, was sodomizing eager throngs of "fanatical Aryan serfs" (EC, 272). Although the author himself deplores the acquiescence of his compatriots, he is not in the least surprised to find his fellow Aryans— with whom he is antagonistically identified and whom he describes as "lumbering, useless cretins"—in such a passive stance, as they are "no longer willing to do a damn thing" (BD, 8) about anything, much less about the crisis at hand.

Céline generally dismissed biographical interpretations of art, holding "that a work cannot be 'explained' by knowing its author" (CC1, 41). Efforts to discover the pamphleteer's motivations by acquiring knowledge of either the writer or his representative "narrator"[4] lead to just such forms of biographical speculation. The dynamic between fictional "play" and narrated reality is complex and somewhat confusing in the pamphlets, where the first-person voice speaks simultaneously for Céline (the celebrated novelist), Destouches (the physician), as well as for a textual persona as "fictionally" misrepresentational (i.e., nonautobiographical) as the narrators of the author's first two novels, *Voyage au bout de la nuit* and *Mort à crédit*. Although not necessarily "explaining" the oppositional relationship between the narrator and the textually constructed "other"—be it the Jew or the directly addressed narratee—this aspect of his political discourse merits closer examination. As Henri Godard has noted (1985, 349), the aggressive "I"/"you" dialogue that is such a prominent trademark of Céline's late fiction first emerged as a narrative technique in his political pamphlets, writings in which the "reader" (or "narratee" as the narrator's textual addressee is properly termed) is asked to join forces with the narrator in order to fend off Jewish influence. Céline's typical narrator does not wish to establish an intimate bond with his addressee, yet the author, like his narrator, finds it imperative to conceptualize a narratee through direct speech in order to engage his listener (both real and imagined) in his oppositional polemics.

With his powerful "atomic" pen (LA, 39–40), Céline erupts with raw emotion that he stylizes into a dazzling verbal delirium. He constantly ridicules and trivializes beliefs to which he does not himself subscribe and refers to them pejoratively as mere "ideas"; the pamphlets illustrate nonetheless that his own writing does indeed present a body of thought, much as it may appear to be grounded in an impassioned irrationality. Recourse to rational modes of thought is actively discouraged as an approach to reading these texts. As he clearly states in *Entretiens avec le Professeur Y* and in *Bagatelles pour un massacre*, Céline wished to be considered an "emotional stylist"; for him, "A style is first, foremost, and above all, an emotion" (B, 121). The pamphlets flaunt Céline's desire to deviate aesthetically from "standardized" literary forms prevalent in which he finds a (Jewish) "cycle of international robotization of minds" (B, 134). He rejects all rational thought emanating from "the head," for he is a man of visceral emotion: "Good dreams come from, issue from your guts [la viande], never from your head. Only lies come from the head" (B, 139). Opting for the expression of passion rather than reason, his works resist comprehension in purely cognitive terms. Jean-Paul Sartre argued that anti-Semitic passion can be expressed in a "*seemingly* reasonable discourse" (1945, 444; emphasis added). Although unequivocally condemning the anti-Semite's ideological commitment, Sartre nevertheless sought to formulate a rational explanation for anti-Semitism.

Incensed by Sartre's accusation in "Portrait de l'antisémite" that he had been paid by the German authorities for authoring his anti-Semitic pamphlets, Céline retorted with his inflammatory essay, "A l'agité du bocal." Having anticipated such accusations, Céline had already countered the charge of ideological panhandling in the pamphlets themselves, noting, for example: "from every front I'm told I've received huge sums from Hitler" (EC, 298). He explains that he had, in fact, no need for such remuneration (EC, 298–99), stating: "What I write, I think up myself, no one pays me to think it, no one incites me . . . At 71, I'll still hound [j'emmerderai] Jews, Freemasons, editors, and especially

Hitler if he asks for it" (EC, 99; B, 209). Céline adds that he might well have sold out to the Soviets and portrayed their society in a more positive light (B, 245) were he as unprincipled and venal as his critics charged. He was, however, clearly not a typical anti-Semite who would "pimp" his creative wares to a well-endowed ideology: "I'll think as I like [and] as I can... out loud" (B, 38), and "I'll open my big mouth however, whenever, and wherever I please" (EC, 299). Céline did receive royalties for his publications, of course, but consistently maintained that he had not, because in so doing he would have to have relinquished his intellectual and financial autonomy: "Buggered by the English or the Krauts, *it's all the same* to me. I didn't suck or jack off anybody. I'm a lady of the world. I screw with whom I want, when I want, how I want. And I decided not to fuck with *anybody. I wasn't turned on.* And that's that! But this is hardly conceivable for people who are forever EMPLOY-EES with their rumps always waiting for some golden dick—'honey-sweet anus'" (CC6, 100; Céline's emphases). This "lady of the world" thus sees herself as both financially and ideologically free to lie in the bedsheets—*les beaux draps,* as it were—of her choice.

Still, one cannot assert that the racist, misanthropic ideology Céline formulates in the pamphlets was unmotivated, no matter how conspicuously befuddled the logic of his extravagant show of anti-Semitism. Judging by their sales both before the war and under the Occupation (see Roussin 1987; Dauphin and Fouché, 1985), these texts circulated widely, reaching hundreds of thousands of potential sympathizers with their electrifying (re)presentation of emotion. Despite his adamant claims to the contrary, Céline was clearly cashing in on his hateful diatribes; he even authorized their republication during the German Occupation. Although Céline argued in *Bagatelles*: "I don't force anyone to buy my books" (B, 153), he nonetheless profited from the anti-Semitic inclinations of his public, inducing his readers to identify their own frustrated hopes and ambitions with those of his narrator by incorporating their identities, like his own, into the text and by suggesting they adopt his narrator's posture of defiance against a perceived victimization.

The short *Mea Culpa* Céline published in 1936 displays neither the violence nor the racist rage of the lengthy pamphlets it precedes. Intended mainly as a critique of the Soviet Communist system, it focuses chiefly on humanity's stupidity and self-imposed servility, a recurrent theme in Céline's writing: "Man has never had, in the skies and on earth, but a single tyrant: himself" (Mea, 341). Céline's refusal to join any political party was already well known; he had nonetheless volunteered to make public proclamations of his deliriously lucid political convictions as early as 1933. In a speech entitled "Hommage à Emile Zola," for instance, he proclaimed: "Hitler won't have the last word, we'll see far more epilepsy, perhaps even here [in France]" (CC1, 79). Foreboding of this sort typifies Céline's general cynicism regarding all political systems and organizations, including German totalitarianism. The publication of *Mea Culpa* indeed marks Céline's definitive break with the communist Left, if, in fact, he can be seen as ever actually having been affiliated with the communists (Morand, 1972, 193). Although Céline may have disavowed the expurgated Russian translation of *Voyage au bout de la nuit*, his first novel was actually lauded in some French and Soviet communist intellectual circles for its searing indictment of the capitalist order.[5] Published shortly after Gide's *Retour de L'URSS* (November 1936), Céline's anticommunist *Mea Culpa* (December 1936) differs sharply from Gide's assessments of the new Soviet system; the latter's criticisms were intended to be constructive, whereas Céline was illustrating the futility of *all* political efforts to improve the lot of humanity. In Céline's view, "Prolovitch"— the pejorative term used to characterize the Soviet working class—had succeeded in eradicating the ruling bourgeoisie only to create a new totalitarian order governed by "Police, Propaganda and Army" (Mea, 345). In sum, Céline's central ideological aim here is the indictment of what is seen as an ill-conceived strategy for ameliorative purification: the proletariat rids itself of one scourge only to replace it with another.

Focusing specifically on the failings of the Soviet system, Céline also chides humanity as a whole, which, he asserts, is its own worst enemy: "Man is the worst breed!... he generates under any conditions his own torture, like syphilis does its tabes" (Mea, 345). For Céline the hygienist, mankind breeds its own consumptive disease: utopian delusions of future bliss; in his words, "the great pretense of happiness [is a] monumental sham" (Mea, 342). He treats inane optimism of this sort with a sizeable dose of his own fatalism. Purifying the human species of its "disease" is, in Céline's sardonic view, either impossible or, in his vision of the "purified" Soviet political structure, a total farce. In *Mea Culpa*, this "prologue" to the subsequent pamphlets, Céline does not make use of the first-person singular narrative voice, nor does he introduce his own name ("Céline" or "Destouches") into the text. He also avoids use of the direct "I" and "you" address that is so prevalent elsewhere in his published works. Yet, thematically, *Mea Culpa* acts as an introduction to the subsequent pamphlets by presenting the figurative notion of pervasive "bacteria" that he is intent on eradicating.

Céline often prided himself on his candor, that is, his willingness to call a spade a spade. When everything one sees becomes a spade, however, even when it's not, one begins to wonder if the designation is in any way meaningful. In Céline's eyes, Jews are everywhere, and everyone has become a Jew. In his Manichean universe ("Jews against anti-Jews" [B, 174]), the choice must be made either to side "with the Jews or against the Jews" (EC, 253). For Céline, "'to be or not to be' Aryan? That is the question!" (EC, 222, in English in the text). Such polarization clarifies racial, ethnic, and ideological differences and encourages opposition to "Freemasons" and Jews: "A choice must be made, one type of perversion must be selected . . . Aryan or Masonic, Jewish or anti-Jewish" (EC, 198). As Kaminski observed after having read *Bagatelles pour un massacre*, Céline was, quite curiously, the only individual in his purview who was *not* a Jew (106), a psychological trait that is common to all anti-Semites, according to Sartre: "The external object spares him [the anti-Semite] from having to look within himself for his personality; he has chosen to focus only on the exterior, never to look to himself, and to be nothing if not the fear he inspires in others: more than Reason, what he flees most is an intimate awareness of himself" (1945, 450). In the pamphlets Céline chooses principally Jews as the object of such external focus. Having named the other, he makes a paranoid universalization both of Jewish identity and of his fear of Jewish domination. In his postwar novels, the object of his invective will shift when the position of the other is filled by a personified narratee ("you"), a textual addressee without whom the author is clearly unable to carry on his intersubjective banter and bluster.

In *L'Ecole des cadavres*, the anti-Semitic wrath of Céline's first major pamphlet, *Bagatelles*, has been largely eclipsed by the dread of impending war. Frantically struggling to arrest the inexorable march toward a new war, Céline admonishes everyone, but principally Jews, for the warmongering that, he insisted, was once again propelling France, indeed the entire European continent, toward bloodshed. In Céline's portrayal of this international powder keg, major power brokers, from Franklin D. Roosevelt to the Pope, become Jews: "Vatican policies are always propitious to Jewry... We've had Jewish bishops, popes" (B, 215); "Nothing more Jewish than the current Pope.[6] From his real name Isaac Ratisch. The Vatican is a Ghetto" (EC, 266). With no apparent logic, the term "Jew" becomes a preposterous designation for Aryans, alcoholic French cretins, the British intelligence services, bankers, Freemasons, and France's elite "200 families" (Kaminski, 1938, 31–35). His universalizing invective also implicates Communists, blacks, the bourgeoisie, literary critics and publishers, and even the presumably Aryan addressee of the text itself. Although Jews are the principal target of Céline's wrath, particularly in *Bagatelles*, they are by no means his sole adversary.

The product of an obvious persecution complex, the paranoid traits discernible in Céline's writing extend well beyond the pamphlets. The narrators of Céline's novels are often suspicious and distrustful of others, even when this sparks an ideological confrontation of one against all. In *Voyage au bout de la nuit*, for instance, the narrator displays his grandiosity by stating that his adversaries could be "nine hundred ninety-five million and [against them] there's me alone, they're the one's who are wrong . . . and I'm right" (R1, 65). Similarly, the pamphlets' narrative persona proclaims his willingness to confront all opposition, stating: "After all, I didn't care if I had the whole world against me in the anti-Semitic crusade" (B, 45). In the prosecution's briefing at Céline's postwar trial, it was observed that the author "never worried about pleasing anyone, either before or during the war, which earned him both his unique and separate position in the world of Letters as well as enemies in every camp" (cited in Gibault, 1981, 206). Criticizing everyone in *Bagatelles*, including himself, Céline invites all of society, even potential French Aryan sympathizers, to become his foes. This persecutory posture will function as his chief defense against bellicose "kikes" (youtres) who, quite ironically (and again, projectively), are described as "the biggest cud-chewing paranoids on the planet" (B, 49).

Bagatelles pour un massacre is the first of Céline's texts in which the narrative voice is named "Céline" in addition to the previously used "Ferdinand" (Godard, 1985, 292). As the author stated in a 1957 interview, *Bagatelles* was "perhaps the only book I wrote for the French and in which I speak personally, without reservation."[7] The "reservations" he presumably had in his two previous novels can be found in the guise of an apparently more generous attitude toward Jews (i.e., derision of the father's diatribes against Dreyfus in *Mort à crédit* [R1,600]) and in his use of a less autobiographical narrative voice. In the pamphlets, the author forthrightly takes on the identity of "Céline." Taking the pseudonym Doctor Destouches, he simply dons another masquerade.

Although the narrator ("Céline") addresses interdiegetic characters in the pamphlets, much of his speech is addressed to an unspecified narratee, referred to as "you" (B, 118). This direct form of address—i.e.,

"I assure you!" (B, 60), "I swear to you!" (B, 60), "I affirm to you" (B, 61), "I tell you" (B, 99)—places a metanarrative focus on the act of communication. It also signals or reinforces the pamphleteer's authorial intentions regarding the information he seeks to convey with force and immediacy to its receiver (B, 65). In *Bagatelles*, the narrative voice bearing the name "Céline" engages in dialogue with three parties: Léo Gutman, the artist Gen Paul ("Popol" or "Popaul"), and a cousin, Gustin Sabayote. The narrator addresses these textual characters with the familiar (*tu*) form in contrast to speech directed to the extradiegetic narratee (the "reader") with *vous*. In the opening segments of *Bagatelles*, "Céline" forewarns his "sadistic" cohort, Léo Gutman (who stifles his "excitement" and "tears out [his] balls" [B, 34]), that he is about to launch into a spectacular anti-Semitic tirade: "Ah! you're going to see anti-Semitism!" (B, 34). Curiously, Céline augurs his own fate (while also subtly lauding his own temerity) when he has Gutman caution: "Ferdinand... You'll end up in prison" (B, 51). Gutman attempts to calm the novelist's anti-Semitic fury, exclaiming: "but Ferdinand, you're delirious!... I'm going to have you put away! I swear!... You'll return to your novels" (B, 224). Appearing at the beginning and again at the close of *Bagatelles*, Gutman's remarks frame the anti-Semitic discourse uttered throughout. Claiming that Céline is deranged, Gutman (a character identified in the text as a Jew[8]) mocks the narrator's irrational, anti-Jewish hysteria, saying, "You're some sort of a reasoning fool... you're just a dirty failure [sale raté]" (B, 227). In the pamphlets, the anti-Semitic novelist becomes a self-described "failure" who covets the success and power he attributes to Jews.

Although the pamphlets can be viewed as an exercise in the expression of hatred, on closer observation, it is apparent that envy is a more prominent and pervasive emotion in *Bagatelles pour un massacre*. Not simply a manifestation of irrational antipathy, Céline's envy of Jews stems from what he perceives to be their disproportionate dominance in the arenas of politics, finance, commerce, publishing, intelligence, and culture. His principal aim, then, is to outperform and outdistance his rivals: "I've got to get ahead of the Jews!... all the Jews!" (B, 23). It is particularly in his role as racist that he hopes to surpass the Jews whom he, once again, rather ironically and projectively portrays as "racists, they've got all the gold, they've seized all the levers, they've grabbed on to all of the controls" (B, 51). Céline claims that critics—and everyone else for that matter—would find him more appealing if only he were Jewish or, as he puts it, "Rabbi-esque" (Célineman rabineux [B, 14]). Although he is an unqualified success as a novelist, the Aryan writer suffers both from criticism and, as he bellows in the opening passages of *Bagatelles*, from Jewish obstructionism that has prevented him from selling his prized ballet scenarios.

Curiously, the character traits manifested by Céline's narrator in *Bagatelles* often mirror those attributed to the Jews he presumably despises. Gutman, for example, reproaches Céline for his arrogance, proclaiming: "You're boasting like a Jew, Ferdinand!" (B, 15). The author closely identifies with what he sees as inherent characteristics of Jews: "Always anxious and persecuted, Jewish lords will be perpetually traveling from one end of the planet—their planet—to another" (B, 49); "In film, the Jew—as a 'Jewish character'—will never appear before us except as a 'persecuted' being, a touching character quashed by the perfidy of things, by misfortune" (B, 160). Elaborating on the persecution complex from which he claims, stereotypically, all Jews suffer, Céline refers to an essay in which a presumably Jewish man describes his childhood experience as a member of the "martyred race" that later led to a full-blown "persecution complex" (B, 181).[9] Like this persecuted Jew, Céline himself is loath to take personal responsibility for his misfortunes (such as his failure to sell his ballets) and searches everywhere for a cause and explanation of his failings except, as Sartre noted, "within himself."

Céline himself is known for possessing numerous other qualities that he projects on to a Jewish identity, including entertaining public performances, paranoia, and especially "racist nonsense" (turlutaines racistes): "At least the Jews can still put on a good show, be funny, amuse us with their racist nonsense and their endless martyr ploys, their jabbering, their petty words, paranoid ventures and their ever-wagging tails [queues] [which are] caught in doors over and over again, crushed and rehabilitated in thousands of trances and contortions" (B, 165). Céline even claimed that he came to write "in Jewish" (B, 83) when laboring under the supervision of "Yubelblat" at the League of Nations in the 1920s. He would later abandon the "debauchery of such dialectically pretty shit" in favor of the "violence and frankness of French Belles-Lettres," which he took up after being professionally "martyred" at this job (B, 83). When referring to a fellow doctor (described as a "clumsy little Yid" [B, 212]) who criticized his writing in a medical journal, the pamphleteer once again sketches a portrait of the other that is remarkably similar to the image he projects of himself (except perhaps that Céline renounces all use of "Freudian" gibberish): "This coward's racist rage, his craze of envy, were dressed for the occasion as scientific vituperation. This foul infection slobbered over with insults in his psycho-Freudian, delirious pluri-moronic gibberish. Judging from all his verbiage, his fool's scepter and his pathos, this imbecile must be a psychiatrist" (B, 212–13). Providing examples of Jewish rage and racism, Céline seeks to justify his own and, as evidenced by direct address to the narratee, hopes to influence his interlocutor. In *Bagatelles*, for example, he directly quotes Jewish writings, either verbatim or with careful modifications, in which the slaughter of Christians is actively encouraged: "'If you Christians haven't hanged us all in fifty years, you won't even have enough left to buy the rope to do it.'"[10] These numerous quotations from texts he claims were authored by Jews, expressing anti-Christian or "anti-Aryan" sentiment, are provided for his reader's much-needed instruction: "I'll no longer explain anything to you... Now I hope you know how to read 'Jew'" (B, 186). Céline implores his presumably Aryan reading public to educate itself on the deep-rooted causes of its own impending "slaughter" and is given the address where appropriate documentation can be procured ("where you will find a very well-stocked French library," i.e., the Information Center of the Anti-Jewish Party—Rassemblement Anti-Juif—[E, 35]).[11] In the event his reader is inadequately informed or has not yet procured such documentation, Céline quotes extensively from anti-Semitic writings he has culled from these resources.

Judging from the quantity of epithets hurled at Jews (always referred to in the third person), it would seem logical for the pamphlets' narratee (the second-person addressee) to be a non-Jewish Frenchman. The first-person plural pronouns designate narrator and narratee as "us"; the Jews, therefore, are "them." Discussing the problem of impending war and the need for front-line fodder, *Bagatelles'* narrator proclaims: "We ought first to ask that Jews sacrifice their own guts, first! in person-!... before we enlist our own" (B, 66). Seeking to heighten his Gentile interlocutor's awareness of his own persecution and to minimize that of the Jewish community, he repeatedly warns that "they" are out to get "you," thereby establishing an intrinsically adversarial relationship between his Jewish opponents and his disempowered Aryan narratee: "Those nasal-labial corners always worried... flexing, furrowed, rising again, defensive, hollowed out with hate and disgust... for you!... for you, the abject beast of the enemy and accursed race, to destroy.... It's your blood these ghouls thirst for!... This ought to make you shriek" (B, 208). Just prior to calling openly for an alliance with Hitler[12]—in his mind the only means of preventing war—the narrator cozies up to his narratee, choosing the familiar form of address for "you" (*tu*), a unique instance of the second-person singular for the narratee. The familiar *tu* is justified when the value and status of the Aryan addressee is condescendingly diminished to that of an animal: "So croak, impossible animal!... Scum! You no longer even jump in fright at the sight of such monsters! Can't you see your torture and death spelled out for you, furrowed in their faces? So *what mirror do you need*? to fathom your own death? . . . Learn to read, on the faces of Jews, the warrant they have out for you, the Warrant, the living, scowling Proclamation of your massacre" (B, 209; emphasis added). As this passage illustrates, the French Aryan (the "Français de race" [B, 173]) Céline addresses is treated, as are his Jews, with abuse. The French are presented alternately as "stupid" (B, 78), "alcoholic" (B, 106), and consummate "cuckolded drunken Aryans" (B, 131) who are "devoured by mutual hate" and "envy" (B, 52–53). In a typically projective mode, the Aryan (like the Jewish) identity Céline constructs is as obsessively hateful and envious as the narrator himself proves to be. If Céline intends his reading public to be Aryan (or at least non-Jewish), any attempt to foster ideological complicity, emotional empathy, and trust between Céline (the author/narrator) and his addressee is undermined when the potential ally is directly and colorfully assailed as a moron, blind to the imminent war. One such diatribe ends when he tells the credulously submissive Aryans: "You don't have heads, all you have are coconuts, and you know how they're opened! one sharp blow!" (B, 178). Remarkably, it is with such effrontery that Céline sought to spur his reading public—these ignorant, mindless and apathetic Aryans—into action against his warmongering Jews.

The "massacre" to which Céline's racist, persecuted, and bellicose Jews were herding his Aryan brothers is one to which he would have liked to usher the Jews: "If lambs are needed in the Aventure, let's bleed the Jews!" (B, 222). As much as he appears to empathize with the persecution complex from which he believes Jews typically suffer, he is convinced that their paranoia is rushing Aryans into another calamitous war. As a preventive measure, he verbally launches a preemptive strike against them; singled out for direct (verbal) attack, the flustered Aryan is provoked by insult and thus obliged, however reluctantly, to take sides in the conflict: "What are you waiting for, dead as a door nail?... Waiting for a death rattle?... Come on, [muster up some] courage!... You're an obstruction! You're grotesque! You're obscene! . . . Can't you read the signs?... The tea leaves?... Come on, let's go! wake up!... The pistols are on the table!" (B, 192). The narrator-narratee relationship is caught in a power dynamic: the narrator occupies the position of "top man," lording his authority over a passive, dim-witted narratee he is egging on so that the latter will stand up against the (Jewish) forces he believes are propelling the world toward war. The virile bravado Céline displays here toward Aryans is noteworthy since it is much the same phallocentric demeanor he adopts toward an array of "other" social categories he disparages including Jews, women, non-Europeans, and peoples of color (primarily "black" and "yellow"). What is the force that Céline, like Molière's Arnolphe, finds so alluring on "the side of the beard"? As I will demonstrate, Céline's preoccupation with male anatomy as a marker of sexual difference (and value)— namely, a focalization on penises and, particularly in relationship to Jews, on foreskins (prépuces), or a lack thereof—is indeed closely related to his racist valorization of sameness over difference (which also frequently affirms simultaneously the primacy of male, [hetero]sexual identity) as well as to the phallic assertion and counterassertion of power (i.e., virility) in both the persecutor and the persecuted.

As early as *Voyage au bout de la nuit*, the Célinian narrator's admiration of phallic power is evidenced by his envy of another man's "thing" (truc)—"endowed as he was, the lucky devil, with a tremendous penis" (R1, 360)—and in the veneration of his own "thing" (machin [410]). In *L'Ecole des cadavres*, one of "Céline's" old flames, the sharp-tongued mermaid who appears in the opening chapter, refers to him appreciatively as "Pretty Dick!" (Belle bite). Moreover, the "author" appears to be proud of his manly capacity to stir up everyone's anger. "I'm one of those authors who's got gusto, good reflexes, muscles. I piss off the entire human species with my frightful retorts, my fantastic pair of balls (and by fucking God I'm proving it!). I spurt, I conclude, I triumph, I soak the page with genius." (E, 213). For Céline, sexual and verbal prowess are, quite obviously, interrelated. Once again, the first few pages of *L'Ecole des cadavres* (in which he tersely, but graphically, vaunts his anatomical endowment) illustrate the intertwining in Céline's political writing of the scriptural and the sexual, of the political and the phallic, of erotic impulse and emotional rage: "So, pass me the ink of the Seine... You'll see what I have to say... how I soak my dick in vitriol!" (EC, 15). Coincidentally, the "tempting" mermaid of this opening scene escapes, in a splash, his threats of virile verbosity.

Céline was in fact circumcized,[13] an unusual practice among European Christians of his generation. This circumcision, a literal as well as symbolic castration of sorts, certainly must have encouraged his psychic identification with a ritually circumcized ethnic group he frequently refers to as the "foreskinless" (non-prépucés). When Céline bellows, "Till the end of time, the Jew will crucify us in order to avenge his foreskin" (B, 98), he may be speaking as much about himself as he is about Jews. The blustering *machismo* that is so conspicuous in his works, both political and literary, is particularly relevant to the discussion of Céline's anti-Semitism; he portrays his Jewish foes as both emasculated (because they are circumcized and thus, like their bourgeois lackeys, have had their capacity for emotional immediacy "castrated" [B, 123]) and emasculating (because of the enormous political and economic power they wield). As mentioned, Céline's aggression toward Jews also includes the sentiment of envy. Jews present not only the frightful spectre of his own castration (circumcision) and mirror his own persecution complex but are also worthy of his envy because of the virile force of mastery and influence that they represent for him and that he clearly seeks for himself.

The identity of Jews and blacks is closely tied in Céline's racist diatribes. In his postwar novels, Céline shifts attention away from these racial or ethnic groups to magnify the threat of an imminent invasion by an Asiatic, or "Yellow Peril." As Sander Gilman points out, however, "the very concept of color is a quality of Otherness, not of reality. For not only are blacks black in this amorphous world of projection, so too are Jews" (1985, 30). In likening blacks to Jews, Céline is in fact drawing on a long and well-developed tradition of European iconography that, Sanders notes, can be traced to the Middle Ages: "The depth of the association of the Jew with the black enabled non-Jewish Europeans during the nineteenth century to 'see' the Jews as blacks" (34). Céline's physiological descriptions of blacks amplify imagery of anatomical endowment and prowess that, as in the case with Jews, affords them considerable (and much envied) powers of sexual mastery. As in his portrayal of other ethnic and sexual antagonists, Céline's construction of racial difference relies heavily on standard stereotypes. Blacks are thus physionomically configured as "frizzy-haired ones [who] fuck hard"; these burning "volcanos" are "dicks made human!" which entice weak-willed Aryan women ("Women lose themselves over niggers"[14]). Unable to compete with their sexual rivals, the very existence of the relatively feeble white male (and thus the entire race) is threatened: "Kinky is King of the day... He's on the rise... the white's in decline" (B, 228). Céline proceeds to identity negroid traits in the Jewish population and to confound (and ultimately animalize) both groups: "Messieurs kikes, semi-niggers" (B, 133); "the Semite, in actuality a nigger, is but a perpetual brute on his tom-tom" (B, 136); "the Jew is nigger already" (EC, 284). He also wishes to see both expelled from France and returned "to their own homelands" (chez eux): "Give or take a nigger, I prefer the cannibals... and then, not here... in their own country" (B, 145). In his third and last pamphlet, *Les Beaux Draps*, the "nigger" is viewed as ruling the entire world by dint of his imperious penis whose brawn surpasses even that of the Jews: "The nigger, the Jew's real daddy, who has an even bigger member, [is] the only one who stands out, after all the spoilage" (BD, 196). As seen in his attitude toward Jews, Céline envies the power, in this case phallic, he attributes to blacks while despising them for the emasculating effect they have on the white (Aryan) men (and women) they subjugate.

For Céline, sodomy is the most abject form of sexual submission and humiliation. He scorns the *enculés* who occupy the position of passive sexual object although, unlike his characterization of Jews and blacks, his demeaning attitude toward them is not tinged with envy but rather fear, the fear of himself becoming an *enculé de Juif*. Although his narrator clearly views himself as the prototypically masterful, hetero-sexual male, Céline's political diatribe is replete with far more than casual allusions to "buggery" and "cocksuckers." In *L'Ecole des cadavres* the narrator ("Céline") quotes a letter from an individual he identifies as a "Jew," who, incensed by *Bagatelles pour un massacre*, responds by calling him a "faggot face" (figure d'enculé) and tells him: " 'if you feel like getting buggered, all you have to do is let us know. If you're thirsty, there's some hot cum for your manure snout, you'll be smacking your chops, you'll take it for cream'" (EC, 17). Céline positions his textual identity in what he would consider to be the lowest state of abjection, an *enculé de Juif*, even as he recognizes the source of his flux of retaliatory and venomous "cum": his pamphlet, *Bagatelles pour un massacre*. In her study of abjection, Julia Kristeva recalls from biblical law that all bodily excretions are considered abominably impure (1980a, 121); it is perhaps not surprising that Céline chooses to portray himself in this graphically threatened position as recipient of body fluid, which, in his view, is abhorrent not only because its origins are presumably Jewish but also because to receive it, as a man, is deemed a most abject sexual humiliation.

The narrator's first two interlocutors in *L'Ecole des cadavres* are a woman who eludes his grasp (the mermaid who denigrates him through domineering invective, calling him a "shameful, prostatic old cum eater!" [E, 12] and screeching: "I'll fuck you" and to whom he retorts: "I'll impale you alive" [je t'encule vive, E, 15]) and a Jew whose contemptuous letter throws its recipient, " 'Céline, the disgusting one'," into a fit of rage that will spew forth for some 300 pages that follow. The insult of insults thus represents an ignominious threat to his masculinity and sexual predominance, especially when uttered by a member of the ranks of Céline's objectified, inferior beings (i.e., a woman, a Jew, etc.): "The Kikes *fuck* you (t'enculent), *piss* and shit in your *dirty, stinky, pig snout'* " (Céline's emphases, EC, 17). As fiercely antiwar as it is anti-Semitic, Céline's second pamphlet addresses the Frenchmen who have allowed themselves to be taken politically and diplomatically by the rear, most particularly by belligerent Jews: "It's a new Alsace-Lorraine to get buggered by the Jews! every true patriot is firmly resolved, for the glory of France!" (EC, 181). Although his Semitic adversaries, he claims, have enslaved and sodomized willing throngs of "fanatical Aryan serfs," Germany, quite the contrary, had been admirably successful in preserving "her" autonomy: "Germany has always stayed away from latinism. She's managed to do splendidly without it! She's never been prone to the marvelous buggery by haughty Roman armies, by athletes of rhetoric, prelude to the other precious buggery of conspiring, wildly fanatical Jews" (EC, 252–53). Céline paints a picture of the peoples west of the Rhine as diametrically opposite to their eastern neighbors, whose Nazi ideology emphasized sexual "restraint" and "discipline" (Mosse, 1985, 160).

The Aryan "narratee" is not always directly addressed in *L'Ecole des cadavres*: Céline at times will speak in third-person generalities, for example: "men need hatred to live"; "it's in their nature. They just need to have [this hatred] for the Jews, not for Germans. . . . Hate for Germans is unnatural. It's an inversion" (EC, 284). One of Céline's central aims is that of informing his compatriots of the frightfully emasculating effects of "inversion." A diplomatic and military alliance with Germany is, in his mind, more in accordance with "nature" and sanctioned virility.[15] As such, the subject he ideologically challenges, both directly and indirectly, is expected to ally him- or herself with the narrator's effort to fend off all forms of enemy penetration of the most sacred orifices of the French body politic.

Along with intense envy and hatred, the spectrum of Céline's emotions regarding Jews includes an intense fear of being sexually overpowered; Aryans are seen as especially vulnerable prey. French literary and political figures such as François Mauriac and Pierre Laval are ludicrously identified as Jews; in reference to such "kikes" (youtres), Céline asserts: "When you're blond and blue-eyed, it's easy to see yourself buggered by such people... [their] ponderous gaze puts you on the defensive" (R2, 1036). In *L'Ecole des cadavres*, Céline will use direct address to forewarn of the threat of "Jewish buggery," encouraging his addressees to protect their menaced virility: "The Jews will snap up our jobs . . . shit in your beds, bugger your sons. That's how it is and will be! Let's sing the Kike-a-doo-da-loo [la Youpipignolle]" (EC, 42). Paradoxically, the omnipotent Jewish aggressors actively sodomizing French Aryans are themselves an embodiment of weakness because they are circumcized (i.e., castrated) individuals whom Céline characterizes as being stripped (emasculated) of all human emotion, which makes submission to their will all the more demeaning. Céline's response to such abject humiliation is an appeal to the Frenchmen's sense of virile integrity, despite their own lack of "authentic" emotion and the fact that they have already been "perverted (inverti) to the bone" (B, 136). Céline struggles against all nonemotional, devirilized forms of art: "flys without dicks! loose sphincters! fake tits, all the dirty tricks of imposture" (B, 130–31).[16] Emotionless art, he repeatedly claims, is the direct result of "Jewish standardization" (B, 141) in the arts and the media. Although he is assured of his own capacity to resist "robotization," he is nonetheless extremely fearful of becoming victimized by ever more powerful Jews.

The preoccupation of Céline's narrator with shoring up defenses against a rear attack by his foes is evidenced not only in his obsessive fear of becoming an *enculé de Juif* himself but also in his marked concern for strengthening his verbal and moral vigor. Alice Y. Kaplan has noted that in *Bagatelles pour un massacre* the process of "Jewification" and "contamination by Jews" generally takes place "up the ass." In Kaplan's reading, "Jews are excrement incorporated—the 'ex' become 'propre'; the dirty, clean" (1986, 107). She neglects, however, to explore the sexual ramifications of Céline's use of the expression *enculé de Juif*. The attitudes Céline adopts with respect to Jewish identity vacillate between a fear of the passive as well as the aggressive traits of his adversary, as they fluctuate textually according to the narrator's capacity to control his sphincter. In his earlier works, Céline makes much ado of his heroes' anal fixation. In *Mort à crédit*, for example, the narrator frequently refers to his childhood trauma of having a perpetually soiled bum as a result of always defecating "like a bird, between two storms" (R1, 566). The victimized child of this novel, constantly harassed and terrorized by his parents (particularly his father, Auguste), loses all control after bludgeoning his father with his typewriter; he then suffers from an intense, Oedipally charged bout of diarrhea: "My asshole is convulging... I'm shitting in my pants" (R1, 824). Céline's predilection for scatological description is also evident in page after page of *Guignol's Band, II*, where Ferdinand (like his father, he says) loudly erupts in a verbal (oral) as well as physical (anal) delirium (R3, 588–91). In contrast to his painstaking and punctilious method of composing his literary works, Céline wrote all of the pamphlets very quickly. Interestingly, it is when his verbiage is the most free-flowing and expurgatory that Céline focuses most obsessively on the thematics of *la race d'enculés*.

Céline's verbal output slows considerably in the closing segments of his last pamphlet, *Les Beaux Draps*, the only tract first published during the war. A colloquialism describing the situation in which France finds itself in the aftermath of the defeat in June 1940, its title—in English, "This Fine Mess"[17] or "Some State of Affairs" (Knapp 1974; 124)—aptly conveys the exasperated tone pervading the work. Taken literally, *les beaux draps* also suggests the sullying of French national honor as a result of the stupendous, frightful defeat, one of diarrhea-inducing proportions for both the military and the civilian populations. As Céline observes in his prologue to *Guignol's Band, I*, the routing of French military forces during the German invasion of May 1940 produced a "mush of panic cow-pies in human slugs running for their lives" (R3, 91).

The forces against which the narrator of the first two pamphlets fought—the Jews, humanity's innate stupidity and masochism, racial impurity, persecution, alcoholism, to name but a few—are once again thematic staples in *Les Beaux Draps*. The chief innovation of Céline's third major pamphlet is derived from the historical conjuncture itself, that is, the effects of the monstrous war in progress that had been predicted in his two previous publications. The expression "Nous y sommes" (we're in the midst of it), recurrently uttered in *Bagatelles pour un massacre* (124, 127, 130) and signaling the deplorable state of affairs resulting from "Jewish robotization," has become the "fine mess" of the military and domestic predicament in *Les Beaux Draps*. The narrative persona "Céline," on whom the author relied in *Bagatelles* to present his politico-artistic views, gradually begins to recede from the textual fore in *L'Ecole des cadavres* and by *Les Beaux Draps* has been virtually eliminated as a characterized narrative entity. In its stead, one finds a first-person "narrative" voice who makes extensive extratextual reference to the identity of Céline, the author and medical doctor.

In much the same ideological vein as the earlier pamphlets, in *Les Beaux Draps*, Céline proclaims his belief that Jews and Freemasons were endeavoring to eradicate from the earth everyone but themselves; with the possible exception of a few "poor, inoffensive maniacs" (BD,

42), himself included, who, (like his farcical character Jules in *Normance*), were guilty of nothing more than their "inoffensive" theatrics, brandishing "pamphlets, fools' scepters and noisemakers" (BD, 42). His relationship to Jews is as complex and confounding in his last pamphlet as it is in the two that precede it; his own subjectivity, like that of the Catholic Aryan hordes he reviles (who "regret [they were] not born Jewish" [BD, 70], remains inextricably tied with (and in this example, becomes the negation of) Jewish identity: "The rest of us, we were born backwards, born for catechism, the angelus of onion skins [pelures], the breviary of sirloins, men of consumption, brutes for battle" (BD, 102).

In *Les Beaux Draps*, the narratee-"reader" is directly addressed with great frequency and continues to be the object of scorn and abuse: "I'm telling you, you gang of bastards, all you're still good for is Hell" (BD, 26); "Take my word for it, pinhead" (BD, 57). It is in the pamphlets that Céline's narratee is first given the prerogative of speech. In *Bagatelles*, the utterances of this textual interlocutor are conveyed through the speech of the narrator: "You'll tell me that all this is a bunch of blabber, Ferdinand's off his rocker again" (B, 64); "Ah! so you'll say... it's all overstated... This kid's exaggerating!" (B, 238). The uncharacterized narratee of *L'Ecole des cadavres* implores "Ferdinand" to end, or at least shorten, his "pretentious . . . imprecatory paradoxes" (EC, 283). In *Les Beaux Draps*, the narratee will dialogue with the narrator for several pages, challenging his program of "Labiche Communism"[18] (the sweeping wartime reforms proposed in a mockingly serious manner that were designed to provide all French citizens, "even the dictator," with a modest living wage [BD, 135–37]). Addressing "Céline" quite respectfully as "Sir (Monsieur)," this unidentified persona chides the author and disputes his policymaking credentials, exclaiming: "You can't understand anything about anything! Your dream has no substance . . . like all flops!" (BD, 180). Indifferent to such naysaying, Céline unilaterally advocates his program of "petty-bourgeois Communism" (BD, 137): "Do you agree? yes or shit? No petting! Time for action! If you refuse, then too bad!" (BD, 200). First introduced in his pamphlets, hostile, contentious exchanges between narrator and narratee are a common occurrence in Céline's postwar novels, an innovation whose origins can be traced, in both ideological and narrative terms, directly to these volatile texts that marked a pivotal change in Céline's textual representations of "self" and "other."

Even as his own words continue to gush forth in *Les Beaux Draps*, Céline describes the state of overwhelming disgrace into which the French body politic has fallen as an intestinal ailment, similar to the constipation from which his narrator suffers: "Confined, constipated, sly, raging, fearful, demanding, cheating, deceitful, brushing over everything and liking nothing, blabbering about everything and understanding nothing, ah! the arid little phenomenon!" (BD, 169). The theme of physical and moral costiveness repeatedly invoked in his last pamphlet will recur in subsequent works (i.e., *Féerie pour une autre fois, I* [F1, 140–41, 191) that are laced with imagery of and reference to oral as well as intestinal blockage. In purely formal terms, the motif of corporal retention is not accompanied by the reduction of Célinian verbiage. During his imprisonment in Denmark, Céline's narrator in *Féerie* (I), like the author himself, suffers for extended periods from severe constipation and gives us a detailed account of his physical discomfort. Prior to and following his imprisonment, however, Céline had perfect mastery of his bodily functions, verbal and otherwise, and was able to purge himself at will of all obstructions to his creative expression, be it a prewar Jewish literary critic ("I shit out a Jewish critic every morning and it doesn't hurt my ass!" [B, 213]) or subsequently, "Jean-Baptiste" Sartre, who, in a tape-worm characterization, Céline succeeds in expelling from his bowels but who continues to aggravate him with unfavorable commentaries (for which he is, of course, repaid in kind).[19]

The mastery of anal expulsion, consistently maintained when Céline is most prolific, parallels the virile posture the author adopts throughout his writing, particularly with respect to the identity of male homosexuals whom he scorns for their willingness to submit to an "inverted" invasion. His narrator in *Guignol's Band, I*, views association with homosexuals to be the ultimate affront (le comble) to his masculinity and vocalizes his homophobic aggression toward them: "Bunch of pansies! You've got nothing in your shorts!" (R3, 118). Céline's nostalgia for French valor is expressed in the pamphlets in terms of the male anatomy he so greatly reveres: "Oh! If only we still had any balls at all [left] in France" (B, 204). References to male homosexuals—such as "queen" (tante), "fag" (lope), and the *enculé*—using pejorative terms designating not only the male homosexual but also any abjectly emasculated male, are in fact strewn throughout his writings, both political and literary. Céline's scorn for effeminate men is exemplified with Titus Van Claben (of *Guignol's Band, I*) who worked his shop every day in "Oriental drag" (en grand travesti oriental [R3, 181]); Van Claben is ridiculed and insulted through the use of demeaning feminine adjectives such as *folle* and *conne* (R3, 184). Moreover, the narrator openly declares, "I don't like homos!" (R3, 217).[20] He dreads having his masculinity sexually assailed, particularly by Van Claben, who, with the menacing female figure, Delphine, is eager to rip off his pants and "smoke his pipe" (R3, 215). Notwithstanding the "affection" shown the narrator by the homosexual Dédé in *Guignol's Band, II*, and the adolescent "jerking off" (branlage) and "sucking off" (sucettes) at the narrator's English boarding school in *Mort à crédit* (R1, 731–32), Céline's narrators insist on flaunting their heterosexual inclinations (e.g. MS, 83) as proof of their invincible masculinity.

Other than the parallel Philippe Muray has drawn between Céline's mythical trepanation and a castration complex (1981, 108), and Julia Kristeva's terse commentary on the relationship between Céline the anti-Semite's "anal eroticism" and his obsessive fear of submission to Jewish power (1980a, 216), very little has been made in Célinian criticism of his sexuality and its relation to his writing. It is evident, however, that the psychoanalytic links between the author's anal eroticism and his verbal as well as social aggression are quite significant. One could trace, for instance, the author's stunning intolerance of difference to a developmental immaturity expressing itself in an anal obsession, a particularly suggestive hypothesis when one considers Céline's choice of adolescent narrator-protagonists in the two novels he authored from the mid-1930s through the 1940s, *Mort à crédit* and *Guignol's Band*, contemporary in their composition to the sophomorically unconscionable pamphlets. Such reflection might also illuminate the source of the violent, explosive impulses to which Céline gives free rein, especially in his pamphlets where the historical, literary, ethical and, above all, political issues he raises are the most starkly presented.

Antiwar sentiments pervade all of Céline's works; they stem from the author's firsthand experience of both world wars. In *Guignol's Band, II*, for example, a work composed during World War II but set in London during World War I, Bigoudi asserts that war reduces men to sodomized servitude and robs them of their manhood: "In those days!... Yea!... men were respected! . . . They didn't go off to get buggered at war!" (R3, 704). Similarly, in the first two pamphlets, Céline makes frequent reference to "The Next One" (La Prochaine [B, 198]), which, of course, ultimately became World War II and resulted in the millions of fatalities Céline had predicted (EC, 78). Even his post–World War II writings continue to denounce, and are replete with allusions to, the "next" conflagration, a Third World War he believes will be an "atomic one" (R2, 750), with "the H... V... Z... bomb" (R2, 166). Céline's pamphlets have been defended by some of his admirers precisely because of his consistent denunciation of reckless militarism. The Jewish-American critic Milton Hindus, for instance, although he perhaps overstates the case for distinguishing between

Céline's "imaginative faculty" and his ideological stances, continued to laud the author and his pacifist efforts even in the late 1940s when he had full knowledge of the pamphlets and of their fiery anti-Semitism. Hindus in fact critically corroborates Céline's own statements that the chief intent of his first two pamphlets had been that of preventing another war (1986). Up to the very end, Céline argued quite disingenuously that his pamphlets were principally antiwar rather than anti-Semitic documents. In one of his last interviews (published in 1961), he exclaimed: "I wrote nothing against the Jews... all I said was that 'the Jews are pushing us into war,' that's all... I have nothing against the Jews... it is not logical to say anything good or bad about five million people" (cited in Stromberg, 1961, 104). Disclaimers of this sort notwithstanding, even the most superficial reading of these texts reveals that Céline had indeed engaged in exclusionary politics, ranting against Jews both before and during the implementation of the Nazi regime's Final Solution, a policy in which France's Vichy government fully participated. These anti-Semitic texts, however "pacifist," may have a childishly taunting quality about them and stem clearly from feelings of envy attaining paranoid proportions, but they also give candid expression to sinister human passions in a historical context with far from innocuous consequences.

The fact that Céline's three major pamphlets are not available to the general public perhaps contributes to the controversy they continue to generate a half century after they were last published. This unique publishing status does not, however, minimize their significance in the corpus of Céline's writing. Although his "purely" literary works never attain the racist frenzy of the pamphlets, both his fictional and political writings are marked by his characteristically negative views of humanity and its ills. His pamphlets signal an important evolution not only with respect to his subject matter, which becomes more crudely bigoted, but also in his narrative technique, which becomes more candidly self-representational, as well as more engaging of his reader (through the personified, directly implicated, narratee).

Although he scorned the expression of rational "ideas," it is clear that Céline availed himself of literary media to publicize many of his own, suggesting what French society should or should not be. Often formulated in "scientific" and "medical" language, Céline advanced racial theories and established explicit categories and hierarchies of value that had a slot for all human beings, including his fellow Aryans (BD, 68). In the final novels, the so-called German trilogy, when Céline shifts the focus of his racism from Jews to blacks and Asians, he openly plays on his reputation of being "extremely racist" (R2, 161). In these later texts, the antipathy, fear, and envy of Jews expressed so violently in the pamphlets is generalized to all of humanity with which the writer is now thoroughly (and consistently) disgusted. As with his anti-Semitism, the intense negative feeling toward the "other" he chooses to loathe (i.e, the Jews to whom he refers in the third person or the Aryan narratee he addresses in the second) is conspicuously projective and thus more telling of his sense of self than it is meaningful with respect to his view of others. Whether they are described by his admirers as antiwar or by his adversaries as anti-Semitic (as well as antidemocratic, antiforeign, antiblack, antihomosexual, antiwoman, antibourgeois, antiproletarian, etc.), these writings are, in the end, unquestionably "anti-Céline" for, as *Bagatelles'* narrator saw it, he himself was "absolutely one of the planet's most consummate cretins" (B, 75). Céline the writer perhaps should have asked himself—as he so tragically and compellingly communicated to his reader—the question we have seen the narrator of the pamphlets pose to the narratee: "What mirror do you need?" (B, 209). The identity that will mirror his own in *Bagatelles* is both that of the emasculated/emasculating Jew and that of the Aryan simpleton he alternately scorns and pities; it is one that vacillates widely from victim to persecutor and back again, a verbal, visceral battle driven by primal emotions of hate, fear, and envy.

Jennifer Forrest

▼

The (Con)Quest
of the Other
in *Voyage*
au bout
de la nuit

▼

CÉLINE'S DEDICATION of *Voyage au bout de la nuit* to the American dancer Elizabeth Craig invites the reader to establish biographic links between his one-time companion and his fictional American character Lola. The complex interrelation of Elizabeth Craig's name, the construction of America, and the gender problematics raised in *Voyage*'s narrative itinerary has yet to be fully explored.[1] A close reading of this central episode in the novel illustrates that his protagonist's American adventure involves not only an effort to comprehend the logic and mechanics of this new American order but also, perhaps more important, a will to conquer its entirely different breed of women. In *Voyage au bout de la nuit*, as in many of Céline's subsequent novels, female characters are often given what are deemed to be specifically American traits, such as an Amazonian stature, stony facial features, and muscular physiques. In this respect, Céline is not entirely original because the discourses of New World exploration and the nascent technological order America came to symbolize in the last quarter of the nineteenth and in the first quarter of the twentieth century typically relied on imagery of this sort. In my discussion, I examine the relationship between Céline's idealization of the American landscape and his conceptualization of feminine identity, a textual dynamic that is as revealing of modernity's imagination of urban industrialism as it is of the gender specificity of Céline's narrative topography.

New World, New Woman

As stated, the valorization of the muscular woman is a constant in Céline's novels and is also a recurrent image in his pamphlets and correspondence. But this alluring model of femininity must be contrasted with the more menacing vision of the preying, bestial woman who entices men and draws them into her essential nothingness. These two types of women are distinguishable in the very materiality of their flesh. The desirable woman possesses a firm, almost stonelike body that is impervious to decomposition, whereas the body of the invasive female is distinctly flaccid and viscous, viscosity being an elementary feature of the process of decomposition. This reductionist view of femininity can in fact be traced to the fundamental rift Céline discerns between past and present, Man and Nature. For instance, in the opening chapter of *Voyage au bout de la nuit*, France is seen manufacturing the image of itself as a locus of dynamic transformation, whereas in Bardamu's view, it is actually a monumental anachronism. France is described as a galley ship steeped in the mythology and values of an unproductive and stagnant past: "The century of speed! they call it. Where? Great changes! they say. For instance? Nothing has changed" (J, 3). When Bardamu asks, "Where [can this be found?]," he is formulating a purely rhetorical question. But he is also situating his query within the aspirations and ambitions of his own worldly travels. If the fruits of modernization cannot be savored in an obsolete France, he surmises, then they must surely be attainable elsewhere. Bardamu imagines this other place to be America, that legendary Land of Progress where he will put his own imagination of the modern ideal to empirical test.

The dialectic between Old and New World that Céline introduces in *Voyage* necessitates the comparison of two societies and leads eventually to the negation of one. It is in the first stages of the empirical test that Bardamu, still in France, establishes the polarity between France and America. As with Michel de Montaigne's "noble savage," and the territory he inhabits, America is traditionally seen as Europe's uncivilized other. In the early twentieth century, however, America emerges from its isolationism and begins to take on international significance both as an economic powerhouse and as a political force with which to be reckoned. No longer the icon of primitivism, America has become a bustling hallmark of modernity, now the colossally productive "other" of a declining, impotent Europe (Collomb, 1987).

The overlapping of the apparent geographical (and hence, ideological) purity of America's past and of its as-yet-unscathed industrial present resuscitates the thematics of New World exploration that are fused with notions of the new technoindustrial world order. Mythically, America is cast as a cultural blank page, and for Bardamu, this blankness is a positive quality. Prior to his journey, stereotypical assumptions regarding America's lack of cultural refinement are perceived as a sign of purity. In a sociohistorical context, the *tabula rasa* of America's eternal present redefined European conceptions of the machine. The nefarious machine, introduced first in alienating factories and later as the weaponry of modern war, is viewed quite differently from the admirable American machine that not only enhances industrial productivity but also provides material comfort and improved hygiene for its population. Paradoxically, America was seen by Europeans as being closer to both nature and technology, a view that negated the standard distinction between nature and artifice. In this context, American know-how incorporates nature while transcending its limits.

Bardamu is merciless in his indictment of European civilization, depicted in imagery connoting irreversible decay. The scene at the war front in the first chapters of the novel is a repulsive mixture of natural (mud), human (blood, body pieces, vomit), and animal (blood, fat, intestines) muck. Not surprisingly, his denunciation of the European woman also exhibits a similar preoccupation with corporeal disintegration in that she is frequently presented as an amorphous mass of decomposing flesh. A negative foil to the myth of the vibrant American woman elaborated in the early period of New World exploration and conquest,[2] the figure of European woman as emblem of her civilization's decline is revived in twentieth-century writings such as Céline's in an effort to justify the European male's flight from the Old World and its putrefying femininity.

Throughout his fiction, Céline has recourse to numerous turn-of-the-century feminine models that enjoyed, and continue to enjoy, wide currency. The women his protagonists encounter belong to the gallery of negative female clichés that emerged in fin-de-siècle art and literature: the "whore of Babylon" (Musyne in *Voyage*), the man-eater (Mme Gorloge in *Mort à crédit*), the Ophelia (Nora Merrywin in *Mort à crédit*), the nymphomaniac (Sosthène's wife in *Guignol's Band*), and the pedophile (Ferdinand's mother's clients in *Mort à crédit*), to name but a few. The introduction of these stereotypes allows us to situate Céline's portraits of women within the range of turn-of-century male responses to a growing feminist awareness and quest for empowerment. Chief among these responses was an effort to codify perceptions of women with quasi-scientific prototypes while striving to reinforce and uphold the symbolic force of long-established myths of feminine identity. Linking the failure of European modernity directly to repulsive imagery of the female body sets the stage for a masculine revolt against the bourgeois order that was viewed as having emasculated him. As Bram Dijkstra notes in his *Idols of Perversity: Fantasies of Feminine Evil in Fin-de-Siècle Culture*, it is the devouring European woman, however, who initiates this process by drawing a defenseless male subject into the sludge of her being and inhibiting his "transcendence of the flesh" (1986, 398). Similarly, Céline emblematizes the successes of American modernity in the body of the American woman whose vitality and strength symbolize Bardamu's will to escape from a declining Europe.

While maintaining the outer forms that correlate female biology with organic matter, Céline's feminine ideal is entirely distinct from the forces of nature. Céline takes the degenerative and parasitic elements that he attributes to the general category of woman and completely domesticates and civilizes her by striving to contain her expansive being; one could even say by casting her into a mold as one would molten metal. In a move that is reminiscent of Fritz Lang's formulation of the robot-woman in his film *Metropolis* (1926), Céline sketches the contours of a new kind of woman, one who is composed of flesh and blood but who is also forged with sturdier, man-made materials. As in *Metropolis*, Céline's American model merges with the materiality of the modern city; she is icy, resistant, and angular like a monument of concrete and metal. The New Woman is the product both of nature and of man's technological ingenuity. Bardamu, the narrator of *Voyage*, thereby eludes engulfment by women not only through their reification but also by creating an entirely altered experience of woman, one that is mediated by the very materials of modernization with which she is fabricated.

This fusion of female corporeality and industrial substance in *Voyage* is distinct from Céline's characterization of women in his other novels in that it modifies the practice of voyeurism, a standard avenue for his medical sexual experience of women, often realized through stolen, secretive glimpses.[3] The physical as well as psychic distance provided by openings such as wall holes, key holes, and windows, combined with the relative anonymity of the gazer, allows for innocuous erotic escapades. There are numerous references in Céline's work to such voyeuristic encounters. In *Mort à crédit*, Ferdinand and his coworker, Robert, climb on to the stove in the Gorloge kitchen to spy on Mme Gorloge and Antoine during their love-making in an adjoining room.

But the wall or door that separates the voyeur from the person(s) on the other side does not always guarantee the safety of distance. The object of the voyeur's gaze can still turn the tables and take control. Mme Gorloge, for example, is aware of Ferdinand's propensity for peeping and turns it to her advantage by forcing him to cross the line of demarcation separating indirect participation from direct involvement in the sexual act.

In *Voyage*, however, such conventional forms of voyeurism fail to satiate the protagonist's desire for the feminine ideal. More satisfying to him are the cinematic experiences described in the American episode that offer the potential for less threatening autoerotic moments, such as those in which he indulges before silent celluloid goddesses similar to the one Céline's narrator will later describe so graphically in *D'un Château l'autre*: "Anybody who remembers those good old days remembers Suzanne... what a screen artist! and her vaporous negligees against a background of 'soft blue light!' of 'moonlight'... what a sublime artist, absolutely silent, no talkies in those days... it's the word that kills!... a woman that talks softens your pecker, ah, they came up hard at the silent pictures!... Take a look at the movie houses today! the trouble they have filling up!... blah-blah-blah... crushing soporific... gloomy balls... soft cocks!... smiles, vaporous negligees! tender music! we'll be returning to all that!... and moonlight!" (C, 49–50). The glutinous quality of the contacts Bardamu typically has with women disappears entirely in that juncture between viewer and film, dissolved by the cinematic medium itself. Bardmu's actual physical distance from the screen allows him a margin of safety he is not granted in his normal erotic encounters with women. In the passage cited, for instance, the materiality (however illusory) of Suzanne's female body is minimized. References to her "vaporous negligees," softness, and the lulling effects of the moonlight illustrate not only the effectiveness of visual techniques used by early filmmakers to create the sultry beauty of female screen idols but also draws on the "floating woman" imagery so prevalent, according to Dijkstra, in late-nineteenth-century visual art forms (1986, 87–89). The mistiness surrounding these women in early cinematography creates the impression that they are but atomized particles about to evaporate into thin air. Their volatility further reinforces in the male viewer a sense of his own corporeal solidity and of his ability to exert power over the viewed feminine object without actually advancing to direct physical contact.[4] As Dijkstra notes, the allure of the original screen goddesses depended in large part on this sort of "feminine unsubstantiality" (89), which the introduction of sound greatly affected. More closely approximating the real thing, talking pictures had a disruptive effect on the flow of male fantasies and dramatically altered the sense of feminine plasticity, a development that Céline's narrator contends emptied all the movie houses, presumably frequented only by fantasy-craving male viewers.

In the first quarter of the century, film was, as it remains today, a powerful ideological instrument. Although French and German films enjoyed a good deal of financial and critical success in this period, American cinema quickly gained on its European competitors (Collomb, 1987, 76). This was in part due to its valorization of spectacle over art. Having far greater resources, American cinema was able to assert itself internationally through large-scale distribution overseas (77). Hollywood productions quickly became the standard for measuring cinematographic success as well as the model for generating a mediated sexual experience. Hollywood's ascendancy hastened the normalization of American taste and style in Western cinema. For instance, Suzanne Bianquetti, the film starlet to whom Céline refers in *D'un Château l'autre* (R2, 1075), is prototypically American and bears a striking physical resemblance to the New Woman configured in *Voyage au bout de la nuit*.

However, it is not only alluring celluloid images that help to forge the Célinian protagonist's relation to the New Woman. It is the entire cinematic experience, enhanced by comfortable seating, climate control, muted lighting, and music, that shapes this relation: "It was warm and cozy in the movie house. An enormous organ, as mellow as in a cathedral, a heated cathedral I mean, organ pipes like thighs. They don't waste a moment. Before you know it, you're bathing in an all-forgiving warmth. Just let yourself go and you'll begin to think the world has been converted to loving-kindness. I almost was myself."(J, 173–74). Going to the movies becomes a wholesome activity in which Bardamu revels in warmth and affection as opposed to being traumatized by his typically tacky and sooty contacts with women he encounters in the brutalizing outside world. Inside, the filmic embrace frees him of his inhibitions ("all-forgiving warmth")[5] and allows him to absorb "a small dose of [the cinema's] admirable ecstasy" (J, 174). He likens the spectacular female thighs projected on the silver screen and that he beholds with such wonder to organ pipes (174), an imaginary construct that plainly decarnalizes the woman. In replacing and containing female body parts with metal, he converts a woman's erotic attributes into enduring qualities. Bardamu the film spectator performs a hygienic alchemy of sorts, transforming woman's base carnality into either impervious substances (the concreteness of movie house furnishings such as the organ pipes) or sheer evanescence (the women he views on screen). In this highly mediated atmosphere, Bardamu experiences a euphoric sense of self, deriving from the specific ways in which early cinema constructed the male heterosexual viewer.[6]

It is with notions of femininity such as he envisages at the movies that Bardamu sets out to conquer the American Woman. Constitutionally, she is a far cry from the French women who belongs to the "race" that Bardamu reviles in his discussion with Arthur Ganate in the opening scene of the novel. This is not to say that the American woman is the source of the Célinian protagonist's desire but, rather, that she comes to embody the protagonist's conviction or "faith" that the object of his desire actually exists and he might one day possess her. The dedication of the novel to Elizabeth Craig suggests that the ideal is more than mere fantasy. But by its very foreignness, her name also situates the object of desire at a geographic remove, thereby underscoring the fact that it is attainable only well beyond Europe's borders. As such, turn-of-the-century Europe's fantastic projections of America and its women, representing the sole viable alternative to Europe's creeping physical as well as ideological decrepitude, simultaneously raise and dash hopes for a better tomorrow. This is the case not only for war-weary soldiers such as Bardamu but also for a large sector of Europe's intelligentia. As Michel Collomb observes, America at this time stood out for Europeans as the yet-to-be-written other of the European psyche: "Let us remember that, beyond its actual intervention in the course of European affairs, America constituted for Europeans a conceptual frame, a projected and anticipated outline on which was virtually written the scenarios of their future. The crisis of the infrastructures is serious in the Europe of 1925, but it is nothing, it seems to us, compared to that of the spirit, that is to say of the intellectual, moral and political models that could permit Europeans to visualize their future" (1987, 85). America, he adds, is not solely an abstract symbol of Progress but also its very incarnation: "Supported by Fordist theories and grounded in powerful ideological motivations, the idealization of America reaches its pinnacle: abstract social space, purified of all the contradictions in which Europe is floundering, it becomes, in the language of liberal intellectuals, a euphoric norm, a concretized anticipation of Progress" (1987, 87). It is here, at the high point of Europe's "idealization of America," that Bardamu's desire for the American landscape converges with his belief that New World women are a source of renewal. His desire to travel to America is sparked by his wartime encounter with Lola's body, an object on to which he projects his aspirations for, and through which he visualizes his fantasies of, the future. His desire to travel to America is fostered by both his frustrating and failed relationship with the French prostitute Musyne and his devastating experience of war. Abandoned by Musyne, he remarks: "from that time on I became harder and harder to please. I had only two thoughts in my head: to save my skin and go to America" (J, 69).

The American objective, formulated in response to his pressing need to flee both Europe's military conflict and its degenerate women, echoes an earlier sentiment expressed in his first experience of the war: "I'd lost my virginity" (J, 10). The metaphorization of war as whore ("You've got to be pretty much alone with her as I was then to get a good look at her, the slut, full face and profile" [J, 10]) parallels the disparagingly feminized images introduced in descriptions of the countryside through which Bardamu roams during the war, an unsightly, frighteningly expansive, and chaotic terrain with "roads that don't go anywhere" and "endless fields of mud" (J, 8). The presence of an American woman's name on the dedicatory page of the novel prepares the reader for the role America will initially play as counterforce to this ghastly reality, one that directs the protagonist's hopes toward an "other," more life-affirming sphere of existence where the female body, or so he imagines, is an organized and fully contained landscape from whose "depths" no "horror" can erupt (J, 9).

The Anatomy of the American Body

One of the most revealing passages regarding Bardamu's (con)fusion of the American landscape with the American woman's body can be found in his erotic encounter with Lola during the war. "It was," he unabashedly states, "in the immediate vicinity of Lola's rear end that I received the message of a new world" (J, 44). The most intimate parts of Lola's body carry a message from this "new" world and ultimately compel him to undertake his "pilgrimage" (J, 44) there. But the message is essentially nonverbal, not only because of the specific human orifice from which it obviously derives but also, perhaps more important, because Lola herself is reticent to expound on her homeland: "Lola made me curious about the United States, because of the questions I started asking right away and that she hardly answered at all" (J, 40).

Bardamu's notions concerning America are not in the least tainted by Lola's reserve and her vapid remarks concerning New York society. Her silence is not interpreted as a deliberate attempt to hide and preserve America's treasures. Lola does not withhold information so much as she unwittingly exhibits her limited intellectual faculties. Her inability to express thoughts other than those she gleans from war propaganda and the society columns only heightens Bardamu's curiosity about America. Like an automaton that interacts with humans only according to programmed instructions, Lola regurgitates an endless stream of patriotic drivel that, although eliciting a visceral reaction from Bardamu,[7] fails to dissuade him from enjoying her sexual favors: "Nevertheless, since she was sexually accommodating, I listened and never contradicted her" (J, 42). The lack of detail in her responses to his questions concerning her native land invites him to fill in the gaps with information he can either provide himself or locate elsewhere. Consequently, he impulsively projects a trip to the very source of that information. As for the lacunae in their daily conversations, Bardamu actively fills them either with his own prattle or by engaging his American paramour in sexual activity.[8] Their love-making does not trigger his dread of the torrential female fluids linked in his mind to the inundating European woman. And although Lola's room in Paris is filled with photographs of her numerous suitors, this is more a decorative album of friendships that may or may not have been intimate than a grandiose display of her erotic conquests. There is no evidence of sexual excesses that would divest her of a certain hygienic purity. Hers is not a threateningly assertive and wanton body; she is passive and thoroughly "accommodating."

Although Bardamu credits Lola with being the inspiration and motor force behind his journey to America, he does not view his physical domination of her as an adequate substitute for the thing itself. Through his contact with Lola's body, he indeed forms his notions of what America has to offer, but it is clear from the generally unfavorable portrait the narrator sketches of her character that his protagonist does not expect Lola to provide sufficient knowledge of the tantalizing New World he so avidly desires.

In her essay "Castration or Decapitation," Hélène Cixous compares the dynamics of the male/female relation to that of the Sphinx and Oedipus in Sophocles' *Oedipus Rex*. It is a relation that relies on one individual (here, the woman) being compelled to formulate the questions meant to elicit information from another person (the man) who is in a position to provide or withhold the knowledge being sought:

And so they want to keep woman in the place of mystery, consign her to mystery, as they say "keep her in her place," keep her at a distance: she's always not quite there... but no one knows exactly where she is. She is kept in place in a quite characteristic way—coming back to Ocdipus, the place of one who is too often forgotten, the place of the sphinx... she's kept in the place of what we might call the "watch-bitch" [chienne chanteuse]. That is to say, she is outside the city, at the edge of the city—the city is man, ruled by masculine law—and there she is. In what way is she there? She is there not recognizing: the sphinx doesn't recognize herself, it is she who poses questions, just as it's man who holds the answer and furthermore, as you know, his answer is completely worthy of him: "Man," simple answer-... but it says everything. (1981, 49)

Lola plays the role of the "watch-bitch," the sphinx, who is meant to stay in "her place" "outside the city." Although Bardamu may express some frustration at Lola's reticence in speaking about America, his demeanor is feigned. Lola is, in fact, not actually thought to be capable of producing answers to Bardamu's questions, precisely because, as Cixous's commentary on the Sphinx-respondent dynamic suggests, she is a woman and is not expected to "know" anything; that is, to possess the knowledge required in order to respond appropriately to Bardamu's queries. Her answers, even if they were forthcoming, would therefore be devoid of meaning.

The precariousness of Lola's literal and figurative position at the moment when Bardamu receives his message from the New World is better understood when one examines the positionality of Bardamu, both character and narrator. First, there is the Bardamu who experiences events firsthand and for whom the yet-unvisited America is still the pristine New World. He uses Lola's body not as substitute for the "real" America but as one of America's enticing export commodities. He momentarily and imaginatively transports himself to that far-off land through an immediate sensory contact with (and consumption of) the product. His experience of Lola differs little from the early-twentieth-century European consumption of other American exports such as jazz, cocktails, American bars, and cinema (Collomb, 1987, 74). His yearning for America reflects a desire to go to the source of production of the New Woman. Because the city of New York is often synonymous with the entire American nation in early-twentieth-century French novels and poetry, it is imagined to be the exclusive site of this sort of production.

As mentioned, Lola's role is that of Bardamu's Sphinx. She is much like the Statue of Liberty towering over New York's harbor and addressing new arrivals prior to their entrance into the city proper. Lola is to New York what the Sphinx is to the city of Thebes. Bardamu's insistence on acquiring knowledge of America and Lola's apparent inability to provide it initially reflect a reversed dynamics of the classical relation between Oedipus and the Sphinx. In this conventional dramatic schema, it is Lola who should be formulating questions and Bardamu who should be granting the answers. Because of this role reversal, the meager information that she is able to furnish is wholly unreliable: "I often asked Lola questions about America, but her answers were vague, pretentious, and manifestly unreliable, calculated to make a brilliant impression on me" (J, 45). Her answers are less indicative of resistance to being incessantly prodded for desciptions of America than of her genuine incapacity to answer his questions clearly, rationally, and truthfully. The details she offers regarding her girl-friends, like "the potpourri of dollars, engagements, divorces, dresses, and jewelry that seemed to have made up her existence" (J, 45), identify her with the prototypical female consumer. Her allusions to marriage in the same utterances in which she covets consumer goods, such as clothing and jewelry, reduce the notion of matrimony to that of a commercial transaction. Lola is a decorative American-made product and little else. The information concerning America that she might be capable of providing Bardamu is mere commercial trivia.

Lola's mouth, much like her behind, becomes the "place of not knowing." Nonetheless, she remains, as a conventionally constructed woman, a mystery waiting to be solved by man, spurred on by his all-consuming "desire to know": "So in the end woman, in man's desire, stands in the place of not knowing, the place of mystery. In this sense she is no good, but at the same time she is good because it is this mystery that leads man to keep overcoming, dominating, subduing, putting his manhood to the test, against the mystery he has to keep forcing back" (Cixous, 1981, 49). In an inversion of their actual relations, it is Bardamu, not Lola, who is supposed to produce meaning. Lola's com-ments with respect to the America that "produced" her make a "brilliant impression" on Bardamu, simply by virtue of their impreci-sion. Feeling that he has already been duped by his own country's patriotic call to arms, he is initially wary of the alluring impressions of America Lola leaves on him. Whether that vision is the product of Lola's patently evasive answers to his questions regarding America or is rather an illusory image, it is nonetheless transformed into something desirable because this "mystery" challenges Bardamu, in Cixous' words, "to keep overcoming, dominating, subduing, putting his man-hood to the test." He has already become skilled in distinguishing the image from the thing itself.[9] Lola is not America. But the impressions created by the initial message received in the general vicinity of Lola's *derrière* set in motion the process by which he will come to "test his manhood." Functioning as a sort of lyrical voice summoning Bardamu, the message is quite similar to the song of the sirens who seduced Odysseus, strapped securely to the mast of his ship, with the promise of the gift of knowledge. However, Odysseus learned from Circe that "their song would steal his life away" (Hamilton, 1969, 214). Unlike Odysseus, Bardamu is not obliged to resist the temptations of this "song," to resist the promise of "ripe wisdom and a quickening of the spirit" (214). He must recognize that any knowledge Lola or America might provide will be misleading and therefore unreliable. If knowledge is to be found, if an answer is to be furnished, it is Bardamu who will acquire it himself. Fleeing the amorphous European female body that is so difficult to contain and control, Bardamu envisions the American body as a concrete entity, not only so she can be easily stabilized and mastered, but also because this concretization will stand as the symbol of his own transcendence.

It is the older Bardamu as narrator who establishes Lola's body-to-be-known as a receptacle of meaning. When Bardamu tells us how painstakingly he explores Lola's external anatomy ("I never wearied of exploring that American body" [J, 44]; Bardamu the narrator is retrospectively combining the language of the explorer used by his younger self with that of the physician that he has since become in order to appropriate the "American" female body as his own "profound and mystically anatomical adventure" (J, 54). Thanks to a degree of spatial and temporal "hindsight," the area that constitutes a compelling mystery for both Lola and her citizen-soldier becomes a wellspring of signification for the mature doctor.[10] Bardamu the protagonist can exclaim: "To me her body was a joy without end. I never wearied of exploring that American body" (J, 44). Yet, it is the seasoned doctor, using his powers of deductive reasoning, who concludes: "And I formed the pleasant and fortifying conviction that a country capable of producing bodies so daringly graceful, so tempting in their spiritual flights, must have countless other vital revelations to offer, of a biological nature, it goes without saying." (J, 44). Here, it is the doctor who understands the "biological nature" of his object. Through his position as privileged observer in society, the doctor, like other "men of science," thus "presumes to be an objective arbiter of the social and existential realities of others" (Tiffany and Adams, 1985, 5). His social status is defined by the parameters of masculine power. And Céline's narrator in *Voyage* deploys this power of observation indiscriminately in his descriptions of his women clients. In *D'un Château l'autre* Céline's narrator also makes liberal use of the discourse of appropriation when describing the pregnant women under his care at Sigmaringen as "my pregnant women" (C, 191). They are viewed, young and old alike, as wild animals with voracious sexual appetites who require around-the-clock policing to keep them in check. He further describes Von Raumnitz's daughter, Hilda, in the language of the professional observer (doctor, veterinarian, professor, anthropologist, "racist," etc.): "Ah, but getting back to Hilda Raumnitz, let's give her a mark... conservatively, she'd have rated sixteen out of twenty in our feminine dog show... I agree with Poincaré: 'If you can't measure a natural phenomenon, it doesn't exist' . . . Hilda, the little bitch, was one of Nature's sur-prises... absolutely no defects!... a well-turned minx, full of spunk! ... perfect?... well, anyway, sixteen out of twenty!... I'm speaking of all this as a veterinarian, a racist so to speak. . . . Hilda was also remark-ably gifted in bitchery (a secondary feminine trait)!" (C, 190). It is interesting to note that the "secondary" in "secondary feminine trait" does not refer to an attribute stemming from other primary traits. Nor does "bitchery" (*la garcerie* as he calls it[11]) derive from other essential qualities. It is something that he has observed and knows to be almost second nature in women, that is, an acquired trait. Yet, contrary to this last assertion, if he is speaking as a "racist," as he so brazenly acknowledges, this second nature is actually nothing other than primal, instinctual, and ultimately coextensive with the very notion of femi-ninity. The women described in the train station orgy in *D'un Château l'autre* are not judged by the socially marginal character that Céline has set himself up to be; they are more closely scrutinized by Céline, the knowledgeable physician and social observer, who finds that female sexuality is instinctively aggressive, voracious, and bestial. Prostitution is, in the end, indistinguishable from *la garcerie* as a line of work to which only a small percentage of women actually resort. In Céline's discourse, the notion of *la garcerie* is used interchangeably to designate woman as an entire category of social beings. In his view, prostitutes (*les garces*), in fact, all women have the same motivations. Money is not the primary exchange value of prostitution, it is one of the fringe benefits. Prostitution is therefore not a vocation but an instinct. It is Céline the self-proclaimed "racist" who draws this generalizing, essen-tializing conclusion after "observing" the young Hilda and the scores of other women exiled at Sigmaringen: "The girls in this very particular place... homesickness, the constant danger, the rutting men on every sidewalk... weren't the only ones... same thing on the rue Bergère or the place Blanche!... for a cigarette . . . for two cents worth of blah blah... Heartbreak, idleness, and sex go together... and not only the kids... grown women and grandmothers!" (C, 184).

Similarly, during his bitterly disappointing reunion with Lola in New York, Bardamu comes away reducing all women to the status of prostitutes, openly declaring that, as she appears to be doing very well for herself, she must, like any prostitute, be engaging in some form of illicit, but highly lucrative erotic exchange. The means by which a woman ascends socially, he has us understand, are not limited to the unscrupulous deeds of a few corrupt women but include all forms of opportunism in which women generically engage. In fact, he asserts, one need only look to the biological sciences for an explanation of this degenerate female conduct. Contemplating the sober elegance of Lola's apartment, Bardamu directly links the constitution of the prostitute's identity with the nefarious influences of nature: "There always seems to be a certain magic about getting rich quickly. Since the rise of Musyne and Madame Herote, I knew that a poor woman's ass is her gold mine. Those sudden female metamorphoses fascinated me, and I'd have given Lola's concierge my last dollar to make her talk" (J, 182). It is not self-preservation but rather natural processes that compel women to use their bodies as means of escaping the degradation of inferior class status. In this regard, Céline's discourse as proponent of egalitarian "Labiche Communism"[12] is systematically cancelled out by his racism (and this in late-nineteenth-and early-twentieth-century usage of the term, which claimed to have scientific foundations). Lola, like Mme Herote and Musyne ("those sudden female metamorphoses"), sheds her opportunistic hide in order to cloak herself in an alluring, yet deadly erotic form. This oblique reference to the late-nineteenth-century construction of the reptilian female identifies social climbing and gold digging as functions that, as Dijkstra points out, come as naturally to women as the shedding of skin does to snakes (1986, 313).

Bardamu, the doctor, takes Bardamu, the vagrant-turned-social critic, and repositions him in the social world. This retroactive reading, no doubt a product of the narrator's acquisition of a medical degree, allows him to establish a fundamental difference between his own social marginality and that arising from "true" female corruption. In fact, he transforms his own position as social outcast into something of a positive value by stripping women of their voice and individuality, of their "veneer of civilization" (Dijkstra, 1986, 237). As such, Bardamu's own self-styled marginality simply becomes a form of rather innocuous social deviance that pales in comparison to the depravity of the entire feminine gender.

Bardamu's language makes it clear that he presupposes knowledge of the self that Lola herself cannot posses by virtue of the location of the source of that knowledge, that is, in the hidden portions of her body (her *derrière*). For Bardamu, the practitioner of medicine, the general region of her "behind" is no longer simply a "hole," an "abyss," or a "mystery." Adjectives denoting forms of viscosity are remarkably absent in his description of Lola's anatomy. His language presupposes a knowledge of her and of America that even Lola cannot possess, because that part of America is located outside her field of vision (namely, *derrière*) yet well within his own. Bardamu's use of medicoscientific language is another means by which the male narrator guarantees his own superiority and means of transcendence.[13]

In his first description of Lola, Bardamu claims that his relation to her is not solely physical: "Of course Lola wasn't all body" (J, 44). But in the same utterance in which he affirms that their relationship possesses a fuller, more spiritual component, he nullifies his own statement and reduces whatever "spirit" Lola might have to the inconsequential matter (*l'esprit*) churning in her head, that is, within the purely physical entity that contains and from which derives her incessant chatter. Far more intriguing is her "wee little face that was adorable and just a bit cruel because of her gray-blue eyes that slanted slightly upward at the corners like a wildcat's" (J, 44). Bardamu describes Lola as purely sensual, bestial matter; her "savage" animal magnetism, while making her more enticing, also makes her less than human. Paradoxically, her less-than-humanness renders her more alluring just as her stonelike qualities seem to enhance her eroticism: "Just looking at her made my mouth water, like a sip of dry wine, that flinty taste" (J, 44). The hardness in her face as well as its flintlike properties contribute to the overall impression that Lola possesses a statuesque form. The movement toward total petrification proceeds with a snuffing out of the life in her eyes, body parts characterized as "hard" and "inanimate," "barely alive." The wild, uncontrollable impulses in Lola's nature are negated when they are solidified (and thus immobilized) in stone. She is transformed into a work of art, not because Bardamu's aim is transcendence over reality through art but because his aim is mastery of woman through reification. America becomes the promised land precisely because it is said to manufacture them in an endless production line, proof of the successful transformation of physical, erotic attraction into concrete, pliable matter. Bardamu's description of the endless row of women with crossed legs in the lobby of the Laugh Calvin Hotel is just one in a string of production line images. In this scene, the visual effect of the serialization of identical, fragmented body parts suffices to create the impression of man both as product and as machine.[14] It is in this context that we can best understand Bardamu's euphoria when he beholds the beautiful women who gush into the streets of New York at lunch hour. His cry is that of the explorer who has at long last discovered the hunted treasure:

> There erupted a sudden avalanche of absolutely and undeniably beautiful women. What a discovery! What an America! What ecstasy! I thought of Lola... Her promises had not deceived me! It was true. . . . And yet, what supple grace! What incredible delicacy of form and feature! What inspired harmonies! What perilous nuances! Triumphant where the danger is greatest! Every conceivable promise of face and figure fulfilled! Those blondes! Those brunettes! Those Titian redheads! And more and more kept coming! Maybe, I thought, this is Greece starting all over again. Looks like I got here just in time. (J, 167).

In thus realizing his American dream, Bardamu anticipates not only the dawning of a new age of artistic (re)production ("those Titian redheads") but also, even more augustly, a second coming of Greece. Bardamu as narrator makes frequent reference in this passage to the grandeur of Greek statues that testify to the symbolic emancipation of man from the realm of organic degeneration and death. From a mythological perspective, he can be seen here to be countering the curse of the man-eating Medusa who wields her powers, indiscriminately petrifying men with her sinister glance. Conversely, in Céline's *Voyage*, it is the masculine gaze that immobilizes women and turns them into stone so that they can presumably be shaped and molded to his own liking. In her new statuesque form, the female gaze is emptied of nearly all human content, her eyes becoming "lifeless," "point animés" (J, 44).[15]

In correlating Lola's body with that of the (North) American continent, Bardamu reactivates "sexual metaphors of lust and mastery" so prevalent in discourses of New World exploration and conquest. To the image of the Sphinx, he adds those of the siren and the Amazon, each of which is "experienced and dangerous" (Tiffany and Adams, 1985, 71). The rhetoric of conquest is at work on several levels of Céline's narrative. On the one hand, he invokes the lexicon and logic of New World exploration by having Bardamu sail to America on a Spanish galley ship, the *Infanta Combitta*, that can only be gliding toward rather than away from the newness of New World. The language of

Homer's *Odyssey* is also invoked in this segment. Implicitly, Bardamu becomes a modern Odysseus who has conditioned himself both mentally and physically for the encounter with the American "siren" who is expected to bestow on him the transcendence he seeks. Bardamu assumes that in having *known* Lola's body, he too will come to know and thus conquer the American body.

When Bardamu makes his journey, he is perhaps cognizant of some of America's more disconcerting myths and realities, such as its growing women's liberation movement, its relaxed mores, its gangsters, and its obsession with quantity over quality (Collomb, 1987, 70). Even greater is his desire to participate in its optimism and in its fundamental otherness from which a new man might emerge, one that has not only "domesticated technology and put it into application for [his] use" (77) but also harnessed the energies and mastered the workings of the female body. This notion of man manipulating and orchestrating modernity is instantly debunked when Bardamu is directly faced with Detroit's industrial machinery, where, to his horror, he discovers that it is the machine that is actually molding man. Bardamu realizes that "at the machines you let yourself go," "you give in to the noise." From the moment one submits to the dictates of the machine, he continues, "everything you look at, everything you touch, is hard" and "everything you still manage to remember more or less becomes as rigid as iron" (J, 194). He emerges from this technological nightmare "a different man... a new Ferdinand" (J, 195). He may enter New York as a conqueror, but he leaves Detroit a broken spirit.

Prior to these disturbing revelations, however, he still envisions a successful technological conquest of the American female and its urban landscape. The American woman is like the American city that has been forged from materials that are hardened (concrete and steel) and vertically erect. Seen from its harbor, New York is not, as might appear at first glance, phallic, in the sense that the city is transformed into something masculine.[16] The image of New York, far from disappointing Bardamu, conforms to his great expectations. The Amazonian quality of the city's verticality acts as a powerful sensorial stimulant as it challenges him to enter. This description of New York superficially presents a clearly masculine image of the city. But if the American woman is to be the inverse (l'envers) of the European, if she is to be unlike any other woman, she must, diacritically, be "stiff as a board . . . terrifyingly stiff" (J, 159). America's verticality is its siren song.

Bardamu must become the masculine corollary of the Amazonian city/siren, the modern woman, the New Woman.[17] Like Odysseus's crew whose ears are jammed with wax to protect them from the menacing seductions of the sirens' song, Bardamu's companions are protected by fear and mistrust of Americans from the siren call of New York's splendor. Bardamu attributes their reluctance to disembark to their sexual impotence: "But one thing is sure, you've all got ladyfingers between your legs, and limp ones at that" (J, 161). Taking on the adventuresome persona of the New World explorers, who proceeded him with a bravado that both amplifies his own prowess while ridiculing the impotence and inertia of his companions, Bardamu is now confronted with the "experienced but dangerous" (Tiffany and Adams, 1985, 72) American Amazon. For women unlike any to be found elsewhere, Bardamu must rise to the occasion.

To what better models and authority could one appeal than those of New World explorers and conquistadors? Although he does not display the cultural supremacy and arrogance with which the European explorers generally encountered the New World, his attitude toward the city/woman mirrors the male domination and mastery with which they colonized the New World. Bardamu's defiance of his shipmates bespeaks his conviction that although the stature of the American city/woman implies the presence of an autonomous subject distinct from the European, it is undermined by an essential deficiency that only he can overcome. She may not be the reclining woman that passively awaits to be taken by force, but she is still vulnerable through her mythical craving for gold (Dijkstra, 1986, 367–71). Women congenitally lust after gold (or, as in the case of *Voyage*, the Dollar) because it functions as a substitute for the social and cultural power from which they are structurally excluded. The land of Progress and Plenty, Bardamu insists, is typified by its love of the dollar and it is monied maleness that he intends to wrest from the American woman/city.

Urban Decay and Feminine Degeneration

The American city had everything to dazzle and disorient the European traveler. The New York that Bardamu finds is not symmetrical, nor is it "warm, welcoming, and peaceful."[18] New York is not like European cities that "lie along the seacoast or on rivers" and "recline on the landscape, awaiting the traveler" (J, 159). In his first glimpse of New York, Bardamu implicitly defines the American city in terms of the Amazon. He contrasts the image of New York with that of the European city, a passive, flaccid, organic feminine object. Unlike her European corollary, the American city/woman is capable of making a clean break with nature. She emblematizes a new form of urban construct, the metallic and concrete modern city. Once inside this new order, however, Bardamu encounters an unintelligible and inhospitable urban environment. He seeks solace from the human alienation surrounding him in the people he observes from his hotel window in the Laugh Calvin, but his calls for help go unheeded, an unresponsiveness identical to that which he experienced in his relationship with Lola. In the face of such profound human estrangement he is forced to reevaluate his optimistic vision of America's urban modernity.

Michel Collomb notes that French writers in the first quarter of the century were dismayed by "the lack of solidarity amongst [America's] inhabitants" (1987, 93). Similarly, Bardamu's American adventure reveals the profound human alienation produced by the processes of industrialization and urbanization that developed unchecked across the entire American terrain. The City of Progress may be fabricated from metal and concrete, it may be organized according to the laws of rational production, but it cannot be contained within the limits of the obsessive rationality it seeks to impose on the chaos of nature. It overflows. It bears the mark of excess. As Collomb recognized, many French intellectuals reacted just as Céline did to the excesses of American modernization: "Excessive mechanization and standardization, disproportionately large cities, cultural impoverishment, general decline of individualism, these are the prominent features of the anti-American polemic in which French intellectuals engaged in the interwar period" (1987, 95). The America that represented a spiritual New Jerusalem for some continental travelers was a highly concrete New Babylon to others. For Bardamu, America is a crushing disappointment because the reified image of the city, like that of the woman, cannot altogether rid itself of organic matter. He encounters the return of the repressed organic when he walks aimlessly through Wall Street, noting that it "was like a dismal gash, endless, with us at the bottom of it, filling it from side to side, advancing from sorrow to sorrow, toward an end that is never in sight, the end of all the streets in the world" (J, 166).

This dismal "gash" is a wound in the flesh of the modern city; it signals an end to the narrator's hope that transcendence might be achieved, simultaneously presaging the triumph and pull of the abyss. And it is this specter of doom that will later shape the Célinian narrator's vision of the Apocalypse,[19] a vision that conflates imagery of the modern city with that of woman and urban decay with naturally feminized forms of organic decomposition. From the portrait of Rancy in *Voyage*, where the sky is "the same as in Detroit, a smoky soup" (J, 204) and where buildings are coated and oozing with a viscous, jaundiced matter, to *Nord*'s apocalyptic descriptions of Berlin in ruins, the vision of the modern city is no longer that of New York's "suspended deluge" (J, 177). The deluge is upon us. It is henceforth impossible to distinguish between the metaphors used to describe the engulfing woman and those in which Céline discursively figures urban decay and decline. The American women Céline constructs in the early passages of his first novel is unable to function as the instrument of male transcendence she was thought to be. This points as much to the author's view of female inadequacy as it does to the antimodern sensibilities with which his aesthetics and ideology are so closely identified.

Rosemarie Scullion

▼

Choreographing
Sexual
Difference:
Ballet and
Gender
in Céline

▼

Once a human being reaches the fundamental conviction that he must be com-
manded, he becomes "a believer." Conversely, one could conceive of such a pleasure
and power of self-determination, such a freedom of the will that spirit would take
leave of all faith and every wish for certainty, maintaining himself on insubstantial
ropes and possibilities and dancing ever near abysses. — FRIEDRICH NIETZSCHE

I'm completely taken by the dance. Dancers bewitch me.
— LOUIS-FERDINAND CÉLINE

IN *Eperons: Les styles de Nietzsche*, Jacques Derrida asserts that art
and style cannot be dissociated from "the question of woman" (1979,
71). Nowhere is the validity of this claim more appreciable than in the
writing of Louis-Ferdinand Céline, a novelist who consciously endeav-
ored to make his words prance across the page with the graceful drive
and staccato precision of a corps of ballerinas sprinting across the stage.
Céline's critics have frequently commented on his obsession with
dance, often equating his style with the compelling force, soaring
rhythm, and formal rigor of classical ballet. Few students of Céline's
aesthetics have, however, examined the signifying process that implicates his writing in matters of sexual difference, that is, in "the
question of woman."[1] Indeed, the vast corpus of commentary that has
accrued since his death in 1961 has paid but scant attention to the

Figure 1.   The entrance of the corp de ballet, led by Bettina Sulser, of the American Ballet Theatre in Act II of *Swan Lake*.
     Photo © Paul B. Goode, used by permission.

discourse on gender enunciated throughout Céline's literary and political writing.[2] In the discussion that follows, I propose to explore the relationship between Céline's celebration of dance and his thoroughly essentialized view of the female body, especially that of the ballerina whose refined muscularity and grace of movement make her one of the author's most highly prized objects of aesthetic consumption and erotic preoccupation. My central aim is to illustrate that Céline's aesthetic principles and practice are entwined with the dynamics of sexual difference and domination and thus bear cultural meaning extending far beyond the semantic field of the famed "emotive subway" that the author so imaginatively conjured in describing and hailing his own high-velocity writing.

   The extended commentary on literature and art contained in his postwar correspondence with Milton Hindus is generally thought to complement the aesthetic vision Céline elaborated in *Entretiens avec le Professeur Y* (1955), the treatise on style that defines his conception of writing-as-emotive subway. The Hindus correspondence,[3] along with the American critic's account of his meeting with "the crippled giant" in Denmark in the summer of 1948, are especially pertinent to the discussion of ballet and gender in Céline. Documents that repeatedly foreground the author's fascination with dance, they also baldly mark sexual differences and construct the female body as a delectable surface to which his male gaze is obsessively drawn. And there is no doubt that Céline's love of dance is gender-specific, for the ballet dancers he relishes are invariably female, that is, *danseuses* whose femininity is an essential component—if not a defining trait—of the art form he venerates. Recent advances in theorizing gender identity and male spectatorship help to illustrate, however, that the type of aestheticizing, cryptomedical gaze that Céline brings to bear on the artistry and anatomy of the ballerina is far more coercive than the adulation he showers on her suggests. Drawing on the insights of film and dance critics, we can see that Céline's overvaluation of the ballerina's body, both as transcendental aesthetic ideal and object of his own erotic desire, ultimately relegates the dancer to an entirely subservient position in a scopophilic economy in which the male spectator[4] continually asserts his primacy, remaining, nonetheless, a subject that is always already lacking and foundering in relation to the feminine other he strives to appropriate.

"To hell with morality... give me beauty," Céline thunders to Hindus, going on to proclaim that "all of art [is] the translation of the lines of the dancer's legs" (1986, 38). In addition to foregrounding the centrality of dance in his aesthetic vision, this statement evinces the author's rhetorical skill in glossing over the weighty ethical issues raised in the post-Liberation juridical proceedings in which he became entangled in December 1945.[5] In placing such great emphasis on the Beautiful, which, Hindus observes, the author "always identifies . . . with the feminine (86)," Céline deflects attention away from the two other metaphysical categories—the True and the Good—with which it is typically bound: notions that were very much at the ideological fore of France's postwar purge. Far less politically charged than the questions of morality and truth, which the Fourth Republic so authoritatively brought to bear on his polemical writings, Céline's preoccupation with things beautiful in the post-Liberation era effectively curbed critical interest in the issues of authorial accountability these texts starkly raised in the war's aftermath. That his predominantly male critics have generally followed Céline's lead in depoliticizing and dehistoricizing his prewar and wartime textual practice by so readily acceding to the notion that his art translates the lines of the dancer's legs is perhaps attributable to the allure—aesthetic and otherwise—of the feminine imagery the author frequently invoked during the postwar years in showcasing his literary achievements. However, rather than transcending the malicious racial and ethnic politics he embraced in his pamphlets, Céline's recourse to the ballerina's body as aesthetic icon can be seen as a sublimated reinvestment of much the same animus toward the other he freely vented in those writings; an enmity that is artfully cloaked in his exaltation of the dancer's form.

In *Dance, Sex and Gender*, Judith L. Hanna goes far in demystifying classical ballet's feminine aura and in deconstructing the gender codes enunciated in what she terms its "mute rhetoric" (1988, 165), of human motion. The feats of corporeal suspension and curvature that so enthrall ballet's spectators, she observes, involve far more systemic violence than meets the viewer's eye. In much the same manner that modern cinematography occults the enunciative apparatus of filmic narrative,[6] classical ballet conceals its modalities of articulation that bend the human body in contortions whose neurological effects—wrenching physical pain—are never signified on the surface of the performative text. For female dancers, whose carefully constructed feminine allure has become synonymous with the art itself, ballet's mode of regimenting the female body is fully in step with patriarchal culture's efforts to constrain women and restrict their movements,[7] ample historical evidence of which can be found in such culturally diverse practices as Victorian corset-lacing and Chinese foot-binding (the latter having a faint resemblance to the distorting ballet toe shoe).

That ballet—particularly since the early nineteenth century[8]—has been considered a distinctly feminine art form is evidenced in choreographer George Balanchine's assertion that "ballet is woman" (cited in Hanna, 1988, 144). Yet, despite the fact that women generally outnumber men and until recently have eclipsed the masculine presence on stage, throughout its history, male elites have artistically and managerially dominated the art:[9] "Although women came into the limelight and appeared to reign supreme, ballet continued men's three-hundred-year dominance. . . . On the ballet stage, males were literally behind the females, not merely in partnering roles, analogues of patronage by the stronger of the weaker sex. Offstage, men retained control as ballet masters, choreographers, directors . . . producers, and theater directors" (Hanna, 1988, 126).[10] Accorded a certain specular primacy in the dance performance, the ballerina is often a mere instrument of the typically male choreographer's aesthetic will. Perhaps more palpably than in any other art form, the female body is subjected to manipulation and deployed according to male artistic desires and directives. Ironically, in creating the visual impression of feminine frailty, delicacy, and languor, ballet relies on the woman's extraordinary physical prowess, endurance, and agility, strengths that must be camouflaged in order to sustain the signifying effect of her wispy evanescence—just as the excruciating pain wrought by straining the body's joints and muscles beyond their natural limits must also be masked. For instance, the toe dance, introduced in the 1830s at the Paris Opera by the celebrated Italian ballerina Maria Taglioni, allowed female dancers to elevate themselves *en pointe* and to scale to new balletic heights. Stretching the naturally angular leg and foot nexus into an anatomically perverse, but visually striking, straight line (see Figure 2), the toe shoe, so instrumental in executing this and other breathtaking moves, significantly "restricts natural movement and perpetuates the ethos of female frailty and dependence upon male authority" (Hanna 1988, 125). Considered too effeminate for male dancers, the toe dance and footwear accompanying it, as well as the *en pointe* position, are reserved for female dancers whose bodies endure great stress when obliged to sustain the pose for extended periods of time. The punishing character of the moves and stances taken up by dancers, while never visible to spectators, resurfaces in the language of ballet itself, which features such technical terms as *fouetté* (whipped), *frappé* (stricken), *battement* (beating) and underscores the subservience of the body to the exigencies of the art through a preponderance of passivity-marked grammatical constructions such as *jeté, chassé, dégagé, pas de bourré, fouetté*, and *frappé*. Physical standards designed to foster a sense of female weightlessness and fragility further impose on women dancers a draconian nutritional regimen that promotes, indeed glorifies, the anorexic:

Contemporary ballet choreographers and directors . . . almost always male . . . mold ballet's young women to the ideal of femininity that equates beauty and grace with excessive thinness, an aesthetic that is punitive and misogynist. . . . Pert-breasted, narrow-hipped women evoke the male fantasy of deflowering the virgin. Relentless pursuit of the unnatural "ideal" female body arrests puberty, imbalances hormones, contributes to hypothermia and low blood pressure, and often leads to psychosomatic disorders of starvation, vomiting, and use of laxatives that are related to injury. (Hanna, 1988, 128)[11]

That choreographers and their aesthetic values are the reigning force in professional ballet is evidenced in their superior position within a "prestige hierarchy" (121) that grants them the authority to "selec[t],

Figure 2. Marcia Haydee of the Stuttgart Ballet ascends with seeming effortlessness to the *en pointe* position in *Sleeping Beauty*, balancing herself on a roughly one-and-a-half-inch narrowing wedge of glue- and heat-treated canvass.

Photograph by Max Waldman, © Max Waldman Archives, Westport, Conn. All rights reserved.

manipulat[e], combin[e] and structur[e] specific components [of the dance]. [These components] are treated in such a way that they exhibit the character, qualities and meanings pertinent to the choreographers' own purposes" (Hodgens, 1988, 61-62). Close reading of ballet's visual text reveals that the selections and combinations choreographers have historically made in elaborating the beliefs and stories they render with the dancer's body exaggerate forms and perpetuate norms of male agency and female passivity, of masculine authority and feminine submission (see Figures 3–6). Female dancers, patronistically referred to as "girls," are obliged to show deference to the choreographer and submit to his artistic will and authority. Gelsey Kirkland, a ballerina who worked under George Balanchine, the Russian émigré maestro who ruled over the New York City Ballet for four decades, describes the aesthetic tyranny to which he regularly subjected his dancers, recalling how, on one occasion, Balanchine "halted class and approached me for a kind of physical inspection. With his knuckles, he thumped on my sternum and down [my] rib cage clucking his tongue and remarking, 'Must see the bones.' . . . He did not merely say 'Eat less.' He said repeatedly, 'Eat nothing'" (cited in Hanna, 1988, 128). Another Balanchine dancer, Toni Bentley, describes rather melancholically her experience of the male choreographer's objectification and exploitation of the female form by contrasting its inspirational function in impressionist painting with Balanchine's artistic use and abuse of her flesh: "It's a pity [Balanchine] needs 100 individuals as his tools rather than paint brushes. What would have happened if Van Gogh's brushes one day had refused to be manipulated because they wanted better living conditions?" (cited in Hanna, 1988, 128). Natasha Lesser, a woman who studied ballet seriously between the ages of 6 and 14, recently shared with me her stark recollections of childhood experiences as a member of the junior corps in the Washington Ballet Company, where she witnessed professional ballerinas serenely tiptoeing offstage. Out of the spotlight, these women swiftly removed their footwear revealing maimed and bleeding toes that had to be hastily bandaged in order to ready themselves to return once again to the stage. An ethic of stoicism prevailing in the profession prevents any outward expression of physical pain, conditioning dancers to conceal their suffering not only before spectators but also, indeed especially, before peers and impresarios.[12]

Although Céline was merely a dance enthusiast who loitered about Parisian dance studios ogling ballerinas, he was as despotic as Balanchine in his evaluation of their form. Consonant with the 1948 statement made to Hindus in which he declared "anatomy is my god"

(HER, 129), in a discussion ten years later with Georges Cazille, Céline chastised postwar youth for their hedonism, sniping:

They drink, eat, live high on the hog; which takes the place of everything else. There's the music hall, the strip-tease joints, which doesn't mean they have any expertise in the area. I scrutinize all of these pleasures.... These strip-teases. You can tell they know nothing about it. I'm speaking from a veterinary perspective. On a scale of 1 to 20, I give these dames a 3, they're rotten with defects, thighs in a pitiful state. In general, it gets 4, 5, 6 out of 20, and even then, [only] in a dance [studio]. I've never tired of [watching] dance lessons. It's my specialty. (CC/, 419)

In this statement by Céline women are generically depreciated through the reduction of their status to that of mere object (i.e., "*it* gets" [*ça* fait] emphasis added) to be ranked according to his own erotico-artistic standards. Their value is further diminished by the "veterinary" science Céline the physiologist introduces into his "expert" evaluation of their physical condition, the criterion that mattered most to him when it came to assessing female worth.

The male dancers who share the stage are, of course, subjected to many of the same physical demands, as well as to the choreographer's paternalistic authority. Yet, once again, although they have not, until very recently, taken up quite as much of the spotlight as the ballerinas they tossed and escorted about, the ballets in which they figure grant male dancers significantly more physical and narrative force in advancing the kinetic tale being told. They initiate and execute lifts, tower over twirls and guide the ballerina as she dashes across the stage. However, simply by occupying ballet's performative space, male dancers—generally presumed, according to Hanna, to be homosexuals—are themselves feminized and thus relegated to a subordinate position in the heterosexual power structure governing the profession as a whole.[13] That its male practitioners have since the early nineteenth century been marked by the art form's essential femininity is illustrated in a brief passage of Marcel Proust's *A la Recherche du temps perdu*, one of the many portions of the novel in which a drifting of the marks of sexual difference is perceptible. In this particular scene, Robert de St. Loup is chatting backstage with his mistress Rachel, a prostitute-turned-actress. In the background, a gifted dancer, thought to have been modeled after Russian virtuoso Vaslav Nijinsky, is warming up for a performance. Relishing the dancer's poise and his supple hand gestures, Rachel flirtatiously bubbles: "Oh, he is truly splendid with his hands. Even I, a woman, couldn't do what he's doing" (2, 477). In a not-so-subtle attempt to incite St. Loup's jealousy and to humiliate him

Figures 3 and 4. Suzanne Farrell and Sean Lavery of the New York City Ballet strike stereotypically gendered poses (i.e., active/passive, high/low, vigorous/limp, dominant/submissive) in *Romeo and Juliet.*

Figures 5 and 6. Natalia Makarova of the American Ballet Theatre bows and bends her faceless body into bird-like contortions in *Dying Swan*.
Photographs by Max Waldman, © Max Waldman Archives, Westport, Conn. All rights reserved.

publicly by flaunting her moral turpitude, Rachel approaches the dancer as she takes leave of the Marquis and coyly inquires: "Those little hands of yours, can they do that with women? . . . You actually look like a woman, I think we would get along quite well, you and one of my [girl]friends" (2, 478). Along with the homoerotic implications of Rachel's rather provocative proposal, the overtly feminized portrait Proust sketches of this "célèbre et génial danseur,"[14] draws the world of dance theatre into *La Recherche*'s vast reflection on and literary transgression of the heterosexual norms of Western culture.

But unlike Proust, who so artfully played with sexual difference and unsettled seemingly immutable gender categories, Céline strives to contain his balletic desire well within the signifying limits of patriarchy's heterosexual symbolism. In a July 1947 letter to Milton Hindus, Céline writes: "I'm terribly sensitive to certain physical beauties—dancing girls (*danseuses*), etc., and out of them I shape a sort of artificial paradise on earth. I've got to be close to Dancing to Live. As I think Nietzsche wrote, 'I'll have faith in God only if he dances'" (1986, 107). The instrumentality he grants himself ("out of them I shape") closely parallels that of the choreographer whose principal task is to see that the moves his dancers perform are transformed into a semblance of effortless human motion; a process of naturalization whose "artificiality" Céline entirely disregards when he explains to Hindus that "what we call *ballet* is more natural than what we call *danse libre*—which reeks of mechanization" (1986, 101, Céline's emphasis). That Céline fails to consider the punitive effects the "mechanics" of ballet have on the bodies of the dancers whose "natural" grace he worships is not in the least surprising, given the comfortably aloof position of male spectatorship from which he visually consumes the art's finished product.

Céline readily acknowledged the scopophilic impulses that drew him to the ballerina, indicating to Hindus on several occasions that his sexual predilections were more those of a "voyeur" (1986, 119; HER, 118, 131) than a "rapist" (1986, 119). The presumably reassuring distinction the author draws between the act of rape and the visual pleasure he procures in simply "looking at" women should not lead one to construe his voyeurism as an entirely innocuous pastime. Although Céline presents the scopic satisfaction he derives from contemplating the ballerina as an uninvasive activity, it is quite telling of his underlying malice toward women that he so cavalierly considers rape, the most violent form of male appropriation of the female body, rather than consensual adult sexuality, to be the alternative to his voyeurism.[15] Indeed, although he appears to glory in the erotic delights his specular object provides, his statements regarding the female body display considerable sexualized aggression toward women and a conspicuous desire to humiliate them. In his postwar discussions with Robert Poulet, Céline, arguably the twentieth-century novel's most renowned "leg man," amply exhibits what his American paramour Elizabeth Craig recently described as his "rather peculiar obsession" (Monnier, 1988, 25) with the female anatomy:

I've always been interested in the female body. As a technician, you understand; from the "veterinary perspective." Like a horse breeder who relishes the forequarters and pasterns of his stable boarders. Ah, the way the muscle flexes in relation to the others, the movement of the joints, the frisky foot, the Knee-cap!... Especially the legs, as you can see. Nothing is more genuine than the legs. You bring me a woman, I give her the once-over. A pretty face, it goes without saying; but that's chicanery. What counts are the lines of the body, which alone give definition to the physical personality. And especially long lines, low lines. Ankle, heel, knee... the inner contour of the thigh... How it all moves, how it tenses up and slackens. The veterinary point of view concentrates on the hips and the calves. Of course, in the past, there were still other things interceding in my pleasure, like when I watched young damsels in tutus: the erotic penchant. I was a great enthusiast, terribly Priapic!... With an imagination drawn to the texture of the limbs, the blessed curve that bends and unfolds and the rays of light which bounce about, dainty islands of pallor and gentle sleekness. That's why when I met ballerinas... Ahh, I was at last beholding *some legs*! (Poulet, 1971, 38–39; Céline's emphasis)

Viewed through the prism of Western civilization's current system of values, in which the animal realm is systematically depreciated and exploited, Céline's hippocentric discourse of the female body and dancer is clear evidence of the abysmally low esteem in which he actually held the ballerinas he professed to cherish. It should be recalled, however, that ballet itself borrows vocabulary from the animal world in terms such as *pas de cheval* (horse steps) and *pas de chat* (cat steps), language that imprints a certain animality on those who are called on to perform the moves. But what stands out most in the quote just cited is a phenomenon film critic Mary Ann Doane refers to as the male "drive to specularize" (1983, 157) the female form, whereby the scopophile visually appropriates the terrain of feminine identity. Doane's analysis of the operations of "The Clinical Eye" and the medical discourses on female identity and pathology circulating in the "woman's film" of the 1940s, a genre of classical Hollywood cinema, offers insight into the erotic and

152 ▼ *Rosemarie Scullion*

epistemological energies driving Céline's scopic manhandling of his female object:

When [the female body] is represented within mainstream classical cinema as spectacle, as the object of an erotic gaze, signification is spread out over a surface—a surface which refers only to itself and does not simultaneously conceal and reveal an interior. . . . The medical discourse films attribute to the woman both a surface and a depth, the specificity of the depth being first and foremost that it is not immediately perceptible. A technician is called for—a technician of essences, and it is the figure of the doctor who fills that role. Medicine introduces a detour in the male's relation to the female body through an eroticization of the very process of knowing the female subject. Thus, while the female body is despecularized, the doctor-patient relation is, somewhat paradoxically, eroticized. . . . The [woman's film] narratives thus trace a movement from the medical gaze to the erotic gaze in relation to the central female figure, activating a process of despecularization/respecularization. (154–56).

Remarkably, in his conversation with Poulet, Céline prefaces his commentary on the feminine specimen he is "examining" by flaunting his expertise as a "technician," who, in repeatedly imputing horse anatomy to his female object (Poulet, 1971, 38–39; R2, 160), demotes himself from physician to veterinarian (Poulet, 1971, 38–39; R2, 160; CC7, 417). As Doane notes with respect to Hollywood's filmic representations of the male medical gaze, one that is quite similar to that asserting itself in Céline's writings and public statements, the male "technician" continually vacillates between an erotico-aesthetic and a medical stance, fluctuations that typically lead to an amorous coupling of female patient and male physician (or in Céline's case, between horse and veterinarian) in which the "language of medicine and the love story become interchangeable" (169). The following passage from Céline's postwar novel *D'un Château l'autre*, in which the narrator exuberantly details the German maiden Hilda's anatomical virtues, offers a prime example of this entwining of the medical and the carnal:

One thing you can say for Hilda, had she lived at another time, she would have been married. She was sixteen years old . . . medically speaking... I give grades for "achievement," on a scale of 1 to 20... even searching diligently, you won't find one decent girl in a thousand. I'm telling you!... vitality, muscles, lungs, nerves, charm... knees, ankles, thighs, grace!... I'm finicky, alas, I admit it... the tastes of a Grand Duke, of an Emir, of a breeder of thoroughbreds! (R2, 160)

The tension between Céline's aesthetic overvaluation of female body parts and—as is plainly evident in his metaphorical horsing around with the female form—his concomitant desire to debase his specular object brings to mind the psychodynamics of the imaginary register that psychoanalyst Jacques Lacan argues are of primal significance in the formation of human subjectivity.[16] In the early months of life, Lacan theorizes, the human infant revels in symbiosis with the mother's body. Sometime between the ages of six and eighteen months, the child, not yet in command of its body movements, happens upon its mirror image. Bolstered by an adult who thereby assists in prefiguring the motor coordination it has yet to master, the infant catches sight of its mirror image, which provides an incipient sense of its distinctness from the mother and leads it to (mis)recognize and (mis)take the gratifyingly whole, more kinetically accomplished specular image for the self. "Caught up in the lure of spatial identification" (4), however, the "jubilant" infant, fascinated by the visual *Gestalt* it promptly introjects, also intuits this imago's exteriority, drawing the nascent subject into a dialectic of idealization and negativity that henceforth binds the "narcissistic libido and the alienating function of the I." It is this bond that initially spawns a marked "aggressivity in relation to the other" (6), the earliest form of which is the mirror image whose agility and perfect wholeness become the toddler's unattainable ego ideal and the basis for all subsequent imaginary identifications. It is no doubt this dialectic of idealization and animosity that Céline's narrator Bardamu is conveying in *Voyage au bout de la nuit* (1932) when he philosophically muses: "We spend our time in this world killing or adoring, both at the same time. 'I hate you! I adore you!'" (R1, 72). Lacan's thinking on the specular foundations of human subjectivity and on the affective oscillations introduced in the imaginary register has had a considerable influence on contemporary film studies, a discipline whose theoretical advances greatly illuminate the problematics of visual pleasure and its relation to the construction of sexual difference.[17] Borrowing from these contributions, Célinian criticism can grasp more fully the psychic and broader cultural implications of the author's vacillation between the deification and vilification of feminine identity, thus moving analytically beyond descriptive and moralizing accounts of his misogyny.

In "Visual Pleasure and Narrative Cinema" (1986), Laura Mulvey analyzes the satisfaction motion pictures provide spectators, emphasizing that cinematic gratification derives much from the imaginary register and from memory traces of its scopic delights. The viewing subject relishes the sight of human images amplified and projected onto the silver screen in which s/he recognizes a likeness to the self; an experience relaying back to the mirror stage that gave "birth [to] the long love affair/despair between image and self-image which has found such joyous recognition in the cinema audience" (202).[18] In addition to purely narcissistic pleasures of this sort, aspects of the cinematic experience are plainly scopophilic and lend themselves to voyeuristic projections. Involving the specular appropriation of the human form as an object of erotic desire, scopophilia is a perversion wherein sexual energies are diverted away from "normal" erotegenic zones and, in its most extreme forms, become invested solely in the subject's sight. Voyeurism distinguishes itself from scopophilia in that it entails forms of sadism, that is, the viewer's deriving of gratification from the spectacle of an erotic object's torment. Both scopophilia and voyeurism establish a clearly demarcated spatial distance between viewing subject and viewed object, codified positions that are typically gendered and hierarchized into those of the male spectator who takes pleasure in looking at the female's exhibitionist poses, an activity that Céline clearly fancied. In his February 1948 response to a letter from Hindus in which the American scholar had apparently made reference to a sexually explicit publication, Céline wrote: "Send me the erotic book of that cucumber! Let's have a good chuckle! . . . I've lived by Priapus my whole life, either as a pimp or as a doctor and have always had great fun! . . . I have always liked beautiful lesbians—very nice to look at and [they] don't wear me out with their sexual demands. Let them carouse, get each other off, devour themselves—I'm a voyeur—It tickles me pink! and how! always has! Definitely a voyeur and, on occasion, an enthusiastic consumer, but very discrete!" (HER, 137).

Mulvey observes that the narcissistic and sexual impulses that cinema simultaneously activates are, in fact, quite contradictory. The viewing subject's identification with an imaginary filmic signifier of the same tends to collapse the boundaries between self and specular object, a spatial distance on which both scopophilia and voyeurism rely.[19] Much of the enjoyment the cinema provides arises from the tensions between ego libido and sexual instincts that are magically reconciled in the genre's "perfectly complementary fantasy world" (Mulvey, 1986, 202). In classic Hollywood cinema, the sexual pleasures of looking are generally reserved for the male spectator who appropriates the female image projected on the screen as erotic object. Yet, if in its imaginary form the female body being exhibited and scopically mastered by the male viewer offers him an erotic *frisson*, in its content, this corpus of signs also presents a considerable threat, for it remains a "point of reference that continually returns to the traumatic moment of [the male subject's] birth: the castration complex" (202).

In Lacanian psychoanalysis, the castration complex is a symbolic rather than anatomically centered moment in the history of the subject. Entry into language introduces a third term (the "nom/non du père" or paternal metaphor) that breaks up the mother/child dyad, creating lack and engendering loss that is more monumentally "Other" (Autre) than the slighter forms of difference ("objets petit a") encountered in the imaginary register. In her fascinating critique of Freud's essays, "Some Psychical Consequences of the Anatomical Distinction between the Sexes" and "Fetishism"—key psychoanalytic texts in which the notion of lack and its relation to gender identity is theorized not in symbolic or linguistic terms but rather in concrete reference to human genitalia[20]—Kaja Silverman argues that both Freud and classic cinema manage male castration anxiety by projecting onto feminine figures their own lack "in the guise of anatomical deficiency" (1988,1). Rather than acknowledging the structural and symbolic forces that universally engender alienated desire, male subjectivity strives to disavow the loss of presymbolic plenitude by projecting that Other-induced lack onto female characters and their phallus-less bodies, a terrifying absence whose traumatic psychic and emotional effects the male subject represses, only to have them return in the form of fetishism.

According to Freud, the fetish "is a substitute for the woman's (the mother's) penis that the little boy once believed in and . . . does not want to give up" (Freud, 1953, 21: 152–53). In disavowing the "horror of castration" (154)—graphically described in "Some Physical Consequences of the Anatomical Distinction between the Sexes"—the child who has been traumatized by the sight of the mother's absence of a penis attempts very early to cover over or veil that frightful deficiency by shifting his scopic energies elsewhere, a displacement that will later account for his adult preoccupation with the female breast, face, foot, or even, as Freud notes, with a "shine on the nose" (152). In Freud's mind, fetishism is, then, a strictly male phenomenon, for, he surmises, "*no male* human being is spared the fright of castration at the sight of a female genital" (154, emphasis added).[21] In this moment of crisis, the male child is confronted with the "unwelcome perception" of the mother's missing phallus, knowledge he psychically registers but then immediately disavows. To resolve this tension between knowing and not knowing, he retains the belief that "the woman has a penis, in spite of everything; but this penis is no longer the same as it was before. Something else has taken its place, has been appointed its substitute, as it were, and now inherits the interest which was formerly directed at its predecessor" (154). In this process of displacement, the male fetishist develops an aversion to actual female genitalia, loathing that stands out as an affective trace of the castration trauma:

We can now see what the fetish achieves and what it is that maintains it. It also saves the fetishist from becoming a homosexual, by endowing women with the characteristic which makes them tolerable as sexual objects. In later life, the fetishist feels that he enjoys yet another advantage from his substitute for a genital. The meaning of the fetish is not known to other people, so the fetish is not withheld from him; it is easily accessible and he can readily obtain the sexual satisfaction attached to it. What other men have to woo and make exertions for can be had by the fetishist with no trouble at all. (154)

Although one might expect, as Freud himself suggests, that the fetish would bear some formal or metaphorical resemblance to what the child construes as an absent maternal phallus, he notes that the relationship between the missing member and the substitute object is often metonymically disguised, that is, contiguously related to rather than symbolically representing the organ that is presumed to have been severed. Frequently, he asserts, "the inquisitive boy peered at the woman's genitals from below, from the legs up" (155). The objects that are fetishized in attempting to manage castration anxiety are therefore often associated with lower body parts or with objects in some way related to that portion of the female body, such as shoes or other items of feminine clothing (155).

As his public statements amply illustrate, in his preoccupation with the female form, Céline's sight is obsessively drawn to lower body parts ("knees, ankles, thighs" [R2, 160], "especially long lines, low lines. Ankle, heel, knee... the inner contour of the thigh... the hips and the calves" [Poulet, 1971, 38–39]). The narrators in Céline's novels are similarly bewitched by hypervalued body parts bordering the site of female castration. *Voyage au bout de la nuit*'s Molly is said to have "long, blond, magnificently strong, lithe legs, noble legs" (J, 196), and *Mort à crédit*'s Nora Merrywin carries a bundle of erotic booty beneath her skirts:

Mrs. Merrywin, before we went back to school, made another stab at arousing my interest in things . . . "The table, *la table*, now come along, Ferdinand . . ." I resisted all her charms. I didn't answer one word. I let her go out ahead of me . . . Her buttocks fascinated me too. She had an admirable ass, not just a pretty face. Taut, compact, not too big, not too little, all in one piece under her skirt, a muscular banquet . . . A thing like that is divine, that's the way I feel about it . . . The witch, I'd have eaten every bit of her, gobbled her up, I swear. . . . I kept my temptations to myself. (D, 225)

From a Freudian perspective, Céline's fetishism is also clearly evidenced in his openly acknowledged penchant for the "beautiful lesbians" he finds "very nice to look at" but who "don't wear [him] out with their sexual demands" (HER, 137). The low-maintenance sexual proclivities of the erotic objects he favors spare him the trouble of having "to woo and make exertions" (Freud, 154), burdens that the more normalized male must bear in seeking sexual gratification. That Céline's idealization of the ballerina's body and her art is related to a castration-induced fetishizing of lower female body parts is underscored in his rapturous proclamation to Poulet: "That's why when I met ballerinas... Ahh, I was at last beholding *some legs!*" (1971, 39). Such male-affirming salacity notwithstanding, in her function as both erotic spectacle and, at least potentially, an object of specular identification, the exalted female body in general, and that of the ballerina in particular, actually presents a significant threat to the Célinian subject's masculine identity. Once again, Mulvey's theory of visual pleasure allows us to see how the ballet "leg show" (Hanna, 1988, 124) works to undermine the male spectator's position of subject mastery.

In her discussion of the woman's function as image and the man's cinematic role as bearer of the appropriating gaze, Mulvey explains that, in order to uphold the binary categories of sexual difference on which patriarchy's symbolic edifice rests, the male spectator of classic cinema must be given access to a diegetic image of masculine likeness with which to identify. Through this process of identification with a signifier of the same, he vicariously possesses (or comes "to have") the passive female he has taken as an object of visual pleasure via the male film protagonist's active narrative mastery of her. The assertion of primacy over the female object allows the male voyeur to continue disavowing both his own passivity and the symbolic (rather than literal) castration to which all human subjects are obliged to submit in the process of acculturation. This traumatic loss of prelinguistic, preoedipal plenitude is, Silverman argues, surmounted in classic Hollywood cinema through the construction of a male subject who, both within the filmic narrative and from the site of male spectatorship, projects his own lack onto subservient female characters (1988, 1–41). Were a signifier of male dominance not available to him, the moviegoing voyeur would run the risk of nasrcissistically identifying with (that is, of coming "to be") the female image from which he derives his visual pleasure, thereby slipping into the space of the deficient, subordinate, and disempowered feminine object.[22]

Although there are obvious structural differences in the technologies and syntax of filmic and balletic discourse, in terms of gender identity, their scopic regimes offer striking parallels. In both art forms, feminine figures function as erotic surfaces that male subjects, both diegetic and extradiegetic, strive to objectify (or again, "to have") as titillating toys. The cinematic split Mulvey discerns between female spectacle and male-driven narrative is also reproduced in the classical ballet. Although the ballerina's *porteur* can hardly be seen as having phallic authority and prestige comparable to that of filmic characters played by a Cary Grant or Clark Gable, he bears signs of "male firstness"[23] in both his teleological agency and his corporeal dominance of his mate. Citing the example of the often sexually charged *pas de deux* that accords the male dancer just such primacy, Hanna observes that:

In the duet, a man manipulates, controls and plays with the female partner. . . . The *pas de deux* draws upon the stereotypic quotidian non-verbal gender behavior . . . in the use of space, time, carriage, gaze, gesture, and quality of movement. . . . The woman "looks up" to the man, rises *en pointe* to meet him. Rising *en pointe* in some positions renders the dancer insubstantial. Unable to stand alone, the male supports and assists her. When a man carries a woman draped around his shoulders like a scarf . . . chauvinistic tones are unmistakable. (1988, 168)

The conflict between the ego identification processes the ballet spectacle activates and the erotic energies it unfetters, tensions that classic cinema reconciles so marvelously for the patriarchal status quo, can also be seen emerging in the ballet narrative, where the meanings it generates in relation to sexual difference are not quite so tidily recuperable within phallocentric signification. For instance, the imaginary structures that in classic cinema allow male spectators to identify with a same-sex protagonist who exerts authority over female characters[24] are mediated in ballet by virtue of the fact that in practicing a dance genre that is conventionally perceived to be a feminine art form, male dancers who advance the ballet narrative are themselves feminized. That male ballet dancers are stereotypically identified as homosexuals also makes this diegetic-extradiegetic male bonding between performer and spectator particularly threatening to the scopophile who is already skidding dangerously close to the margins of heterosexual identity in his fetishistic relation to the female body, whose hypervalued lower extremities are, according to Freud, his only safeguard against a return of the repressed horror at the sight of the mutilated maternal body and a panic-stricken flight into homosexuality (1953, 21: 154).

Like its filmic counterpart, the dazzling ballet spectacle that holds male viewers of Céline's voyeuristic ilk in such thrall is not without its own psychosexual tensions either. We have seen that the ethereal feminine essence ballet constructs relies on gender markers of frailty, delicate volatility, and demure submission to create a visual impression of femininity, signifying effects that Céline poetically describes as "rays of light which bounce about, dainty islands of pallor and gentle sleekness" (cited in Poulet, 1971, 39). Yet, it is important to recognize that the fetishizing scopophile who takes the ballerina as an object of sexual arousal and gratification finds his visual pleasure at variance with his narcissistic drive to identify with the image of the awe-inspiring ballet dancer (male and female) who performs magnificent feats of physical coordination harking back to the masterful ego ideal originally encountered in the mirror stage; a founding moment in human subjectivity whose implications Céline seems to grasp quite clearly when he proclaims: "Alas, only the impossible is admirable" (CC5, 80). That the bodies of both female and male ballet dancers are saturated with femininity makes this identification between spectator and balletic spectacle a particularly menacing one for its male hetero-sexual viewers.

It could be argued that Céline sought to allay the anxieties to which his ballerina watching quite conceivably gave rise by authoring ballet narratives that affirm the logic of patriarchal domination. Three of the five ballets Céline wrote between 1936 and 1948, *Scandale aux abysses* ("Scandal in the Ocean Depths"), *Foudres et Flèches* ("Thunderbolts and Love-Darts") and *La Naissance d'une fée* ("The Birth of a Fairy"),[25] construct crisis narratives in which a foundering male authority is overtly or covertly challenged by an array of evil forces that drive the ballet's imaginary universe to the brink of catastrophe; tragedy is only narrowly averted through some form of supernatural intervention. For instance, Neptune, the mythological potentate of *Scandale aux abysses*, is introduced as a figure whose legitimacy has been "greatly compromised... ruined." This once great "God of the Seas" is openly "ridiculed before his people," who see him as "decidedly impotent... powerless, laughable, forlorn, senile" (CC8, 131). He is thus quite inca-pable of protecting the marine realm he rules from human predators. By the end of the ballet, however, Neptune manages to reassert his authority ("Ah, Neptune trifles no more" [162]), bringing newly recovered powers of divine retribution to bear on the murderous Kaptain Krog, a wicked human being who has wreaked havoc on underwater life:

We find [Neptune] on his throne . . . completely recovered from his weaknesses... from his indulgent attitude toward humans... He, who is by nature so benevolent, usually so accommodating... of all their indignities, of their pranks... pardoning even their insolence!... now, faced with the horror of [a] new affront, regains possession of himself, he is going to lash out without mercy!... Neptune is going to punish frightfully this sort of slime, these sadistic, creeping, heinous monsters... with an insatiable appetite for suffering and crime!... Ah, Neptune trifles no more! (CC8, 162)

Céline's "mythological ballet," *Foudres et flèches*, presents a similar scenario of godly authority in question and in decline. While the cavorting Jupiter slumbers with his aging and vindictive mate Juno, Achilles steals his ruler's thunder, the weapon with which he and his fellow generals plan to wage war on the Cyclopes. Waking to find himself deprived of his thunderbolts, Jupiter "curses and swears, stomps about... No more thunder! The heavens do not reply! No more echo! His anger is frightening. He dances his anger!" (CC8, 192). Although the thunder is returned to Jupiter in short order, the culprit Achilles is condemned by the acrimonious Juno to see his beloved mistress Erythre and the siren Prynthyl—who conspired to obstruct the generals' war plans by hiding the thunderbolts at sea—forcibly wed to a hideous Cyclope. Once again, calamity is averted when the darling divinity Cupid arrives on the scene with ploys and love-darts aplenty ("The war of love is declared! Arrows fly by each other, are exchanged over the heads of spectators. . . . A thousand flashing darts cross each other! Love triumphs!" [203]), weaponry that counteracts the destructiveness of Juno's spite and the generals' bellicose designs. Although at the close of the ballet, Jupiter's authority remains "greatly compromised" by the embarrassing arrival of his Gypsy lover, the collapse of his rule leaves power in the hands of the endearing male god Cupid ("The reign of Cupid begins" [202]), who compels his subjects to make love, not war.

La Naissance d'une fée—one of the ballets whose supposed rejection by the presumably Jewish-controlled organizers of the 1937 Paris Exposition prompted *Bagatelles pour un massacre*'s author to spew forth anti-Semitic bile for more than 300 pages—features a thoroughly conventional scenario of unrequited love between a golden-haired "Poet" and the brokenhearted Evelyne: a maiden who is forsaken by her betrothed when he is erotically (and geographically) swept away by a bewitching ballerina. As in *Scandale aux abysses* and *Foudres et flèches*, issues of male power and prerogative take center stage in this ideologically transparent allegory of Jewish domination and Aryan male victimization, a dance scenario teeming with images of reviled otherness that acts as the overture to Céline's extended racist tirade. In magically obliterating a range of threatening differences, *La Naissance d'une fée* and its divinely inspired dénouement leave no doubt as to the sweeping exclusionary aims of the political discourse it introduces.

It is interesting to note that *La Naissance d'une fée* is situated temporally in France's absolutist past ("Epoch: Louis XV" [B, 15]), a period in which ballet was still considered a predominantly male art form. A proliferation of signs drawn from the semantic field of the premodern era's traditional cosmology (in the form of witches, demons, spirits, elves, fairies, spells, magic wands) further propels the narrative back in historical time, stirring nostalgic desires to recover lost origins and to revive a wondrously "authentic" cultural heritage, one that is unalienated by modernity's deadening rationality and untouched by the influence of Jews. Establishing this historical setting for *La Naissance d'une fée* might also be considered a retrogressive attempt to revirilize ballet, which from the early modern to the modern period had banished the male presence to the performative margins and feminized the few (now seen as deviant) male dancers who still practiced the art.[26] Rather than fully restoring that paradise lost, however, *La Naissance d'une fée* quite skillfully collapses the old balletic order and the new, thus reasserting the male preeminence of the art's courtly forms while punctuating the flow of phallocentric narration with the ballerina-as-corporeal-spectacle favored in postrevolutionary ballet. Although it by no means definitively stabilizes masculine identity, *La Naissance d'une fée*'s rather ingenious temporal *bricolage* effectively shores up patriarchal codes and anchors the balletic text in signs of male precedence and privilege while sacrificing none of the feminine frills and voyeuristic thrills that the surface of the modern ballerina's body so delectably proffers.

La Naissance d'une fée's "Poet" stumbles on his beguiling ballerina one fateful day when a royal carriage passing through town is obstructed by a crowd of villagers whose exuberant jostling of the vehicle provokes a mechanical failure. Forced to stop for repairs, a whip-wielding coachman descends from the vehicle to assess the damage and to determine his course of action. The situation quickly gets out of hand, however, when the crowd clamors to see the "twenty young girls," in tow, all perfectly "charming, [with] pretty, giggling, mischievous faces [and] ringlets" (B, 17). To the great consternation of their curmudgeonly master, the dancing nymphettes eagerly accede to the demand and come pouring out of the rig. In stark contrast to the Poet who is described in the ballet's expository tableau as a blond, curly-haired Adonis clad in seductive attire—quite obviously the figure that invites extradiegetic male identification—the ill-tempered "devil-coachman-ballet master" (18) is presented as "a little man, all dark, all cranky, with a swarthy face beneath his three-cornered hat, with eyebrows and moustache like Mephisto." "Beware!" the narrator alerts his interlocutor, "in reality it's the devil himself in disguise!" (B, 17). That this troll-like fiend exerts control over the enticing troupe is a source of considerable resentment and frustration for the townsmen, who lust with complete abandon after the nubile creatures:

The little coachman Mephisto is outflanked... He curses... He flails about... he nabs them in the crowd. . . . "Hurry, Girls! Hurry"... Having gone to such great pains to reunite, finally gather this mad cargo, he lectures the girls!... He also explains to the innkeeper that he is in charge!... That he is the master! That he is to be obeyed!... [That he is] the "Master of the King's Ballets!" He must drive his frisky troupe to the neighboring castle for the Prince's wedding banquet!... The Ballet Corps! . . . "Mephisto-coach-man"... finally gets the group of dancers together [and] with the crack of his whip, herds them inside the inn. Behind him he closes this heavy door. . . . [With] the door shut, the exasperated crowd scatters. (B, 17)

The discontent of "the crowd," whose scopic drives have been thwarted so high-handedly by the scheming coachman ("Just the same, he's quite shrewd!... He knows exactly what he's doing, the scoundrel!... He's sly!" [17]), appears in actuality to have been most keenly felt by the male contingent, for just minutes after the townsmen are carted off by their irate wives, they all come scampering back to the inn:

One by one they come back on stage (*just the men*) [and] try to see what's going on inside the inn... They knock at the door... No one answers... They try to open the door... Their faces pressed up against the shutter... They've all come back... The poet, the portly magistrate, the notary, the doctor, the professor, the shopkeeper, the blacksmith, the constable, the general, all of the notables, the workers, even the undertaker... You can hear music-... coming from inside the inn... the curious look through holes... They mime in step the "dainty moves" they are watching. The girls from the Ballet are rehearsing a number inside the Inn. (B, 17–18; emphasis added)

All ranks of male society find themselves left out in the cold, reduced by the troupe's cagey taskmaster to a band of peeping toms. Frustrated in their desire to manhandle the dancers themselves, the group settles for nuzzling up to crevices that allow them to watch the coachman thrash his whip about, orchestrating the damsels' dexterous moves. Arousing much more than the male spectators' curiosity, the vaulting figurines are ideal objects of voyeuristic pleasure, for they can be seen at a spatial remove as they are forced to submit to their overseer's sadistic demands. In this scene, it is the ballet master who provides the male viewer with a representative of patriarchal power, a narrative surrogate of masculine likeness that scopically short-circuits the potential for identification with the fetishized object. With an abundance of phallic authority and agency at his fingertips, the Mephisto character transforms the inn into a makeshift dance studio and begins flogging his unruly dancers into aesthetic submission. Because the luscious beauties are placed well beyond their reach, the men gaping at this spectacle from afar are only able to "have" the dancers by visually projecting themselves into a position of male primacy, in other words, that of the brutish ballet master choreographing the performance. As are all specular identifications of this sort, the visual bond established between the characters is fraught with conflicting impulses of idealization and aggression. On the one hand, the coachman's power quite impresses the men, none of whom ventures to counter his directives when he imperiously whisks away their fluttering beauties and cloisters them in the inn—a commanding display of phallic force well designed to inspire awe in male onlookers. But there are also many negative traits assigned to the Mephisto figure, deriving not only from his enviable position in relation to his leaping sirens, but also, more important, because the puny ogre is textually freighted with marks of racial, anatomical, and temperamental deficiency rendering him unworthy of the sway he holds over these erotic and artistic treasures. These riches, it is clearly suggested, more rightfully belong to blond-haired, fair-skinned, statuesque Poets and other meritorious males of the sort. That the "devil-coachman-ballet master" and his wily maneuvers emblematize Jewish identity and character for Ferdinand/Céline, the scenario's creator, is supported not only by the racist argumentation that *Bagatelles* so viciously elaborates but also even more suggestively by a highly coded series of postwar statements Céline made to Milton Hindus regarding the influence of Jews on Hollywood cinema.[27] Closely paralleling both the voyeuristic scenario and identificatory structures presented in *La Naissance d'une fée*, Céline's remarks shift between expressions of admiration for the other and an ever-so-deftly conveyed feeling of spite that that difference generates:

The New Athenians are certainly the great Jews of Hollywood cinema. They did for contemporary Beauty, and in the end, for artists (if only these damned insensitive assholes had a little emotivity and instinct) more than all the textbooks on Aesthetics and all of the muses of the world since the Quattrocento—You have to admit, you have to say—Hollywood Jews and Ziegfeld had a flair for pretty women, the matrix of all art. (HER, 129)

I'm . . . a pagan for my complete worship of physical beauty, health. I hate sickness, penitence, anything morbid. Completely Greek in that respect. . . . [T]hat is why I have loved America so much! the feline quality of women! Ah! Hollywood—Ah—Goldwyn Mayer! I would have given ten years of my life to occupy their chairs for a moment! All those goddesses at my mercy! (Hindus, 1986, 119)

Céline's desire to have a bevy of Hollywood beauties "at [his] mercy" is quite revealing not only of his misogynist drive to exert untrammeled control over the female body but also of his continued postwar racist animus toward Jews, whose taste in women he backhandedly lauds by reviving the traditional anti-Semitic image of Jewish men peddling female Aryan flesh. In the passage cited, Céline the author proclaims that Hollywood Jews have the same unlimited and much-begrudged access to stables of starlets as *La Naissance d'une fée*'s Mephisto does to his dancing darlings. Not only does the ballet's creator—a textual persona named Ferdinand/Céline—specularly identify with the coach-man's position of proprietorship of the troupe, but he also energetically seeks to oust him from it so that he—the gifted poet (simultaneously identifiable as the ballet's protagonist and creator as well as *Bagatelles*'s narrator and author)—can reclaim it for his more worthy Aryan male self. This ambition to repossess Aryan women—along with all of the cultural, artistic, and material patrimony that has presumably been usurped by Jews—is clearly evidenced in the self-celebratory critique Ferdinand offers of the ballet after unveiling the work to his cohort Léo Gutman: "First of all, from now on I am going to be my own critic. And that's that. Magnificently... I must mount my defense without a moment's delay. I must get ahead of the Jews!... all Jews! racist, cunning, narrow-minded, frenetic, evil... They alone... Everything for them!... Always and everywhere!" (B, 23).

Yet all of Céline's focus on the Jews and their narrative surrogates, who possess that which the Aryan male covets for himself, tends to occlude the textual moments in which the problem not of "having" but of "being" the desired object poses a far greater threat to the masculine subjectivity that *Bagatelles*' narrator so stridently defends. At two different moments in *La Naissance d'une fée*'s scenario, the male spectators endeavoring to appropriate the ravishing ballerinas come to occupy the place of the feminine by momentarily imagining themselves not as authoritative ballet masters but as the dancers themselves, fleeting moments of identificatory slippage that threaten to reveal the founding lack in subjectivity that all of this voyeuristic, fetishistic activity serves to conceal. In the first instance, although the "poet, the portly magistrate, the notary, the doctor, the professor, the shopkeeper, the blacksmith, the constable, the general, the workers and the undertaker" avidly peer through the inn's peepholes, they all begin to "mime in cadence, in 'dainty steps,' what they are watching" (18). When the village notables then insinuate themselves one by one into the makeshift dance studio in order to get a closer look at the dancers—much as Céline himself often did—they begin to reproduce the dance moves of their fetishized objects, thereby *becoming* that which they have been so intent on *having*: "They are seated... under the spell of the dance and the dancers... All the representatives of the grand and the lowly occupations... and the notables hypnotized by the lesson... They mime the gestures, the positions, the arabesques... the variations... The devil is delighted." (18).

The devil is no doubt overjoyed at the sight of this primping and prancing because he has succeeded in feminizing the town's male dignitaries, who have allowed themselves to be lured into striking very prissy feminine poses. The ploy of first locking the men out of the spectacle (a position of lack that only heightens their longing) and then gradually allowing them to approach the ballerinas further serves what seems to have been his grand design all along: that of drawing the townsmen to the neighboring castle where the chief demon Lucifer is eagerly awaiting to divest them even further of their male dignity and autonomy. Although the men venerate the troupe's beauty and artistry, in true misogynist form, Ferdinand's ballet narrative places responsibility for the abject humiliation they will soon suffer at the hands of Mephisto's overlord squarely on the dancers' diminutive shoulders, for it is their erotic appeal that entices the townsmen into the netherworld of this contemptible Prince of Darkness.[28] Lucifer's treachery and ravenous appetite for power and wealth is richly signified in the ballet scenario's crowning tableau: "At the top of the stairs an enormous Lucifer, covered in gold... sits alone eating completely raw souls... at a table covered with a cloth of gold... The souls have the shape of hearts... He rips them apart with whetted teeth... He also swallows jewels... He sugars their hearts with crushed diamonds... He drinks their tears" (B, 22).[29] It is worth noting that in this scene both the haughty Lucifer and the hapless Poet who finds himself restrained in shackles are engaging in forms of voyeurism. The Poet is simultaneously constrained to watch his unattainable prima ballerina tauntingly parade her charms before him, to witness the disgrace of his male cohorts, and to observe the satanical creature peering down from above, orchestrating the orgy of sadism he has so merrily unleashed:

From on high, Lucifer relishes the sight of this whole vile spectacle. . . . He orders the little ballet master to make all of the wretched creatures dance... at the crack of a whip. They all dance to the best of their ability. . . . The judge, quite flushed, with his emaciated, iron-clad convicts . . . The old Miser dancing with his lackeys, with bankrupt borrowers... The General with haggard, blood-drenched soldiers dropping dead from war... The Professor and his snotty pupils, his scamps... fingers up their nose... ears like donkeys... The corpulent Pimp with his hookers, perverts and little girls... The Notary with his impoverished widows... the clients he robbed... the Priest with his flighty nuns and little pansy clergymen. (B, 22)

This final tableau of *La Naissance d'une fée* can be read as a condensed version of *Bagatelles'* narrative structure and overarching politico-aesthetic argumentation. All of the male authorities (The Judge, General, Professor, Lender, Notary, Priest) find themselves reduced to the same abject status as the lower orders over which they had lorded their authority before falling into the clutches of Lucifer. The crew of male cronies are now in the same subservient position as the female dancers they had leered at in the opening tableaux, that is, flogged into submission and forced to dance a humiliating jig of servility before a demonic lecher who derives sadistic pleasure from watching their pathetic contortions. The panic-inducing message conveyed here is crystal clear: If you fail to act now, Aryan males, you will quickly find your patrimony and prerogatives usurped by the Jews, while you, in turn, are relegated to the subaltern status of criminals, footsoldiers, students, debtors, prostitutes, and, most appalling, of ballerina showgirls. Hegemonic discourses on class, race, and gender are stitched together in this tightly woven crisis narrative of downwardly mobile feminization, one that brandishes the horrifying prospect of privileged Aryan males being divested of their social, cultural, and political entitlement.

In *La Naissance d'une fée*, the narrative solution to this catastrophe waiting to happen is found in a divine creature of ethereal femininity, the now supernaturally endowed Evelyne who comes to the rescue of her Prince of Poetry in distress just as the circumstances of his captivity are about to take a turn for the worse:

Just then, Karalik opens the door... she comes in... behind her [is] Evelyne and the little spirits of the forest... The demons [are] stunned... Lucifer is not pleased... He snarls... He thunders... Lightening... He demands that the intruders explain themselves... Evelyne makes a move to free the shackled poet... "No! No! No! Lucifer prohibits [it]... Evelyne must dance!... The female demons are jealous... Karalik points out to Lucifer that Evelyne possesses the amulet of Dances.... The golden reed!... One of the demons goes to grab it from her... Then with a gesture... just one... Magical sign!... the whole castle comes crashing down!... and all of this evil is swept away... by a formidable hurricane. (22)

Unlike Karalik, the nasty witch who in an earlier tableau "lamely" dances around ("Elle danse en boitant la danse des 'sorcières'" [16]),[30] in this deus ex machina ending, Evelyne flutters on stage quite literally bearing a fetish in hand. "The golden reed" she has been granted by the charming "spirits of the forest," a gift of gratitude for having rescued one of their own, allows her to fulfill her wish of being able to dance "divinely" (20), which had been shown previously as her only hope of rekindling the fickle Poet's passion for her. Much to the wordsmith's relief, this instrument of magical plenitude allows the ever-devoted Evelyne to rescue him from Lucifer's destructive designs. Although she now belongs to the "other world" and therefore cannot remain with the repentant bard, Evelyne graciously, self-lessly pardons his dalliance and retreats to her never-never land ("She is now a fairy... She belongs to her little friends of the forests... She is no longer human" [23]), while he, in turn, dejectedly retires to the banks of a river to "forever sing the praises of his ideal loves... impossible loves... Forever... and ever" (23). Evelyne's "golden reed" functions as a sort of magic marker of tolerable sexual difference, restoring illusions of lost plenitude and covering over disavowed lack for the multiplicity of male identities constructed in *La Naissance d'une fée*. As Kaja Silverman notes with respect to classic Hollywood cinema's ideological and discursive "suturing"[31] of the male subject position, phallic fetishes of this sort allow the male spectator to patch over the primal marker of sexual difference—female castration—and to keep the phallocentric discourse of mastery from unraveling altogether, thus laying bare the originary divide in his own subjectivity: "Cinematic signification depends entirely upon the moment of unpleasure in which the viewing subject perceives that it is lacking something. . . . Only then, with the disruption of imaginary plenitude, does the shot become a signifier, speaking first and foremost about the thing which the Lacanian signifier never stops speaking: castration. A complex signifying chain is introduced in place of the lack which can never be made good, suturing over the wound of castration with narrative" (1983, 204). Silverman goes on to note that "the more intense the threat of castration and loss, the more intense the viewing subject's desire for narrative closure" (206). This is precisely, I would argue, the dynamics at play in *La Naissance d'une fée*, where the townsmen find themselves gradually stripped of their reason, authority, power, and privilege. The intensity of the Célinian subject's fright over these shattering losses no doubt accounts for the ballet narrative's cataclysmic closure. This in-the-nick-of-time finale "saves" the Aryan poet's world from the nefarious influence of witches, hordes of envious, scheming women, and dark, dwarfish demons, who, with the stroke of Evelyne's wand, are all eradicated from the play of signification—each representing intolerable differences that threaten to expose the Célinian subject's own schism within itself. Remarkably, Céline actually introduces the rhetoric of suture into his balletic discourse via *Bagatelle*'s narrator Ferdinand, who, in boasting of his artistic achievement to Léo Gutman, admires his meticulous weaving of the text's unity and coherence, stylistic traits very much at odds with the fragmentation and dispersion that have become the hallmark of the Célinian aesthetic: "Get a better look at the assemblage of all these marvels... Look a little closer at the piece... It's hand stitched... absolutely authentic... everything blends... in the adornment, the charm, whirlwind... comes together... Variations... repetitions... everything is enlaced... in the embroidery... soars... breaks free... Let's dance!" (23). The tension between Céline's own elliptical, disseminating style and the fastidious concatenation on which *Bagatelles pour un massacre*'s narrator prides himself suggests that when performing pirouettes of fractured meaning on the fault lines of the symbolic order[32] raises the spectre of primal loss, the Célinian subject retreats to the ideological plateau of phallic mastery. From this elevated site of gendered narrativity, he continues to choreograph a *pas de deux* of sexual domination and, when the need arises, of ruthless exclusion of all that is not his Aryan male self.

Pascal A. Ifri

Mort à
crédit:
The
Underside
of the
Belle Epoque

▼

OVER THE PAST twenty years, there has been a growing consensus in France and elsewhere that Marcel Proust and Louis-Ferdinand Céline are, in Michel Tournier's words, "the two greatest (French) novelists of the twentieth century" (1981, 80). Few critics have, however, explored the parallels in Proust's and Céline's writings, most no doubt operating under the assumption that the fictional worlds these authors created are, as Frédéric Vitoux asserts, situated "light years away from one another" (1988, 21). This critical axiom is slowly but surely being reconsidered. For instance, Serge Gavronsky (1979) has studied Proust in "Célinian Trappings," Pierre Robert (1979) has assessed the influence of *A la Recherche du temps perdu (Remembrance of Things Past)* on *Mort à crédit*, and Henri Godard (1974) has studied the similarities in Proust's and Céline's poetics. I, too, have shown (1991) that some of the same theories of art and literature Proust advanced in *Le Temps retrouvé (The Past Recaptured)*, the last volume of *A la Recherche*, are reiterated in Céline's *Féerie pour une autre fois* and that there are parallels in their conception of style.

Proust and Céline reconstituted brilliantly an entire society and era, leaving us valuable documents with discernible sociological and historical affinities. Proust's and Céline's protagonist-narrators (Marcel and Bardamu/Ferdinand, respectively), observe their surroundings with microscopic precision and relate their judgments and insights to the reader. Significant portions of their works are, in fact, devoted to representing the life-styles and *mentalités* of the social classes in which they place their narrators. Odd as it may seem given the radically divergent tone and substance of their works, Céline can easily be seen as the direct heir to Proust's highly class-conscious writing. Just as his predecessor presented a critical, almost clinical, profile of the mores of the *haute bourgeoisie* and aristocracy in turn-of-the-century France, Céline animated, with the same trenchant candor, the lives of the working and lower middle classes at a contemporary or slightly later historical moment. The symmetry between the novelists' representations of French society is all the more striking in that both rich and poor are confronting the same process of decay and decline engendered not only by the ravages of World War I but also by the broader cultural dislocation wrought by the unfettering of modernity's technological and material process. Although Proust's and Céline's characters are drawn from the polar extremes of the social spectrum, they are surprisingly similar in their human vices and flaws, contributing to the overriding impression that Céline's fictional universe is the mirror opposite of Proust's.

In a postwar discussion of stylistic matters, Céline proclaimed: "Proust tended to the upper crust, I dealt with people I could see and observe" (CC2, 68). In this essay, I demonstrate that Céline's *œuvre*, and most particularly *Mort à crédit*—often considered his most socially conscious novel—complements Proust's remarkably, giving voice to a segment of society that was largely ignored by the latter and that is generally underrepresented in French literature: the petty bourgeois milieu of small shopkeepers, artisans, and low-ranking bureaucrats Céline knew in his own childhood. Céline's narrators, variations of one and the same character, hail from this milieu and never escape its mental strictures, despite the possibility of social ascension that training as a medical doctor affords him. If from *Voyage au bout de la nuit* to *Rigodon* Céline's protagonists encounter individuals from other ranks of society, they spend the greater part of their professional life and social existence in the company of class confreres, people of modest means leading tight-fisted, small-minded lives. In *Mort à crédit*, Céline's narrator describes Paris's petty bourgeois world with an acuity and perspicacity that rival Proust's portrait in *A la Recherche du temps perdu* of the decadent life-style of that city's élite.

The social sphere Céline depicts in *Mort à crédit* is diametrically opposed to that represented in Proust's *Recherche* and can in many respects be seen as the underside of the Belle Epoque. It is comprised for the most part of the protagonist Ferdinand's family and a dozen or so secondary characters personifying the increasingly impoverished classes of the turn of the century. The son of an insurance company clerk and an antique lace merchant, Ferdinand experiences the deprivation and austerity typifying petty bourgeois family life during this period. The fact that he is an only child also conforms to the demographic norms of his class. Historians note, for instance, that only 20 percent of the families of shopkeepers and mid-level white-collar workers had three or more children: "In the lower-middle-class, having a number of children meant jeopardizing the future of all, or favoring one child to the detriment of the others" (Braudel and Labrousse, 1979, 434). The situation of Ferdinand's father is also characteristically lower middle class. Although he successfully completed his secondary education, he struggles to earn a living ("a hundred and ten francs a month" [D, 53]—a modest clerk's salary for the period would be around 160 francs per month) at an insurance company where he is subjected to constant humiliation by his employer M. Lempreinte:

My father didn't make much at the Coccinelle Fire Insurance Company. . . . At the Coccinelle office they treated him like dirt. His pride tormented him and he couldn't stand the monotony. He had nothing in his favor but his school diploma, his moustache, and his lofty principles. . . . Lempreinte, his boss, humiliated him in every possible way. . . . My father had style, elegance came natural to him. That vexed Lempreinte. He avenged himself for thirty years. He made him do nearly all his letters over again. (D, 53–54)

Of greater significance than the sense of style his employer finds so annoying is, as Nicholas Hewitt observes, "the fact that [Auguste] is a *bachelier-employé*, a member of a sad cast whose constant tragedy is chronicled in French literature from the Second Empire onwards." As Hewitt further observes, "the *baccalauréat*, by itself, with no other diplomas, is a sop thrown to the petite bourgeoisie which presents no danger of allowing them access to positions of real power" (1987, 101–02).

The situation of Ferdinand's mother is more complex than that of Auguste but no less representative of her class position. Clémence sells lace, furniture, and assorted other items. She is a small shopkeeper who subcontracts manual laborers and artisans, including Madame Héronde, "the seamstress [who] mends all our lace, especially the old things that are so fragile and hard to dye" (D, 50), and the Wurzems, "a family of cabinetmakers, who antiqued all our small pieces of furniture, the kidney-shaped tables, consoles" (D, 51). Clémence is, then, very much part of the petty bourgeoisie, even though she does not engage in the "boutique capitalism" practiced by some two million people at the beginning of the twentieth century. Although in 1906 its market impact was far from negligible, historians note that small business was but one segment of a socioeconomic and sociopolitical structure that made France's middle class an economic monolith (Braudel and Labrousse, 1979, 156). Yet, the profits Clémence's shop earns are hardly phenomenal. After taking up residence in the Passage des Bérésinas, she has considerable difficulty selling her merchandise, so much so that she is forced to pound the pavement in search of customers such as the Pinaises, who, to make things worse, are all too ready to defraud her. She is only able to make ends meet with the "repair jobs" she agrees to do for ridiculously low prices: "We did them for a lot cheaper than anybody else, we'd take them at any price. And we delivered day and night. For a profit of two francs we'd hike out to the Parc Saint-Maur and back" (D, 64).

Clémence does not have the good fortune of times past. In an earlier day, her mother, Caroline, also a shopkeeper, clearly made a better living. At the end of her life Caroline owned two rental properties in the suburbs and was able to leave three thousand francs to her daughter. True, during the last third of the nineteenth century when she was in business, small shopkeepers did not face the daunting problems they would encounter in the first decade of the twentieth, a point to which I return shortly. It is worth noting, for example, that Mme Divonne, an old friend of the family, profited from similarly favorable market conditions to those in which Caroline had prospered. Having made a fortune selling lambskin gloves, she owned two shops and employed eighteen people before her husband lost everything to bad investments in the Panama Canal.

Other shopkeepers residing in the Passage des Bérésinas, such as Mme Méhon the corsetmaker and the Pérouquières, who own a neighboring bookstore, are no more well-off than Ferdinand's mother and are also plagued by "the terror of going hungry": "We were all obsessed with it... As far as we were concerned, the soul was fear. In every room the walls sweated fear of going without... It made us swallow the wrong way, it made us bolt our meals and run around town like mad... we zigzagged like fleas all over Paris, from the Place Maubert to the Etoile, for fear of being auctioned off, for fear of the rent, of the gas man, the tax collector" (D, 152–53).

In actuality, Clémence and her neighbors are not part of the "boutique capitalism" described. *Mort à crédit* represents this sector of the economy in recounting Ferdinand's initiation into the business world, first in Berlope's ribbon company, and then later in Gorloge's smaller, much less prosperous, metalworking shop. Berlope's establishment employs a sizeable number of people, evidenced by the fact that it has a personnel manager (Lavelongue) on staff; Gorloge has only three individuals working for him: Antoine, a worker, Robert, an apprentice, and Ferdinand, the shop's sales representative. Berlope and Gorloge represent business proprietors, a category that in the early 1900s demographically constituted nearly 31 percent of the private sector, a figure only slightly higher—29 percent—than that of independent workers such as Clémence, with wage earners comprising the majority—40 percent (Braudel and Labrousse, 1979, 156).

Although most of the players in *Mort à crédit* are involved in business activity of some sort, the novel provides a sense of the plight of the working class. The material conditions in which characters such as Mme Héronde and the Wurzems live and labor are as desperate as those of the small shopkeepers on whom they depend for survival, although Céline's narrator clearly suggests that character flaws make them partly responsible for their misfortunes. Mme Héronde, the seamstress, lives in a country shack where she works by the light of a kerosene lamp. She is described by Clémence as a godsend ("une vraie fée," R1, 548) but is also chided for delivering her work late and for making mistakes when she is fatigued, errors that in Auguste's mind place them all in financial and legal jeopardy (D, 131–32). Mme Jasmin, a seamstress Clémence hires when Mme Héronde is no longer able to work, is a debt-ridden alcoholic. Wurzem is considered a superb craftsman but also a shortsighted spendthrift who spends more time fishing than filling his orders. He is thus unable to pay his rent and finds himself living with his large family in an isolated shack (D, 51–52).

Mort à crédit also describes the eccentric lives of Auguste's brothers Antoine, Arthur, and Rodolphe; of Clémence's brother Edouard; and, of course, of Courtial des Pereires—characters belonging to less well defined, but not markedly better off, social categories. Auguste's brothers all live in precarious or peculiar conditions. Here again, however, they are characterized as being in some part responsible for their predicaments. Antoine, who has a good position with the Bureau of Weights and Measures, and whose wife is employed by the Statistics Division, should be able to live comfortably, but the couple is so obsessed with saving money that they never have enough to eat. His wife eventually dies from maintaining this "abstinence" (D, 60).

Arthur, up to his neck in debt, works off and on, living "like a regular bohemian, on the fringe of society, in a shanty, shacked up with a housemaid" (D, 60). Finally, Rodolphe, who lives in a hovel and refuses to do conventional work, ekes out a living doing odd jobs and lands on his brother's doorstep when hunger gets the best of him. The case of Ferdinand's maternal uncle Edouard is a particularly interesting example. With a passion for things mechanical, Edouard invents and sells automobile and bicycle parts. He is one of the few characters in the novel who lives comfortably from his profession, although it is true that he works in a specialized area, has good luck, is "mighty clever," and is not in the least "extravagant" (D, 70). As the narrative progresses, we are told on two separate occasions that Edouard, unlike so many others, "was doing better and better" (D, 153, 284).

In *Mort à crédit*, Céline depicts a dynamic rather than stable social order. Ferdinand's world is in a state of deep crisis that has created the material hardships overwhelming his family and the novel's other protagonists. The novel reflects the major social transformations and economic dislocations that characterize the nineteenth and early twentieth century. Historians Braudel and Labrousse describe these changes, explaining that:

At the beginning of the twentieth century, the chasm dividing various echelons of bourgeois society deepened. The middle classes faced a host of problems. Insecurity was chronic among shopkeepers and salaried workers. Employees with the job security provided by the civil service and larger firms were also hard pressed to balance their income with the costs of maintaining their [class] position, of educating their children and with the need to accumulate savings. They were perhaps most wounded in their dignity. Subjected to the sometimes arbitrary decisions of their employers or confronted with the success of big businesses leaving them in the dust, the pride [they once took] in their social standing was no longer intact; they no longer thought of themselves as fully free to make choices nor as masters of their destiny. (1979, 453)

Mort à crédit, and, to a lesser extent, *Voyage au bout de la nuit* document the decline of a social class collapsing under the weight of modern capitalist development. Nicholas Hewitt has explained in some detail how Céline's narrator in the account of his childhood experiences "discerns in the events of the period the pressures which will lead, by the arrival of the inter-war years, to the destruction of that bastion of pre-war French society, the artisanal petite bourgeoisie," adding that the novel clearly constitutes "an exploration and exposition of the reasons for the decline and exclusion of the urban petite bourgeoisie"

(1987, 86). *Mort à crédit* thus "raises the question of the profound psychological symptoms of such exclusion and reflects its cultural implications" (86).

Hewitt observes that the decline of the petty bourgeoisie is aptly represented in the novel by the description of the 1900 World's Fair. This event triggers the free-floating anxiety that grips Ferdinand's family during its visit to the Exposition's Gallery of Machines, a monumental display that is perceived as heralding a potential catastrophe "hanging in midair in a transparent cathedral with little panes of glass that went up to the sky" (D, 81). The exhibition and the images of industrial progress it projects signal the end of a world, *their* world. It is therefore not surprising that Ferdinand's grandmother Caroline, who in his mind represents the gracious world of yesteryear, is highly suspicious of the Exposition and categorically refuses to listen to her son-in-law's spellbinding accounts to his neighbors of his excursions to this exhibit of future technology. Unlike her peers, she clearly recognizes that the entire Exposition, and the Gallery of Machines in particular, stands as a tribute to the new economic order and the class of industrialists that is devouring its small competitors. Caroline's death, which occurs shortly after the family tours the Exposition, symbolizes the descent of the lower middle class to which she belongs, its proletarianization. This proud owner of two rental properties, with several thousand francs in her possession, perishes after "messing around that day in January even later than usual, first in cold water then in boiling water... always in the draft, putting oakum in the pump and thawing out the faucets" (D, 98). In other words, Ferdinand's beloved grandmother—who after a lifetime of work should have been living comfortably off her hard-earned assets—dies from performing the task of a worker.

The direct effects of this social transformation on Ferdinand's parents preoccupy Céline's narrator in *Mort à crédit*. In this respect, the downward spiral of Clémence's commercial life is exemplary. After working as a saleswoman for her mother, she opens her own shop where she struggles to stay in business selling lace and fabric. It is largely competition from major department stores that, according to Braudel and Labrousse, precipitates this decline: "Along with technological innovation, considerable weight must be given to changes in the retail sector which greatly affected the conditions of everyday life, hiring patterns and potential earnings of large numbers of people. In Paris's twelve largest department stores, the number of employees went from 1700 in 1881 to 11,000 in 1913; the value of commercial real estate

rose from 2 to 5 million francs and profits increased dramatically"
(1979, 402). They add that although the earnings of these large stores
soared, those of small businesses were obviously unable to keep pace:

> Economic growth did not benefit everyone. The least favored were princi-
> pally small business owners, especially those operating in large cities most
> directly affected by the rapid expansion of large-scale industrial and finance
> capital. On average, their assets increased, but at a much slower rate than
> those of property holders as a whole. In Paris, for example, small shopkeep-
> ers and master craftsmen owned 17% of the wealth in 1820 [as compared to]
> less than 3% in 1911 while [over the same period] the net worth of their
> assets rose from an average of 28,600 to 44,000 francs, an increase of 65% as
> opposed to 197% for the whole. This is one aspect of what contemporaries
> called the crisis of the middle classes, which was actually the crisis of small
> business. (423)

These economic factors account not only for Clémence's dire financial
straits but also, at least in part, those of Mme Héronde, Wurzem, and
Gorloge. The relatively large size of "Berlope and Son," the adolescent
Ferdinand's first employer, no doubt allowed the company to withstand
the competitive pressures exerted by the large department stores.
Among other advantages, large-scale retailing enjoyed a flexibility that
allowed it to respond rapidly to fashion trends, thereby cutting deeply
into the profits of smaller competitors. This inability to adapt to rapidly
changing market conditions explains why a sudden change in styles
spells disaster for Clémence. When she procures a large stock of Irish
boleros "at great expense," items that her customers shun "in favor of
other styles, other whims" (D, 258), Clémence jeopardizes the viability
of her shop. As Solomon observes, Clémence, in attempting to sell more
expensive hand-crafted goods, must struggle to keep up with the large
department stores that sell only machine-produced merchandise (1988,
82): "Rich people had lost all their refinement... all their delicacy... their
appreciation for fine work, for hand-made articles... all they had left was a
depraved infatuation with machine-made junk, embroideries that unravel,
that melt and peel when you wash them" (D, 272).

The trend toward mechanized production was, to be sure, no great
boon for artisans. Clémence's predicament is indeed worsened by the
fact that, as Hewitt notes, at the beginning of the century, the textile
industry went into a slump, "possibly as the result of the introduction
of artificial fibers from 1891 onwards " (1987, 100–01). The importance
of this development is confirmed by François Caron who establishes
that "the growth in textiles began to flag in the 1880s. . . . The
industry as a whole dropped from 1.77 percent between 1831–35 and

1876–80 to 1.1 percent between 1876–80 and 1909–13. For dynamic fibers (wool, cotton, silk, jute) the figures are 2.3 percent and 1.78 percent" (1979, 149).

In their totality, these various factors explain Clémence's professional decline, which mirrors the downward mobility of countless small businesses that were forced, as Braudel and Labrousse note, to compete during this period with retail conglomerates: "Taking their cue [from the large department stores], emporia and arcades popped up in cities large and small. . . . The idea [of mass merchandizing] spread from novelty items and dime-store goods to other sectors, particularly food processing, with ever greater efforts made to reach customers: stores expanded into towns and villages [while] door-to-door salesmen offered the latest products to housewives [unable to travel] to commercial centers" (1979, 402–403). This is precisely what Clémence does in trying to find her niche in the new economic order. She abandons her inaccessible location on the rue de Babylone and sets up shop in the Passage des Bérésinas. Solomon describes this setting as "a covered street, usually quite narrow, lined with shops and enclosed by gates at both ends" (1988, 79–80). The Passage is, in effect, an arcade in which a number of small business proprietors cluster in an effort to compete with larger stores. Yet, Clémence, who continues, like her neighbors, to encounter serious financial difficulties, finds herself forced to become a traveling saleswoman, working the open markets at Chatou, Bougival, Enghien, La Porte de Clignancourt, and, later, at Dieppe, where going door to door, she manages to sell part of her merchandise. When bad weather returns, she must once again settle for conducting business in her shop, where things were "going from bad to worse" because "the styles never stopped changing" (D, 131).

After the Irish bolero fiasco, Clémence decides to give up on hand-crafted articles and acquiesces to selling mass-produced goods. She takes once again to working the open markets, diligently going door to door until one day, physically exhausted, she realizes that "little shops are doomed" (D, 294) and that it was useless trying to compete with "big stores" (D, 294). She finally resigns herself to relinquishing her independence and going to work for a large retailer where she will show fabric swatches to customers and where she "won't make much, but it'll be regular" (D, 294). But even these plans do not pan out for her. After deciding to work the open markets one last time, she injures her leg so badly that she can no longer walk and is confined to her shop. When her leg heals, she becomes a sales representative for a notions and, subsequently, an embroidery store, all the while tending to her shop. Indeed, much later, after Ferdinand has become a doctor, Clémence still considers herself a small shopkeeper and prides herself on having paid off all her debts.

Auguste, too, is a victim of the new economic order's technological progress and social upheaval. Although he has given twenty-two years of his life to the Coccinelle Insurance Company, in a letter to his son in England, he writes that he dreads a planned move to "reorganize the whole office" that is sure to benefit "a cabal of young clerks who have recently been taken on." They are "endowed with high university degrees (some of them have their Master's)," take "advantage of their influence with the director, of their family ties and social connections, of their 'modern' upbringing (a well-nigh total absence of scruples) and have a crushing advantage over mere rank-and-file employees like myself" (D, 259). To counter this threat, Auguste forces himself to learn how to use a typewriter, but his pitiful efforts do little to alleviate "his fear of being fired" (D, 479) from a job that increasingly torments him. Auguste belongs to a heterogeneous category of white-collar workers to whom the lowliest bureaucratic tasks were assigned and that historians Braudel and Labrousse situate socially "on the fringe of the popular classes." These low-ranking bureaucrats benefited only marginally from the prosperity of the times and were casualties of the same "middle class crisis" from which shopkeepers and artisans were reeling (1979, 422–44). Their status is similar to that of unskilled civil servants, who were also subjected to the whims of superiors. In opposing the "new law of advancement"—in actuality, an open door inviting crony-ism and the abuse of power, white-collar workers decided in impressive numbers to go on strike in 1909, this despite the fact that such an action was, in principle, illegal. This mode of resistance was obviously not an option for Auguste who belongs, nonetheless, to this same social class, one that was "bourgeois in its taste, [in] its [notion of] 'the seriousness of life,' [in] its relatively high level of cultural sophistication, [and in] the sacrifices it was willing to make to raise its children" (Braudel and Labrousse, 1979, 448–49).

If the occupational quandary in which Auguste, a high school graduate, finds himself is frustrating and his future uncertain, Ferdi-nand's prospects for the future are even more precarious, since he is starting out in life with a meager General Education Diploma (*le certificat d'études*) he was granted after taking an exam "everyone . . . passed" (D, 134). His decision to make a career for himself in business is doomed to failure, because this is a crisis-ridden sector undergoing dramatic changes in which hard work no longer guarantees success. The possibilities for advancement in his chosen field become even more remote when, despite his good intentions, Ferdinand makes a number of missteps on the job. After a series of failures in conventional work settings, the youngster enters into Courtial des Pereires's service. Yet, Courtial is no more prosperous than the other characters in the novel. In several respects, the amateur scientist can be seen as belonging to a bygone era. First, the aristocratic pseudonym he adopts at a time when the nobility, as Proust has shown, is in rapid decline, is ludicrous. Moreover, his inventions, however ingenious, are no match for the wizardry of modern technology.

The only character in the novel whose activities allow him to prosper is Edouard, an enterprising mechanic whose special skill working with automobiles brings him greater and greater success. He belongs, in effect, to that "stratum of small entrepreneurs always on the alert for something new" (Caron, 1979, 4), and who made the French automobile industry a particularly dynamic sector of the economy during this period:

The automobile industry is . . . interesting in a number of respects. French production in 1913 was double that of Britain, and French exports in 1911 and 1912 were larger by value than those of the United States. Half of the French automobile output, in fact, was exported and half of this to Britain. Growth was very rapid, but numbers were small. Production grew from 2,000 in 1900 to 45,000 in 1912. The United States was producing 360,000 cars in 1912, when its exports were 154 million francs to the French 212 million. Firms in the industry were larger, on average, than most metalworking branches: 33,000 workers (or one fourth of the working force in chemicals) in 48 factories, for an average of 666 workers per factory. . . . The mechanical industry, led by automobiles, [was] an island of growth in an underdeveloped sea. (Kindleberger, 1964, 300–01)

In sum, just as *A la Recherche du temps perdu* sketches a portrait of upper-middle-class and aristocratic life at the end of the nineteenth century and in the early decades of the twentieth, registering the various transformations and upheavals that technological progress and World War I occasioned, *Mort à crédit* is indeed, as Hewitt observes, "an extraordinarily accurate and relatively rare evocation of the crisis facing the French petite bourgeoisie in the period leading up to the First World War" (1987, 103). Although Hewitt's claims here are beyond dispute, they must be nuanced. We know that the image Céline projects of his childhood in *Mort à crédit* is distorted and blackened as a fictional transformation. Céline's autobiographer François Gibault relates that in 1908, Louis Montourcy, a financial advisor to Louis-Ferdinand's father, "assessed the Destouches's estate to be worth five hundred thousand francs." Gibault concludes that M. and Mme Destouches were far from experiencing the privation Céline so complacently displayed in *Mort à crédit* (1977, 69). Does this mean that the very real hardships of the petty bourgeoisie that Céline depicts in his novel have also been exaggerated?

If it is true that Louis-Ferdinand's father—who was not quite a *bachelier*—had an unremarkable career in an insurance company, where he was undoubtedly underpaid, his mother worked diligently to overcome initial obstacles and lived honorably from her lace business, even though, as Gibault notes, "the large department stores were ruining small business" (1977, 42). In any case, Gibault informs us that Mme Destouches moved to the Passage de Choiseul in 1899, where she "specialized in selling lace, luxury linen and antiques." Later, Marguerite Destouches conducted business as a "hand-crafted point-lace merchant" and then started a business with another lacemaker (1977, 43).

How, one might ask, did Marguerite Destouches withstand the very real crisis conditions that ravaged small shopkeepers like Clémence at the beginning of the century? It should be noted that Clémence exaggerates when she laments that cheap mass-produced goods had flooded the market. J. H. Clapham points out that although in the last half of the nineteenth century, the French textile industry "was equipping itself rapidly with modern spinning machinery," "there were economic reasons . . . which kept the hand loom alive down to 1914. The industry specialized in light women's fabric and always had an export trade in expensive 'novelties.' Such fabrics require delicate [handling] and are produced in small quantities of any one pattern, conditions which favour the hand loom" (1961, 249–50). Moreover, even though small retailers such as Marguerite faced pressure from large department stores, government support allowed them to withstand the competition. Y. Trotignon observes, for instance, that "in 1914, the average business owner was the small shopkeeper determined to fend off competition from department stores. With the imposition of higher licensing fees in 1905, these larger stores do an adequate business, but at relatively high prices" (1985, 51). Social and economic historians of the period further specify that:

A fiscal policy actually favoring small business proprietors over department stores was pursued throughout the Third Republic and was crowned by the 1905 [licensing] regulations. In reality, small shopkeepers were able to find new activities, taking up the slack as domestic production fell off, and benefiting from the development of new technology. Urbanization and the extension of commercial activity into remote areas allowed even traditional occupations to gain significantly more ground than the large stores had forced them to yield. (Braudel and Labrousse, 1979, 156)

It is, in fact, the decline in domestic production that accounts for the bulk of Clémence's repair work, much as it did for Marguerite Destouches. François Gibault relates that Céline's mother was a "tireless worker who singlehandedly tended both to her own shop and household, repairing merchandise and meeting with clients and suppliers" (1977, 49). This image conforms to Céline's own recollections of his mother and her "enormous piles of lace that needed repair, the huge heap that was always spilling over her table—a mountain of work for a few francs" (cited in Gibault, 1977, 49). Small independent operators successfully resisted competition from large stores by adapting to the new market conditions, seeking out customers in the open markets and selling door to door. A general rise in the standard of living and in levels of consumption, along with the protectionist legislation of 1905, also enhanced the viability of small businesses:

The 1905 law . . . taxed stores with large payrolls that sold various types of merchandise. These measures did not apply to small shopkeepers. In 1912, licensing fees for stores with multiple branches were increased. According to figures [compiled by] Landry, chair of the legislative [committee] investigating [the issue], the tax liability for the Paris-France Company went from 13 to 26% of net profits in 1913. For small businesses . . . profits cannot be assessed with any degree of precision, but . . . Landry, [who was] sympathetic to small business notes that "All laws pertaining to the conditions of workers . . . were more of a burden to big businesses than to small ones [since] the latter did not follow them strictly and sometimes, not at all." (Braudel and Labrousse, 1979, 403)

Small business not only withstood the market pressure exerted by department stores but also actually experienced growth, although the presence of these larger competitors cut into their profits. In short, the "commercial and artisanal petty bourgeoisie survived the economic crisis, but the winners [were ultimately] the owners of large companies that were able to adapt to the difficulties and then to profit from the recovery" (Braudel and Labrousse, 1979, 404). Small shopkeepers in fact continued to prosper in France, until the relatively recent emergence of supermarkets and other large chain stores that dealt a disabling, and, in many cases, mortal blow to small independent retailers.

Mort à crédit presents then not a false but, rather, a distorted image of the economic crisis the Belle Epoque's commercial and artisanal bourgeoisie faced. As Céline himself acknowledged, he "transposes" reality in his literary representations (HER, 84). He appears to obey this exaggeratory reflex when he would have his readers believe that Ferdinand's parents, who are presumably on the brink of financial collapse, can afford to send their son to England to learn a foreign language. Although they borrow "two thousand francs" (D, 198) from Clémence's brother Edouard to defray the costs of Ferdinand's English sojourn, they vow to pay him back. Representing nearly two and a half years of Auguste's salary, how can the parents reasonably expect to repay their debt when Clemence's inheritance has been exhausted and her shop brings in but a pittance? At the turn of the century, such meager resources would have precluded foreign travels of the type the young Destouches's parents offered him in Germany and England, excursions that were, historians observe, largely reserved for the wealthy (Braudel and Labrousse, 1979, 443).

Céline's penchant for hyperbole notwithstanding, *Mort à crédit* presents a gripping account of the lives of the petty bourgeoisie and the popular classes during the Belle Epoque and can thus been seen as a striking sociological complement to Proust's *A la Recherche du temps perdu*, which focuses principally on the aristocracy and the upper middle class. Parenthetically, the narrative of *Voyage au bout de la nuit*, Céline's first novel, which opens with World War I and ends around 1930, presents the image of a society that has witnessed the accession to power of the industrial bourgeoisie and, therefore, can be seen as a work that brings closure to the historical narrative he inaugurated in his second novel, *Mort à crédit*. As with Proust's *Le Temps retrouvé*, *Voyage* projects the image of a "world hopelessly cut off from the *Belle Epoque* by the Great War, in which characters like Bardamu no longer have a place and exist only as shadows" (Hewitt, 1983, 15). Many of the poor have been chased out of Paris and live wretched lives in the suburbs where they depend for their survival on a Parisian employer who exploits them shamelessly; for instance, the petty bourgeois (and therefore victimized) Henrouille family, whose head of household is a retired office clerk, scrimped and saved for fifty years to be able to afford a home in which its members continue to lead an impoverished and miserly existence. The Henrouilles have the same mentality as Ferdinand's parents and present an example of what they might have become. Like the Henrouilles, Ferdinand's parents scramble to find a place for their son in the business world, yet live in constant dread of the "financial difficulties" (J, 214) he might encounter. The ruthlessness of this new economic order is felt even in the jungles of French colonial Africa where the Compagnie Pordurière du Petit Congo controls not only the commercial but also the medical institution where "the plebeians of Research" (J, 240) grovel before the authorities in fear of losing their jobs, much like Auguste in *Mort à crédit* submits to the will of his employer, Mr. Lempreinte.

Nowhere, however, does monopoly capital reign more supreme than in the United States. In the Ford factories in Detroit, manned chiefly by foreigners and invalids whose vulnerability makes them more exploitable, human activity has been reduced to the operations of a machine whose sole function is to produce objects of mass consumption. But Céline represents industrial modernity in *Voyage* as teetering on the brink of destruction. The economic crisis has created propitious conditions for the rise of fascism that ultimately led to catastrophe. The disaster about to occur is augured in the decay and slovenliness Bardamu encounters everywhere he goes. The decline of the Western world is particularly discernible in the dereliction of its representatives in Africa whose laxity portends the collapse of the entire colonial regime. Moreover, *Voyage au bout de la nuit*, much like *Mort à crédit* and Proust's *A la Recherche*, can be seen as containing the historical seeds of the apocalyptic destruction recounted in Céline's post–World War II novels: *Féerie pour une autre fois (I* and *II)* and the German trilogy.

It is evident that Proust in the whole of *A la Recherche du temps perdu* and Céline, particularly in his first two novels, have succeeded in documenting the eradication of distinctive cultures at the two extremes of the social spectrum as it occurred in the years between 1880 and 1920 (for Proust's aristocracy) and between 1890 and 1930 (for Céline's lower middle class). Despite the differences in their values, social prestige, and privilege, both classes fall prey to the same historical forces (technological progress, capitalist expansion, World War I, a certain moral decline) that generated an entirely new economic and social order in which they no longer have a place.

It is important to recognize, however, that much as Proust and Céline recognize the structural mechanisms of the great transformation under way, both focus largely on the cultural and human effects of this process rather than on formulating strategies to counter it. This is especially true for the narrator in *A la Recherche du temps perdu*, whose entire social world is reduced to "Swann's way" and "Guermante's way," in other words, to the upper middle class and the aristocracy. Despite the social injustices his protagonists suffer—from their dehumanizing exploitation in the Detroit Ford factory in *Voyage au bout de la nuit* to their total subjugation at the Berlope firm in *Mort à crédit*—despite their keen awareness of the ruthlessness of the new economic order and their constant railing against its inequities, Bardamu and Ferdinand are no revolutionaries. Nor are they interested in exploring the systemic features of a social order in which the rich dominate the poor. In Céline's mind, social and economic injustice appears, in fact, to derive more from humanity's innate malice, selfishness, and greed than from class inequalities. This fact did not escape Leon Trotsky who, after reading *Voyage au bout de la nuit*, declared that "Céline does not at all set himself the goal of exposing social conditions in France" but rather considers the "present social system" as "rotten as every other, whether past or future"; for the author was, he concludes, simply "dissatisfied with men and their affairs" (1989, 30). In reality Céline berates the indigent as well as the affluent, deploring the human traits he finds common to both groups: mediocrity, spitefulness, and unrelenting cruelty. Convinced that the poor are as unscrupulous as the rich, Céline is no more anxious than Proust to see the lower ranks gaining access to and deploying political power. In *Voyage*, through the voice of Princhard, Céline openly derides the democratizing ambitions of the French Revolution, which, in his view, only gave rise to the "free-gratis soldier" (the "*soldat gratuit*") ensuring that they would join ranks with "the first battalions of emancipated maniacs march[ing] off!... the first voting, flagmatic [sic] suckers that Dumouriez led away to get themselves drilled full of holes in Flanders!" (J, 57). Leery of all projects of social change, Céline saw no future for humanity; in the final analysis, as Leon Trotsky observes (speaking of *Voyage*), "there is no hope." Thus, although Céline's general view of French society may seem more realistic and accurate than Proust's, his social conscience gives way to despair and to an overwhelming pessimism with regard to the human condition, which becomes, in the final analysis, atrophic, much like the sociological critique woven throughout Proust's *A la Recherche du temps perdu*.

Translated by Rosemarie Scullion

Andrea Loselle

▼

The History
of a
History:
Franks and
Gauls in
Céline's
German Trilogy

▼

THE GERMAN trilogy is a largely autobiographical series of novels recounting out of chronological sequence Céline's nearly yearlong flight from Paris to Denmark, beginning in June 1944 just after the Allied invasion of Normandy. As the author of another "trilogy"—his violent, anti-Semitic pamphlets, one of which was written and published under the Occupation in 1941—Céline might very well have found his presence in France *de trop* with the Liberation of the German occupied zone. Whether or not prosecution for this publication, as well as for the reprintings of his other anti-Semitic writings, would have occurred had he remained, Céline obviously anticipated reprisal and fled to seek refuge in Denmark. His protracted stay in Sigmaringen on his way to Denmark and his encounters there with German officials and French collaborators only made his proclaimed innocence more difficult to defend. Sigmaringen, the capital of Hohenzollern, is a small town located on the Danube in southwest Germany: it was here the Vichy government was forced by the Nazis to take up residence at the time of the Allied invasions. Waiting for papers permitting him to cross the border into Denmark, Céline spent almost five months (November 1944–March 1945) at Sigmaringen employed as a doctor.

Just prior to and with the appearance in 1957 of the trilogy's first novel, *D'un Château l'autre*, Céline often allowed curious journalists and writers to interview him at his home in the Parisian suburb of Meudon. In these interviews and in the trilogy there is not a single allusion to any feelings of repentance for his hateful verbal attacks on Jews. Instead, Céline complains of his own victimization and regrets that he ever wrote his anti-Semitic pamphlets because he suffered, he claims, outrageous persecution: imprisonment in Denmark for over a year, *indignité nationale*, and bitter exile until his amnesty in 1951. When he discusses his persecution, Céline is often slippery and indirect. In the trilogy, he blames the prewar pamphlet *Bagatelles pour un massacre* for his future woes: "I knew I was cooked... one way or another... everybody agreed . . . that I deserved to be put in cold mud for *Bagatelles*" (C, 251). Céline could, however, only be held legally accountable for the wartime writings (e.g., *Les Beaux Draps* [February 1941]), not *Bagatelles* (1937), and this only insofar as they were intended to incite not anti-Semitic sentiment but rather collaboration with the Germans.[1] The trilogy's narrator predictably portrays himself as an innocent witness to the fall of the Third Reich and as a detached, self-styled veterinarian well versed in human, racial bloodlines.

Céline's periodical references to the "Yellow Peril" in the trilogy suggest, in fact, that little changed in the basic dynamic of an unrepentant racism, because Céline, after the war, simply changed the name of his target from Jew to Asian. But the effect of this substitution would appear, as perhaps intended, to be more derisory than deplorable because it tends to defuse the importance not only of Céline's past political writings but also of the trilogy's more subtle and far-reaching racist statements. Indeed, a closer reading of these novels reveals that Céline's tongue-in-cheek prophesies about the French race being at the mercy of Asian hordes are a red herring for another racial difference he seeks to maintain, one abstracted from history and not from idle prediction: the spurious distinction between Franks and Gauls (or Gallo-Romans) debated by aristocratic and revolutionary factions over centuries of French political struggle. In the trilogy, Céline identifies contemporary Germans with the Franks, the Germanic tribe that invaded and conquered a significant portion of Gaul in the fifth century and who were later claimed by the established French aristocracy as their ancestors. He identifies the majority of the contemporary French with the Gallo-Romans, a race he believes was latinized and undermined by intermarriage with Roman settlers in Gaul and is vulnerable, even to this day, to new linguistic and genetic permutations such as those Céline prophesied in the "Yellow Peril."

Céline does not care much for aristocrats, nor does he care for Germans, but he does care very much about *race*. He sides with the Celtic and Germanic "races," seeing them as fraternal "Nordic" races, and, true to most nationalist groups that take biological hypotheses as axioms, he militates on the side of nation, not *patrie* or the fatherland.[2] Nation and race form his aesthetic in the trilogy in that his famous "emotive" style, reminiscent of popular spoken French, clearly bespeaks a writer who wishes his readers to identify him with a Celtic Frenchman of the soil, not a desiccated "academician" whose latinized language would be, as he calls it in *L'Ecole des cadavres*, an "asshole esperantism" (espérantisme trou du cul) or "copulating Babelism" (babélisme copulateur) (EC, 222). Style, for Céline, must be organic; it must be slangy, emotive, and inventive without linguistic intermarriage (babélisme). Stylistic originality, then, is race specific, autochthonic, and not allogeneous, so that "[w]hat makes [Céline] avant-garde is the same thing that makes him national; this is precisely where his populism verges to the right" (Kaplan, 1986, 118). Céline's racism in the pamphlets is aesthetically grounded and independent of a clearly identifiable political stand. The German trilogy is equally difficult to pinpoint politically because the Frank/Gaul distinction in this later work is aesthetically racial, not political, in nature. This does not suggest, however, that Céline's racial phantasm has nothing in common with the fascisms of the time, for it does: "Rites were the exemplification of history. For almost all fascisms—precisely because they were so nationalistic—looked back to the past and desired both to revive some bygone age of glory and to prove their movements to be the culmination of their country's history. The Teutonic master-race, the new Roman empire, the Turanian Hunters, the Nordic tribes were all motifs on the same theme" (Woolf, 1981, 9–10).

In *L'Ecole des cadavres*, Céline speaks out in favor of a Franco-German alliance for historical and racial reasons (the Verdun Treaty of 843, or as Céline calls it, the "Treaty of Skinning and Dismemberment" [EC, 272]): "The solid part of France, the anti-speechifying part, has always been the Celtic and Germanic part... The non-Celtic part in France chats and pontificates" (EC, 284–85). Céline's racism, however, is always linked with references to language and his emotive style (e.g.,"anti-speechifying"), and in this respect, he differs from other racial theorists and proponents of a Franco-German alliance. Monomaniacal references to his style, which begin to appear in *Bagatelles* and grow in intensity in his later work, should therefore be regarded with suspicion, for Céline's style *cannot* be dissociated from its racially prejudiced underpinnings. Scholars too often pass over that aspect of his style, which Céline himself viewed as organically authentic, in favor of a "purer" notion of style as originality. I propose to counter the growing aestheticism surrounding Céline's work by tracing his historical and historiographic use of racial legends in the trilogy. More specifically, my analysis will be twofold: first, to demonstrate through a reading of the German trilogy the specific nature of Céline's racist, nationalist claims and their continuity with his pamphlets (particularly, *L'Ecole des cadavres*, which, unlike the other pamphlets, is not mentioned in the trilogy but contains, as we have already seen, Céline's opinions of France's racial composition); and second, to show that the trilogy is a clearly revisionist text sharing with revisionist histories and apologies of the immediate postwar period the condemnation of the use of history as judicial proceeding. If the purge trials of the Liberation imposed a separation between textuality and activity by almost uniformly sentencing writers, on the basis not of their literary texts but of their literary activities (Rubenstein, 1990, 141–42, 145), the German trilogy and postwar revisionist texts became rereadings of the Liberation's history of the Occupation as the Liberation's blindness to textuality. The "Yellow Peril" is a feint (an old "prophesy" that, in fact, dates back to Gobineau) inasmuch as the trilogy shifts from the target or victim of the pamphlets toward the subject of Céline's "Nordic" pride, a move that does not, of course, make Céline's work any less "race conscious" and that is figured precisely by the narrator's determined direction northward: "Nord!... Nord!... Nord!" (R2, 877).

The Frankish legend stems from the centuries of historical debate in France over the rights of the nobility and serfs (the Third Estate) and their respective allegiances to the king. The notion that nobles and serfs belonged to two racially distinct groups was used to exclude the Third Estate from the right of assembly and to explain why nobles did not have to pay taxes and members of the Third Estate did. If the serfs were the descendants of the Gallo-Romans, a vanquished race that had, long before the Frankish invasion, been "corrupted" by the Romans, the Germans, and thus, the Franks, were, as Tacitus observed in *Germania*, a pure race of warriors. Or, in the confident, but inaccurate, words of a prominent, nineteenth-century scientific anthropologist: "one knows that during the first half of the Middle Ages, the Franks maintained the custom of marrying principally amongst themselves" (Broca, 1871, 1:

335). Other historians and anthropologists conceded that much earlier on, the Franks intermarried with Gallo-Romans of noble birth and that being a Frank was so important then that high-ranking Gallo-Romans often took Frankish names, making the task of tracing racial descent in many cases impossible. Most contended, however, that during the Dark Ages, Gallo-Romans of low birth, not having intermarried with Frankish warriors (Broca, 1871, 1: 291), had agreed to pledge allegiance in the form of labor to their Frankish conquerors in exchange for armed protection. The right to bear arms was considered a noble privilege and, besides, the Germans, according to Tacitus (and therefore later historians), were not agriculturally inclined. Nomadic hunters rather than propertied gatherers, they even transacted their business armed (Tacitus, 283). "Frank" was also taken to be synonymous with "freedom" because Tacitus had described the Franks in their battles against the Romans as passionately fierce "libertatis autores" (authors of freedom).[3] This description was applied centuries later in rationalizing the economic freedom of the nobles and their exemption from the degrading *taille* as well as all other forms of taxation. It was further elaborated in the claim that the Franks, as the authors of freedom, were the very liberators and founders of France so that the territory they governed was quite naturally named after them. Before the French Revolution, "France" was therefore thought to be named after a specific race or nation separate from the majority of the territory's inhabitants.[4]

Despite historical, scientific, archaeological, and anthropological conclusions proving the groundlessness of these racial legends, the Frankish and Nordic race myths tenaciously persist in bearing a symbolic life of their own. The *franquise*, the double-bladed hatchet carried by the Frankish invaders, reappears during the German Occupation as the emblem of the collaborationist Vichy government. Later, certain critics of Céline's work glorify ad nauseam the author's "Celtic" roots.[5] And even innocent popular literature, such as the comic strip *Astérix*, which first appeared in 1959 when Céline was writing his trilogy, expresses a certain "atavistic pride" (Marny, 1968, 168) by means of discreet Nordic elements.[6]

"France," "French," and "Frank" also gave rise to another notion: *la franchise* or frankness. As Voltaire wrote under this term in the *Encyclopédie*,

This *frankness*, which originally expressed the liberty of a nation, city, body, soon afterwards came to signify *liberty* in speech, in advice that one gives, in the proceeding of an affair: but there is a great nuance between *speaking with frankness* and *speaking with liberty*. In speaking to one's superior, liberty is a boldness, which is either measured or too strong; *frankness* remains more within the right bounds and is accompanied by candor. To say one's opinion with liberty is not to fear; to say it with *frankness* is to listen only to the heart. To act with liberty is to act with independence; to proceed with *frankness* is to conduct oneself openly and nobly. To speak with too much liberty is to show audacity; to speak with too much *frankness* is to open one's heart too much. (1779, 15: 323–24)

The distinction between frankness and liberty in one's speech reveals the socioeconomic separation between the nobility and Third Estate beneath which lies the Frank/Gallo-Roman opposition. It is not difficult to miss the privileging of frank speech as being more open, candid, and emotive, having come not from a social transgression but straight from the heart, a heart that is, however, coldly guaranteed by social class. As indicated, emotive speech forms the basis of Céline's stylistic aesthetic. In *Bagatelles pour un massacre*, he juxtaposes "le franc grossier" and "le franc parler" (frank crudity and outspokenness) with "non-emotive" polite writing such as the style of the nineteenth-century Goncourt brothers ("écrire poli 'goncourtien'" [B, 217]). Politeness, it turns out, is a specifically Gallic (not Nordic) trait according to Voltaire in another important entry, "FRANÇOIS OU FRANÇAIS."[7] Céline elaborates this distinction by shifting the variables so that emotive language will always derive from frank *speech* (no matter how crude) as opposed to polite *writing*. This opposition is in full play when Céline opens the German trilogy by *initiating* the reader into his confidence: "Frankly [Pour parler franc/To speak frank], just between you and me, I'm ending up worse than I started." The narrator, "Céline," speaks a loaded language, frankly Frank. Ironic racial encoding begins with this gesture, which is at the same time a reversal of the social code implied between speaking with liberty and speaking frankly. For Céline, frankness occurs when the spoken word (populism and slang) transgresses and overturns the written law; that is, the accepted codes of polite, written language (= Latinization = Gallo-Roman) as prescribed by the target of many of Céline's polemical attacks, the *Académie Française*. As we will see, the difference between speaking and writing is, for Céline, the difference between French and Latin.

Nowhere is racial encoding more manifest than in the description of the castle at Sigmaringen in *D'un Château l'autre*. Céline takes his reader on an instructive tour of the Hohenzollern castle's gallery of fierce, warrior portraits. The demonic countenances in these portraits are comparable in spirit to two of France's most notorious criminals, Landru and Tropmann, as well as to France's family of hereditary executioners, the Deiblers (all of whom are Frenchmen but whose names sound Germanic). The Hohenzollern family members are, however, "creators" and "founders" of dynasties (R2, 110, 111).[8] Outfitted in arms and armor, these Germanic Landrus are of "pure race," "princes," and "*dauphins*." Next to these austere Nordic monstrosities, Napoléon the conqueror is but an effeminate Latin: "Bonaparte seems more like a young lady—fine features, delicate hands *à la Fragonard*" (C, 133–34). This historic personage is exemplary of a failed conqueror, disastrously defeated, for example, in the "Battle of Nations" at Leipzig in 1813. Not even the real Landru—a small, retiring bourgeois (read Gallo-Roman) civil servant dismembering lonely spinsters in his suburban kitchen—can really stand up to the *démons-gangsters* in the portraits: "not the timid Landru of Gambais!... puny, furtive, with a ramshackle stove picked up at the auction rooms... no!... these Landrus were sure of themselves!... the genuine article [pur jus]" (C, 134). The portraits depict unadulterated Landrus: pure-blooded warriors. The racial encoding of the Hohenzollern visages is finally backed up with a learned reference to Tacitus's *Germania*: "I won't try to outdo Tacitus, but you can imagine that ten centuries of demon gangsters is something!" (C, 136). The Germans, according to Tacitus, were an aboriginal people with fierce blue eyes, red hair, and huge frames, fit only for sudden, violent exertion (Tacitus, 269). *Germania*, admired for its broad-minded account of the Germanic tribes, was also Tacitus's implicit condemnation of Roman decadence (pejoratively construed in a Célinian context as "Latin"). It was, of course, also used in Nazi propaganda to substantiate the racial purity of the German *Volk* and their "innate" warrior attributes (Barzun, 1937, 11). Fierceness and physical height and might are signs of racial purity that the French, even Bonaparte, no longer possess. The purer the blood, it seems, the more daunting the race, so that the French are, by implication, a nation of small-time criminals and sawed-off dictators.

The orthographic reversion in *D'un Château l'autre* of "Sigmaringen" as "*Sieg*maringen" now takes on more meaning. In German, *Sieg*- means "victor" and -*ingen*, "fief." Their juxtaposition evokes the historical distinction in France between nobleman and serf, Frank and Gallo-Roman, "frank speech" and "taking liberties in one's speech." The words also serve to distinguish two countries (i.e., nations) by racial superiority. Such cross-referencing also suggests that the trilogy is, like the portraits, a palimpsest: on one level an account ostensibly about the vanquished (the Germans and collaborators) and on another an ironic account, for the initiated alone, about what the vanquished were, once upon a time, as victors and Franks. The castle at Sigmaringen is also significant not just because this was where the Vichy government was displaced but also because the castle's ancestors, the Hohenzollern-Sigmaringen family, founded "dynasties" and were even at the origin of the Franco-Prussian war, the first modern, Franco-German war that triggered in France a strong wave of nationalist sentiment against Germany (Ragache and Ragache, 1988, 276–77). At that time, Germany was victor and France her subjugated fief. With Germany's subsequent defeats in both world wars, France, for Céline, was cut off from the possibility of a racial alliance that would have protected her fading "Nordic" races. A more schematic representation of Céline's strategy as a chiasmus shows who the "new," postwar victors are:

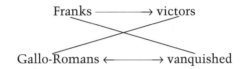

Another favorite classical reference for race theorists, Caesar's *Gallic Wars*, also appears in the trilogy. Céline invokes Caesar's name several times and cites him: "things have changed since Caesar! 'They [the Celts] promise, they laugh, and that's all! hell! they don't forget one thing!'" (N, 264).[9] The French are no longer the easy-going people they used to be; they will not even allow Céline's sins to be forgotten. But Céline has not forgotten his pamphlets either. The same reference to Caesar was used as an epigraph to one of the sections from, once again, *L'Ecole des cadavres* (EC, 284). In this section, he tells us about the future of the French race, doomed to extinction, whether or not the French emerge victorious in the war. Céline predicted: "Neither victory nor defeat can interest us since, in any case, we'll see neither one nor the other; we'll be deceased long before that, crunched, crushed, crumbled in enthusiastic smash-ups, in liberating and fantastically fulminating crusades" (EC, 79). The French, except for Céline and this ambiguous "we," are no longer French (i.e., Celtic and Germanic) anyway. In this same passage, Céline also adds a few thoughts on the disappearance of the Gauls: "We'll disappear body and soul from this territory like the Gauls . . . Christianity's worst cuckolds" (EC, 79). The Gauls no longer exist because they are racially mixed Gallo-Romans or Latins (*méridionaux* or "Southerners") (EC, 284) and, more important, linguistically betrayed through acceptance of the Latin Church; hardly twenty words of their original language, Céline tells us, survive in modern French, which is dominated by another dead language, Latin. Contemporary Frenchmen can count themselves lucky, he says, if in the future the word *merde* (shit) manages to survive (EC, 79). Although he himself as a French speaker owes much to Latin, including *merde*, Céline the stylist takes exception to this fact, just as he excludes himself from the extinction that he claims the French race has suffered as though he were the last "real" Frenchman alive.

That Céline uses the old Frank/Gallo-Roman legend in support of his brand of nationalism and as a revisionist reading of the events of World War II is further demonstrated by the fact that the trilogy is written as a history not as we know it today but as a *chronicle*, a bygone form of history. As I will demonstrate, he adopts the anachronistic idiosyncrasies and narrative techniques expected of a Froissart, Joinville, or Monluc—these being a few of Céline's models for the trilogy. *Féerie pour une autre fois, I* and *II* (1952, 1954), a delirious shower of juxtaposed ruptures and exclamations recounting an Allied bombardment of Montmartre, signals a decisive move by Céline toward history with its references to Pliny the Younger's letter to Tacitus recounting his father's fatal encounter with Mount Vesuvius (F2, 57). If his pamphlets and the outcome of the war put Céline in the losers' camp, then his subsequent writings—obsessive reflections on defeat— become history in more than one sense. The polemical texts written before and during the Occupation were contemporary, largely nonfictional, active diatribes, whereas the texts written after the purges of the Liberation signal a return to fiction as past, a past so remote that literature and history are difficult to differentiate, underscoring once again the racial nuance accorded style because the narrator and his style are coextensive; consequently both are endangered species.

Moreover, his dispute over racial origins parallels the development of French historiography, making Céline's choice of the anachronized chronicle form an overdetermination, a return that recapitulates a very long past of nationalist positions *and* puts modern historical narrative into question. Augustin Thierry's *Récits des temps mérovingiens* (1840), a metahistory of the origins of the French race, recounts historiography's development through these repetitive histories of racial origin, showing how in each rewriting, history advances toward more scientific methodology, "from false to true, from hypothesis to reality" (1: 16), while nevertheless maintaining a nationalist *parti pris*.[10] Each history progressively reinterprets the Frank/Gaul legend like the Hegelian master/slave dialectic, setting first the Franks over the Gallo-Romans (e.g., Boulainvilliers, proud aristocrat), then the Gallo-Romans over the Franks (e.g., Sieyès, patriotic revolutionary). Unlike Thierry's metahistory, the trilogy's chronicler goes generically backward in historiographical time while indicating the direction of the victors/vanquished dialectic of the present: "Think of the stories they tell nowadays about the Gauls, Louis XIV, even Félix Faure!... the defeated are always the scum!" (N, 10). The extended chronological progression from the Gauls and Louis XIV to Félix Faure signals not only the chronicler's impressive grasp of history but also a historical thread of losers with a racially based subtext: the Gallic race conquered first by the Romans, then by the Franks; Louis XIV's absolute monarchy, initiated in part by a Franks-versus-Gallo-Romans dispute only to be overthrown entirely with the French Revolution; and, finally, Félix Faure of the nineteenth century, who was elected by a moderate monarchist coalition and was an anti-Dreyfusard.

In the latter half of the sixteenth century, the chronicle as a genre began to wane precisely at the time histories of the origins of the French race were growing in popularity. Its disappearance was, however, only a reincarnation: it gradually became more of a personal self-defense, more like a memoir (a genre that had gained ascendancy by the seventeenth century) written against times that changed recorded exploits into a defensive response to contemporary political doctrine and loyalty. The chronicle as memoir thus became the discourse of the unofficial vanquished when other histories were being commissioned and written as official, patriotic histories. Monluc, a chronicler of the religious wars of the sixteenth century, accused of disloyalty to the king, is a clear case of this pattern, and although an illiterate, professional soldier always to be found on the battlefield, his dictated *Commentaires* (1592) are just a few steps away from the Cardinal de Retz's highly literate justifications of his court intrigues (another kind of battlefield) in his *Mémoires* (1658–62) written three quarters of a century later.[11] Like Céline, both Monluc and the Cardinal, having retreated toward the end of their lives to the solitude of their country estates to write, felt that they had a lot of explaining to do.[12]

The loser's history differs temporally from that of the winner because the chronicler's "memoir" is his life as he lives it in the telling or, as Monluc puts it in the preamble to his *Commentaries*, his book is "properly the discourse of [his] life" (1964, 22). The trilogy's chronicler is more graphic about his narrative presence: "Without boasting I can say that the thread of History passes straight through me from top to bottom, from the clouds to my head to my asshole" (N, 238). He is the suffering embodiment of history because it is threaded through him as a present perfect continuous history. Simple past, cause and effect, modern history (the opposite of the chronicle) cannot oscillate between the past and the present the way a chronicle can because real events of the past are treated as finished and closed, whereas in the chronicle events are constantly subject to revision and updating, not to final judgment. During his stay at Sigmaringen, for example, having been named governor of an island by Pierre Laval, Céline the chronicler updates: "The main thing: I was appointed Governor... I'm still Governor!" (C, 286). Mostly disappeared or departed persons (corroborating testimony) are mentioned: "Maybe Restif, I thought, and his men... by the way, I never saw Restif again... neither in Germany nor Denmark... nor later here... I asked all over... Marion knew him a lot better than I did... but Marion, you know, is dead" (R, 127). As for the fate of the chronicler's enemies, the morning is cheerfully spent reading the *Figaro*'s obituary notices, a present-day *chronique*: "A slight consolation perhaps, every morning in the *Figaro*, the obits [chronique nécrologique], the departures" (N, 12). The chronicle keeps history open, allowing thus for a seemingly innocent form of revision.

Adapting the trilogy to the stylistic idiosyncrasies of the medieval and Renaissance chroniclers, Céline said: "Brute facts, you won't find any; to reproduce them is without interest. Even the chroniclers, Froissart, Joinville, even they left a lot of room for invention [affabulation], for the power of words, for their music. All this is very important; emotion as style; that's why I called this book a novel" (CC7, 455). Facts juxtaposed with invention parallel Froissart's use of the words *croniser* and *hystoriier* in the prologue to his *Chroniques* (1374–1400, 1972, 35). Froissart's history is the relation of facts in their chronological order (croniser) with embellishment (hystoriier = illustrer) of those facts, but without alteration of factual information. Céline, however, jumbles his chronology and elaborates history to fictional heights. He makes ample use of digression, an important part of his revisions. In his *Histoire de Saint Louis* (1272–1309), Joinville also gets lost in infinite digressions and frequently aggrandizes his role in the crusades and his relationship with the king. Similarly, Céline, chronicler of the fall of the Third Reich, finds digressions or "little asides" (petits à-côtés) essential to the basic interest of his account: "the story of our mishaps may strike you as monotonous" (N, 164). This chronicler also clearly takes liberties with invention, particularly in one passage where he recounts giving Pierre Laval a cyanide capsule and thus fictively links himself to Laval's actual suicide attempt just before his execution by firing squad, a real event that horrified the public. Céline alters history so that, had Laval been successful in his attempt to take his life, Céline, the court chronicler at Sigmaringen, would have been responsible for saving him from the humiliation of execution, a clear case of revision insofar as Céline's account is also an unsubtle commentary on the Liberation Purge trials.

As Céline perceived it, the difference between "chronicle" and "novel" amounts to a difference in name only. They both contain a style and a voice—the style, like Céline's fast-paced "three dots" embroidered punctuation, capturing the fleeting music of a particular era, and the voice capturing a personality. Froissart's *Chroniques* and Céline's trilogy are a certain kind of chronicle: aristocratic as opposed to clerical (although the chronicler is not typically an aristocrat, he adopts these class values in relating aristocratic deeds). Clerical history, traditionally written for the most part in Latin, is more hypotactic, whereas aristocratic history, written in French, is structured by juxta-position and conjunctions (Brandt, 1966, 86–93). Céline's models and fragmented style suggest his preference for aristocratic histories written in French. He privileges this kind of chronicle over "academized" writing, viewing it as a more spontaneous, musical, and less learned use of language: "I could invent, transpose... that's what they all did, the lot of them... in Old French it went over... Joinville, Villehardouin had it easy, they took full advantage, but our French today, so anemic, so strict and finicky, academized almost to death" (R, 161).

Digging himself ever deeper into his role, Céline inscribes his anachronistic voice into the text by using outmoded spellings and, by extension, old pronunciations that privilege the aural, spoken side of his language: *oultre* for *autre* (R2, 139), *François* for *Français* (R2, 311) or *la Télévision françoise* (R2, 580) for *française*. More important, he some-times substitutes for *allemands/Allemagne* and *français/France* their names from classical antiquity and the Dark Ages: *les Germains* (R2, 554), *Germanie* (R2, 170), *les Gaulois* (R2, 488), and *cette Gaule* (R2, 916). Using these designations, Céline alerts his readers to his primary sources: Caesar's *Commentaries* and *Gallic Wars* and Tacitus's *Annals* and *Germania*. Standard reading for Céline, the works of Caesar and Tacitus were also standard reading for medieval and Renaissance chroniclers. For someone like Monluc (who when not on the battlefield was recuperating from his war wounds), Caesar, the conqueror of Gaul, was an example to be emulated: "The greatest captain there ever was, who was Caesar, showed me the way, having himself written his Commentaries, writing at night what he carried out in the day" (22).

The title of Monluc's chronicle is, in fact, taken from Caesar's *Commentaries*. In interviews and in the trilogy, Céline cites the late-Renaissance historian as an authority: "As Monluc, Henri IV's maréchal said: Seigneurs and you, captains, lead men to their death. For war is nothing but this" (CC2, 128). In *Nord*, Céline, as his fictional chronicler Ferdinand, attempts to cite Monluc to doctor Harras, but Harras is distracted by a knock at the door (R2, 398). Monluc is a particularly important model for Céline: a persecuted underdog who could not write but who *dictated* his *Commentaires*, thus achieving a more directly spoken style.

Fictionalized interviews with Céline, the chronicler discussing his work, begin to appear in *Nord*. In the first novel of the trilogy, *D'un Château l'autre*, where no interviews appear, the narrator calls himself in one instance a "memorialist" (R2, 92) but not a "chronicler." The definitive adoption of the more "spoken," chronicler role appears in *Nord*—revealing at the same time the permeability of the real and the fictive, the written and the spoken—with a mimicked interview in the first pages of the novel: "'So you call yourself a chronicler?'/'Exactly!'/ 'Without a qualm?...'/'Don't exasperate me!' I can still hear Madame von Dopf [von Seckt]" (N, 4). Without warning, this "interview" launches a dialogue from the past with Mme. Von Seckt. The inner (memory) and outer (present) ear of the chronicler effect shifts unpredictably between past and present to support the present perfect continuous thread of his aural/oral history.

Interviewers, of course, questioned Céline's anachronistic narrative voice when *D'un Château l'autre* first appeared. In one interview the author explained: "I consider myself a memorialist, a Joinville or Froissart type. Like them, I got caught up in some strange confusions. Believe me, it wasn't by vocation that I found myself at Sigmaringen" (CC2, 38). Describing Tallemant des Réaux's seventeenth-century *Historiettes* (1657–59), Céline nuances his use of the chronicle also to conform to journal(ism): "He tells little stories... it's like a journal, it's like a chronicle" (CC7,433). Therefore, "chronicle" in French has two meanings: a historical, eyewitness account of the past and, as in the case of the obituaries or "la chronique nécrologique," a newspaper that records the present. Céline will later play on this double meaning in the trilogy when he calls his third pamphlet a "chronicle": "The three of us hadn't said a word... just witnesses!... I could remember the stuff people said after *Les Beaux Draps*... which was simply a chronicle of the times" (N, 236). The chronicler traces his own change in perspective from someone who used to write about the present to a witness who, years later, writes his testimony of the past. Here we also see how Céline subtly disinculpates himself from authorship of this important, wartime pamphlet. He was no more than the mouthpiece, a passive recorder, of what the time itself was saying.

Both senses of "chronicle" as seemingly innocent writing absolve the chronicler of responsibility, that is, of authorial intention, because circumstances choose the chronicler, not vice versa. Céline is a doctor and a writer. Circumstances turn a person after the fact into a chronicler but not into a professional chronicler in the way a doctor is a professional. But as a literary writer, the chronicler may have difficulty living off his writing. Céline, the celebrated author of *Voyage au bout de la nuit*, would then resemble Froissart, a poet, who by luck of circumstance always seemed to be on the scene at the right time and was thus able to write his *Chroniques* for his patron, the Sire de Coucy, in order to make a living. Similarly, the Célinian chronicler is forced to make his living by writing the trilogy and complains frequently about having to write in order to pay off the advances extended to him by his patron/editor, Brottin Achille (= Gaston Gallimard): "I've got my chronicle to finish, my enormous debts to pay!" (R, 6). And just as Froissart is present at the foreign English court where Jean II's best knights are being held for ransom, so the trilogy's chronicler happens to be present at Sigmaringen where Pétain and his government officials are being held against their will by the Nazis. Pétain's helpless, captive court sports many of the important collaborationist names of the day (Pierre Laval, Maréchal Pétain, Paul Marion, Abel Bonnard, Fernand de Brinon, etc.) and even comes complete with a pro-fascist, *précieux* writer, Alphonse de Chateaubriant, who makes a brief and tempestuous appearance in Céline's chronicle: equipped with cape, Tyrolian cap with feather, ice axe, and spaniel on a leash (R2,229).[13]

The importance of the chronicle's temporality becomes clearer if we return again to the histories of racial origin. More impersonal, these histories were arguments supporting or criticizing contemporary political institutions (i.e., the power of the monarchy), each rewriting forming a new strategy of appropriation, first in relation to absolutism, then later in relation to the "beheaded" king, that is, as science, when racial anthropologists such as Paul Broca were zealously digging up, examining, measuring, and classifying skulls under ethnic categories.[14] The difference between these histories and a chronicle is temporally epistemological: histories of racial ancestry are about obscure, past events; whence their authors' paradoxical need to appeal to science and attain "objectivity" (Thierry's teleology from hypothesis to reality) in order to gain favor and/or a position in the present. Chronicles, like memoirs, are about lived events, opening the way for "subjectivity" and repetition, that is, different versions of the same event or set of circumstances. Thus, the generic definition of the chronicle as an open-ended, *impersonal* record of significant events in strict chrono-logical succession excludes the historical transformation of the form in France as one that originally corresponded to the generic definition but that gradually became more and more a personalized, self-defensive form relying heavily on its status as an *eyewitness* account. In the end, the chronicle would be viewed no longer as objective but as too subjective, even as literary, and therefore unacceptable next to the new historiography based on cause-and-effect analysis. Céline's strategy in writing a novelistic chronicle in a modern, twentieth-century context is both directed against the "official" postwar form of history and against history as a science of progress. The doctor knows how little science really knows. And the writer knows that no narrative, whether it be historical or fictive, is objective. Céline was not alone in choosing this strategy. Camus's *La Peste*, which appeared ten years before the publication of *D'un Château l'autre*, is also a chronicle written by a doctor (Rieux), whose self-effacing attempt to present his data as objectively as possible does not totalize but instead multiplies versions of the plague experience through the representation and voices of other participants. *La Peste* not only reflects symbolically on the Occupation experience but also questions the Liberation's official version of the Occupation.[15] Coming from the opposite side of the political spectrum, Céline *underwrites* the Franks and Gauls racial legend in his highly subjective chronicle not only to counter historiographical "science" but also to contrast it with the use (and abuse) of history in the service of a new world order that in the eyes of the chronicler paves the way for "democratic internationalism" to the detriment of individuality and cultural and racial sovereignty.[16] Céline's constant references to his style and narrative conceit are gestures on a par with more obvious revisionist histories such as Saint-Paulien's (*alias* Maurice-Ivan Sicard) *Histoire de la Collaboration*: "History has the meaning people bestow upon it. . . . If one admits that the historian writes to make his reader understand (and because he has already understood himself), in the course of his career, he must give different meanings to History" (1964, 4). Sicard's historian is really a chronicler, who, at various stages of his career, revises his history.

As a self-proclaimed chronicler, Céline will give his postwar readers the benefit of his eyewitness testimony, a personal, corrective history of the way it really was: "We'd better get back to Prussia where I've left you out on a limb... to my so cheerless story!... my chronicle of those vast reaches of mud and thatch... the petty comings and goings and fears of those people so long since vanished!" (N, 345). Not only is the trilogy the loser's story, but it is also written under, indeed, predicated on, the disappearance of the chronicler's world and of all those potential witnesses "so long since vanished." In the absence of witnesses, the chronicler of this history, then, is always already anachronistic, harking from a tradition so far back that he is also excluded from present time, which is given over entirely to a miasma of vacations, television, and cars. His history is therefore a dual movement of temporal exile, one that revolves around a set of dubious racial myths and phobias such as those Céline expresses. This exile, however, is much subtler than it appears, as it is a revisionist structure referring to the Renaissance controversy between Italogauls and Francogauls (Kelly, 1964, 226). If, according to Renaissance historians and lawyers, law is the product of history because history evolves into law, then it would be important to agree on the origins of feudal law (Kelly, 1964, 209). Debates centered around whether or not feudal law came from the Romans or the Franks. Céline, as we have seen, sides with the Franks. His position is complemented by revisionists such as Bardèche, who bitterly condemns the Nuremberg trials: "Christian justice was in this respect a law of restitution of the personality against Roman law which is geometric, scientific, material" (1948, 45). Bardèche's Christian justice comes down to Frankish law in opposition to the Roman law that apparently reigns at the Nuremberg trials. The important difference here is that between personal and impersonal history, chronicle and cause-and-effect history, Romans and Franks. If modern history is to Céline and other revisionists juridically Roman in nature, and a prosecutor's *narrative* constructed for the purpose of establishing guilt through impersonal cause and effect, the chronicle is based on personal law, the cyclical, repetitive notion that the chronicler adapts to his vision of human nature and fortune outside the pronouncements and precedents of secular, Roman law. Causes are not linked to a retrospective notion of intention but to circumstances so that the effects, like guilt, are entirely unforeseeable.

Imitating the traditional chroniclers, Céline blames history for his humiliation and defeat.[17] Guilt becomes one's fate only insofar as it is determined by the way things turn out in history, not by what one in fact does: "You're cornered by destiny... caught in a vise!" (C, 203). A sojourn at Baden-Baden with its sumptuous resort hotels complete with gaming rooms predictably evokes another of Céline's reflections on history as a game of chance, the great (roulette) wheel of Fortune: "The 'Everything Goes' Casino of History has a roulette wheel that means business, that doesn't give a shit if you're right, a thousand times... cheat... phony chips... you're in!" (N, 13). Historically guilty but not intrinsically so, the story must be told. Chronicles are often based on this change in fortune, causing the chronicler to reflect on how things do go wrong and how he must record and rectify the facts that misfortune obscures. "For man," Monluc says, "cannot remain in this world without a little bit of misfortune befalling him and, in keeping with this, everyone will then believe the truth" (1964, 9). Like Céline, Monluc refuses to accept personal guilt because adversity is passively received, not actively caused. History then is a simple question of winners and losers, not of the judgment passed by the Liberation.

Maurice Bardèche, who in 1948 published a rebarbative, revisionist condemnation of the Nuremberg trials, appeals as Céline does to a much older law: "One dared not judge this way during Chilpéric's time [Frankish king of the fifth century]. Submission to the law of the strongest was an act of greater loyalty. When the Gaul cries *Vae victis*, at least he does not take himself for Solomon" (1948, 31). Never mind that Bardèche's Gaul is already speaking Latin, the reference to Chilpéric and the Dark Ages is revisionist territory, as is the narrative strategy of Céline's chronicle; for these nostalgic references to the Dark Ages are consonant with the prewar nationalist desire for a Franco-German alliance. A prewar French text on Germany even echoes Céline's strategy by telescoping history and thus establishing the ground for a Franco-German alliance: "For the first time, with Charlemagne and the Franks, Europe was saved and the Empire was reconstituted by a Führer of genius at the head of a great Germanic tribe and of a 'party of the Reich'" (de Reynold, 1939, 104). If "rites were the exemplification of history" (104) for nationalist and fascist groups, then the chronicle is this kind of history's ideal form, precisely because it is a structural and temporal revision, as in a rereading, of Nordic race theories.

The chronicler pessimistically tells Otto Abetz in *D'un Château l'autre*—when, even as Germany and France are falling under the Allied invasion, Abetz proposes erecting an enormous statue of Charlemagne on the avenue de La Défense—"History is written by the victors!" (C, 266). He resembles another bitter chronicler, Commynes, who reflects: "for those who win always have the honor" (387). In coming full circle to Céline's dashed hope for a Franco-German alliance *à la Charlemagne*, one finds the revisionist racial legends in texts by authors such as Bardèche, who expresses hope eternal for a renewal, a historical revision insofar as it is a reversion, of the Frankish legend: "I have no opinion on the Third World War: it doesn't depend on us anyway. But I believe in a harsh battle for control of the West. This battle's victor will be, as in times past, the one the Franks of Germany will hoist upon their shields" (Bardèche, 1948, 269). While he waits, he can pass his time reading *Astérix*, where he may find his victors assimilated into cartoon figures. One of Céline's editors, Roger Nimier, was, indeed characterized as being far-sighted when, in *Nord*, he recommended replacing chunks of the chronicler's history with comic strips. Céline, the old-fashioned chronicler, was, naturally, horrified by the suggestion. With what satisfaction, however, would he have learned that *Astérix* was plagiarized by a German editor to create a Germanic counterpart with victorious (*siegreich*), national-socialist undertones, *Siggi, der kleine Germane* (Marny, 1968, 168)? The comic strip's appropriation is not exactly the alliance Céline had once hoped for but, like the trilogy, it echoes a longstanding and powerful legend.

Philip Watts

Postmodern
Céline

▼

THE RECENT resurgence of critical interest in the works of Louis-Ferdinand Céline, both in France and in the United States, can be attributed to a number of factors: the end of the writer's period of purgatory, the study of fascism and the Occupation by both historians and literary critics, the wealth of texts by Céline relatively free of commentary, and the author's radically innovative forms of writing.[1] Yet, if Céline has become such a powerful force in the contemporary literary field and if his works have begun to attract an expanding number of readers and commentators, it is perhaps because his writing, especially that of his postwar novels, has coincided with the development of new forms of reception. His influence on several generations of writers, including Henry Miller, William Burroughs, Joseph Heller, and Kurt Vonnegut in the United States, and Jean-Paul Sartre and Philippe Sollers in France, has made Céline into something of an *auteur fétiche*. Plurality of forms, fragmentation, simulation, and spectacle, historical borrowings, the rejection of the Enlightenment ideology of historical progress, a breakdown of the boundaries between high and low linguistic registers: all of these characteristics could serve to describe Céline's last works. And although Céline's early texts have been assimilated by certain critics to the tenets and representative works of twentieth-century modernism, increasingly, much of the critical interest in this author has coincided with the elaboration of a postmodern aesthetic.[2]

Postmodernism is, of course, a slippery term, if only because it can designate both a historical period—beginning either after World War II or in the early 1960s, depending on the account—as well as a transhistorical aesthetic sensibility. I do not intend to demonstrate that Céline's last works were postmodern *avant la lettre*, nor do I use this categorization in a valorizing sense. My intention is to examine a critical reception of Céline—as exemplified in the works of Julia Kristeva, Henri Godard, and Robert Llambias—that, while arguing for Céline's radically innovative texts and making Céline into a writer representative of a postmodern sensibility, obviates both the historical context and the political discourse manifest in Céline's literary production.

Though these three critics differ in their approaches and concerns, their readings of Céline nonetheless converge with a particular strain of postmodern thinking interested in evacuating historicity and ideological structures from the aesthetic field. This theoretical basis is perhaps best defined by Jean-François Lyotard's description of the postmodern, where "master narratives"—Marxism, psychoanalysis, critical reason—are seen as surrendering to language games and a "plurality of formal and axiomatic systems" (1984, 43).[3] Lyotard's postmodern framework has certainly fallen under rigorous criticism, most notably by Jürgen Habermas (1987), on the grounds that its rejection of Enlightenment ideology and its celebration of fragmentation come close to the point of departure of fascist thought.[4] Still, the tendencies Lyotard signaled can be found in some of the major critical texts on Céline published during the last two decades. An analysis of the critical reception of Céline's works in France from the mid-1970s to the mid-1980s permits a questioning of what seems to be a central tenet of a certain theoretical postmodernism: namely, that formal traits such as fragmentation and plurality serve to dissolve any precise political ideology in the literary text. If Céline's postwar novels present textual characteristics now associated with postmodernism, historicity and political ideology nonetheless remain essential and inescapable features of his literary production. Furthermore, it is precisely the textual techniques recuperated and accentuated by postmodern readings that transmit the dominant aspects of Céline's political thought.

It is perhaps through readings by members of the *Tel Quel* group in France that Céline's works were first brought back to public attention after World War II. For *Tel Quel*, Céline's writing came to represent what Georges Bataille had called the "experience of limits," a designation facilitated by Céline's status as political pariah in postwar France. In a 1963 article titled "Le Rire de Céline," ("Céline's Laughter"), Philippe Sollers initiated this type of reading, in which he championed the author of *D'un Château l'autre* for having chosen an idiosyncratic, rhythmic style over bourgeois morality. Some fifteen years later, another member of the *Tel Quel* group, Julia Kristeva, turned to Céline using synonymous, if somewhat more analytical, terms and argued for Céline's topicality in the literary scene of the 1970s.

The fact that Kristeva's article, "Actualité de Céline" ("Céline's Relevance Today"), is placed in the 1977 issue of *Tel Quel* between a passage from Sollers's *Paradis* and a study by Harry Blake of American postmodern writers demonstrates the importance Céline had taken as a model for the new aesthetic *Tel Quel* was attempting to forge. Like Sollers before her, Kristeva shows a predilection for Céline's postwar works, in particular *D'un Château l'autre, Nord*, and *Rigodon*, the novels of the German trilogy, symptomatic of what she a calls the "decentering of subjective identities" and the crisis of representation new to postwar capitalist society (1977, 45).[5] What makes Céline an emblematic writer for Kristeva is that his texts elaborate a linguistic practice situated in strict opposition to what she calls a "logico-positivist rationality" (47). In her account, the postwar Céline's rhythmic style goes beyond meaning, beyond the rationality of the unified subject, beyond the institutional and rationalist discourses of universities and political parties. Kristeva's reading of Céline fuses with the larger postmodern project of performing a break with the Enlightenment tradition of rationalism, identified by Lyotard as one of the master narratives of modernity. The rediscovery of Céline, some fifteen years after his death, permits the elaboration of a critical discourse subtly challenging any "institutionalized" and traditional critical language. Kristeva takes particular aim at the politics of Sartre's existentialism, the heir to the Enlightenment humanism *Tel Quel* was attempting to dismantle in the 1970s. What becomes clear at the end of Kristeva's essay is that for her, and, one may surmise, for the *Tel Quel* group, Céline has become the trangressive author who opened the doors to a reading opposed to existentialist politics, "running counter to theories of commitment" (51). As existentialism receded from the foreground of intellectual debate in France, Céline came to replace Sartre as the representative writer of contemporary crisis. By appropriating Céline— a writer of provocatively bad politics—Kristeva and *Tel Quel* were attempting to shift from the discursive mode of rationalism and political responsibility that had dominated the postwar scene to a discourse about delirium, a decentered subjectivity, schizophrenia, and *jouissance*. Céline's resurrection signaled Sartre's demise.[6]

But what of Céline's disastrous politics? What of his anti-Semitic pamphlets and his fascistic impulses? Kristeva's reading of Céline and of what she calls "poetic language" in general is certainly not apolitical, though it admittedly has little to do with the politics of engagement.

Reintroducing a dichotomy favored by *Tel Quel*, Kristeva argues for a radical separation between poetic language and traditional and repressive social and political institutions. Thus, the political function of poetic language would be to prevent the institutionalization of the unconscious (52). In this schema, Céline's novels would reveal the voice of compulsion or instinctive drives, which, without poetic language, results in institutionalized fascism: the state, the family, the fascist camp (47). The hierarchy of styles Kristeva is promoting—from the discourse of institutions to poetic language—can be questioned, however, precisely in a writer such as Céline whose literary itinerary coincided, at times, with the most repressive institutions and whose writings—whether novels, pamphlets, or correspondence—reveal a continuum in both style and thematics.

In her 1980 study of abjection, *Powers of Horror*, Kristeva once again characterizes Céline as a writer whose texts counter all forms of rationalist thought and of any belief in the progressive emancipation of humanity. For Kristeva, Céline's novels permit "neither divinity nor morality . . . neither revolutionary challenge . . . nor skeptical doubt" (1980a, 135–36). Kristeva is certainly right when she speaks of Céline's rejection of revolutionary contestation and history as progress, and it is no coincidence that both of these concepts are associated with traditionally left-wing forms of political thinking. She enters slippery terrain, however, when she equates these forms of ideology with all forms of political discourse and claims that Céline's postwar works are impervious to any type of ideological or political interpretation. Analyzing a passage from *Rigodon* representing the bombing of Hanover by Allied planes, Kristeva assimilates the massive destruction to "the point of departure of scription as the laying bare of meaning" and goes on to add: "No ideological interpretation can be based on his revelation: what principle, what party, what side, what class comes out unscathed, that is, identical to itself, from such a thorough critical conflagration?" (1980a, 154). We are now at the crux of Kristeva's argument: the last works of the author of *Bagatelles pour un massacre* have not only evacuated all meaning but are also incapable of supporting any type of ideological or political discourse. Céline's postwar novels would go beyond politics and history, presenting the "effervescence of passion and language we call style," a style directly opposed to any "ideology, thesis, interpretation, mania, collectivity, threat or hope" (1980a, 206). The postmodern moment, as identified by Kristeva, would thus occur when stylistic innovation replaces political discourse. This stance is, of course, very close to Céline's own insistence on the primacy of style in the postwar years.

Kristeva locates the novels' ideological moment not in political declarations at all but rather in a scene from *Rigodon* representing childbirth. It is here, in Céline's fascination with the abjection of parturition, that Kristeva situates the "economy" of fascism's "drive foundations" (1980a, 155). By evacuating the meaning of such historically significant representations as the bombing of German cities and by locating a maximum of significance in the biological instant, Kristeva reproduces Céline's own interpretative schema. For not only does Céline claim to replace political discourse with a style free of ideology, but also the one political position to which he openly admits after the war is biological racism, a position he constantly opposes to partisan politics and ideology.[7] But what of the passages representing the bombing of German cities? Are they as free of political ideology as Céline and Kristeva claim? If Céline is indeed an antirationalist, this situation no more frees his novels from a coincidence with political discourse than it did his pamphlets. What is more, the horrors of World War II did not produce a radical break in Céline's thought but were the elements to which he would constantly return and through which his writing would be determined.[8]

In a passage from *Rigodon*, partially quoted in Kristeva's *Powers of Horror*, Céline, recollecting his flight through Germany at the end of World War II, sets out to represent a bombed-out Hanover using terminology from the world of dance:

I can see there aren't many houses standing . . . the funny part of it was that on top of every caved-in building, every rubble heap, these green and pink flames were dancing around... and around... and shooting up at the sky!... those streets of green... pink... and red rubble... you can't deny it... looked a lot more cheerful... a carnival of flames... than in their normal condition... gloomy sourpuss bricks... it took chaos to liven them up... an earthquake... a conflagration with the Apocalypse coming out of it! the "fortresses" must have been here... and not just once... two times!... three times!... complete destruction was their idea... it had taken them more than a month, hundreds of them passing over, dropping tons and tons day and night... there really wasn't a thing left standing... (R, 130)

Most noticeable in this passage is the repeated use of a terminology incongruous with the massive destruction it claims to represent. Incendiary bombs seem to have enlivened the city, and fire has turned the usually bleak Hanover into a festive, spirited town, dominated by the topsy-turvy world of the carnival. These dancing flames come back

208 ▼ *Philip Watts*

in the novels almost as frequently as do the phosphorous bombs, and to represent the bombings, Céline uses phrases such as "the dancing flames" as well as references to specific dances such as the "snake dance" (C, 152), the "pirouette" (N, 8), the "farandole" (R, 133), and the "jig" (R, 210)—the last term, one of Ralph Manheim's translations for the French *rigodon*. Through the dance terminology, the representations of the bombing begin to fuse with representations of the writing project itself, as Céline after the war invariably turns to the metaphoric language of dance and music to represent his style.[9] Thus, the "rigadoon" designates at once the narrator's trajectory through Germany, the city's buildings set in motion by the bombings and Céline's own broken but fluid style. Céline seems close to creating an autonomous literary space in which the novel abandons mimesis and affirms its own existence as art. Furthermore, and Kristeva insists on this, the historical destruction of Hanover seems to have given way to the timeless destruction of the Apocalypse, with Céline in the role of witness to the end of the world.[10] Céline's eyewitness account of the historical instant seems, precisely, to have taken him outside the realm of history.

Still, we may ask what it means to represent the bombing of German cities in postwar France. And we may question whether an apocalyptic terminology and a self-reflexive writing strategy really do replace the historical referent.[11] As it turns out, the German trilogy never quite achieves the transcendence of historical reality Kristeva claims for it, for, along with the dance terms and the Apocalypse theme, the novels accumulate historically specific references to an event caught in the web of postwar political discourse. Céline evokes the incendiary bombs dropped by the Allied B-17s, the "flying fortresses," in these terms "the tactic of total squashing and frying in phosphorous" (C, 246); "Hamburg had been destroyed with liquid phosphorous" (R, 191)—phosphorous bombs being specifically linked to the firebombing of Germany. Alluding to the bombing of Dresden, Céline evokes the number of victims— 200,000 dead (C, 243)—making clear that this apocalyptic vision is also based in statistics, although Céline's figures are somewhat questionable. Not only are the streets of Hanover filled with civilians, shopkeepers, women, and children all carbonized by the flames, but also Céline tells his reader that the dead are the direct result of what he calls an "American invention" and the "spreading wings of democracy" (C, 246). As loaded as these passages may be with metacommentary and aesthetic borrowings, they constantly reiterate Céline's history lesson: the most horrifying destruction of the war was wrought on Germany by Allied war planes.

It is through these references that we may begin to reintegrate the passage just cited into the historical context of the postwar period, for, writing about the destruction of German cities by Allied bombing raids is, in 1950s France, a politically marked gesture, and responds to precise rhetorical strategies. Whereas Charles de Gaulle or Winston Churchill, in their memoirs of the war, mention the destruction of German cities only in passing, others, writing during the same period, use the bombings to accuse the Allies of atrocities and to refute charges of collaboration or war crimes.[12] One example of the latter is Maurice Bardèche's 1948 *Nuremberg ou la Terre promise*, an egregiously misinformed critique of the Nuremberg trials at the end of the war. It is difficult but, I believe, necessary to bring this sinister work into a discussion of textual exegesis, for not only did Céline read Bardèche's pamphlet while in exile in Denmark and not only did he integrate certain phrases from this work directly into his novels, but he also seems to have incorporated, though not without stylistic transformation, the use Bardèche makes of the destruction of German cities.[13]

Bardèche's pamphlet opens with the declaration that the history of the war must be revised, that it needs doing over—"the entire history of the war needs to be redone" (1948, 11)—and that the Nuremberg trials have led to nothing more than a falsification of history. In Bardèche's *tu quoque* reasoning, the accusations of crimes against humanity—that is, the Nazi responsibility for the concentration camps—were fabricated by the Allies as a means of diverting international attention away from what Bardèche sees as the true crimes of World War II: the bombing of Dresden, Hanover, and Hamburg by American and British planes. Thus Bardèche can write that the real basis for the Nuremberg trials is the spectacle of the ruins left by the thousands of phosphorous bombs (1948, 17). And Bardèche calls the bombings an "apocalyptic destruction" (1948, 22), prefiguring the very same terminology Céline later adopts. However just the condemnation of this senseless destruction might be, the assigning of responsibility or guilt for the destruction of German cities is problematic. Indeed, the linkage of Allied bombing raids to Nazi concentration camps has become an almost standard feature not only in the condemnation of the Purge trials but also in what has come to be known as Holocaust negationism.[14] The rhetoric of linkage exemplified in Bardèche's pamphlet seeks to eliminate through a series of false equivalences the significance and specificity of the Nazi death camps by transforming the destruction of German population centers into the war's sole specific instance of murder on a massive scale.

To return to Céline, if his last works answer to the imperative of formal innovation, they nonetheless also attempt to rewrite the history of the war and to establish a version of events that runs counter to official historiography. Statements such as "History is written by the victors" (C, 266) and especially "let me tell you: the Nuremberg trials need doing over!" (C, 131) echo and develop Bardèche's revisionist impulses. Furthermore, the linkage of horrors seen in the Bardèche book is not absent from Céline's postwar novels, for when Céline speaks of the concentration camps (and he only mentions one by name: Buchenwald), it is always in relation to other wartime events—the Soviet gulags, the Nuremberg trials, the prisons of the Purge, as though Céline were attempting to minimize any horror he had not witnessed.[15] As for the dance terminology in the bombing passage from *Rigodon*, its force also derives from its function as litotes, or understatement. The reference to dancing flames in this passage is a way of saying more by stating less.[16] From his very first writings Céline uses the ironic understatement, in particular when he chooses to maximize the horror of war. Such is the case in the famous passage from *Voyage au bout de la nuit* where Bardamu describes two recently deceased soldiers: "They were embracing each other for the moment and for all eternity, but the cavalryman's head was gone" (J, 12).

As with the term "embracing," the dance terminology in the trilogy reinforces through its incongruity the impact of the bombing passages. And if such dance terminology leads us to the texts' self-reflexive tendencies, this only reinforces the importance of the historically and politically marked passages. Céline does indeed provide what Kristeva calls an "X-ray of the drive foundations of fascism" (1980a, 155), not only in his fascination with birth and death but also in his impulse to displace the horror of war from the massacres of the concentration camps to the destruction of German cities.[17] To be sure, Céline is offering a personal account of the war, a testimonial to the bombings he witnessed. Yet, this testimony must be integrated into a discursive framework that is both juridical—that is, a condemnation of the Purge trials in France and Germany—and revisionist—the attempt, as with Bardèche, to shift public attention away from the horrors of the Nazi death camps to the Allied destruction of German cities.

It is not by discounting Céline's stylistic innovation that we arrive at a coherent historical or ideological reading of his works. A contextualized reading demonstrates that the diffusion of a revisionist ideology in Céline's last works depends on textual strategies of fragmentation and self-reflexivity. It is precisely when Céline's texts seem most displaced and heterogeneous and when they most consciously draw attention to the writing process—when, in other words, they most distinctly open themselves to a postmodern reading—that they are also most loaded with a troubling historical and political meaning.

Underlying any examination of postmodern thinking is the problematic treatment of history. Either evoked as a heterogeneous composition of different periods or transformed into a depthless and timeless spectacle, the past in postmodern works always seems to be out of place. The eclecticism that characterizes the postmodern aesthetic is most manifest in its historical borrowings, what David Harvey has called the postmodern's "incredible ability to plunder history and absorb whatever it finds there as some aspect of the present" (1989, 54). Beyond eclecticism, the postmodern representation of history has been shown to rest on the transformation of reality into spectacle. It was perhaps Guy Debord who, in *La Société du spectacle* ("The Society of Spectacle" [1967]), first pointed to the omnipresence of spectacle in late capitalist society; although Debord condemned what he saw as the commodification of the image, his theoretical insights have influenced a number of other theorists. Jean Baudrillard (1983), for example, claims that we are living in the era of simulation where the historically real has given way to the image, politics to entertainment, and ideological differences to simulation. Fredric Jameson posits that "simulacra" are indicative of a our society's "depthlessness" and have led to what he calls "a consequent weakening of historicity" (1991, 6). In both cases, whether in the form of borrowings or of simulation, history in the postmodern is always displaced, and this theory of displacement has manifested itself in several important readings of Céline's works.

It is perhaps doing violence to Henri Godard's 1985 *Poétique de Céline* to label it postmodern, for, after all, Godard's acknowledged model is Mikhail Bakhtin's dialogic principle. Still, no critic has more convincingly brought out the eclecticism of Céline's style than Godard, from the historical borrowings to the mixing of high and low social codes.[18] The a priori intention of Godard's study is the radical separation of the literary from the ideological production, of the novels from the pamphlets. Having stated this provision, Godard shows how Céline's verbal inventiveness does not simply arise from his use of a working-class argot, but, rather, from his constant shifting of registers, passing from popular slang to military terminology, from the language of the Parisian shopkeeper to that of literary preciosity, creating a polyphonic text whose ideological thrust, according to Godard, is constantly subverted. Thus, if Godard's reading of Céline can be charted on a map of postmodern readings, it is not simply because he describes the heterogeneity of Céline's style but also, and most important, because, for Godard, Céline's plurivocalism leads inevitably to a semantic indeterminacy. Céline's stylistic eclecticism creates what Godard calls a "halo of uncertainty" in the reading, a "displacement" of the semantic value of the lexicon (1985, 108). This displacement of meaning becomes particularly problematic when the reader attempts to distinguish the historical discourses transmitted in Céline's novels. Godard convincingly points to the numerous historical registers in Céline's texts, from the archaic lexicon to a fascination with medieval legends, and from the nostalgia for the Belle Epoque to the use of the chronicle genre in the last novels.

Yet, for Godard this cannibalization of forms of history leads to the destruction of historicity as Céline's borrowings are set up in opposition to contemporary forms of dominant discourse. Historical references would thus paradoxically serve to detach Céline's writing from a historical context. The use of archaisms, for example, participates in the popular register and as such serves to counter the discourses of social and familial authority (1985, 151). While consistently condemning the politics of Céline's pamphlets, Godard refuses to read the novels as a vehicle for ideology, preferring instead to label the novelist's voice a "counter-discourse" (1985, 197). And because meaning is displaced as soon as the reader attempts to seize it, all political affirmations in Céline's novels are "defused by the writing that carries them" (1985, 207). Godard's landmark study has been crucial for the rehabilitation of Céline's fictional work. Yet, his treatment of history is problematic, for, although he accounts for historical forms in the case of the German trilogy, he performs a questionable separation of the novels from the difficult memories of World War II.

The argument for the displacement of history in Céline's novels finds another proponent in Robert Llambias, whose 1986 article "Guerre, histoire et langage dans le récit célinien" ("War, History and Language in Célinian Narrative") presents simulation and a use of the terminology of the theater as a substitute for history. Calling war the "metasign" in Céline's novels, Llambias sees the language of simulation in the German trilogy as a vehicle for transforming history into a falsification, and events into a gigantic *fête* demanding of its celebrants the complete ability to forget the past (97–99). There would thus be no more memory in Céline, just an endless play of images. Historical references, such as those to the Vichy government in exile at Sigmaringen, would consequently reveal a desire to "deconstruct History" (97). By his reliance upon the language of theater, and by his transformation of history into a spectacle, Céline, according to Llambias, "has evacuated both the story and any meaning this story may have carried" (104). Céline's radically innovative style, when seen in the form of spectacularization of history, inevitably leads to subsequent loss of meaning and detaches the novel from any form of historical representation.

It seems, however, that the wealth of sources on which Céline's German trilogy relies may reveal more for a contemporary reading than does an interpretative schema intent on detaching Céline's texts from problematic political positions. To demonstrate this, I refer again to a passage from the trilogy, in *D'un Château l'autre*, where Céline uses the vocabulary of the operetta to evoke the town of Sigmaringen in which Maréchal Pétain, Pierre Laval, and the remnants of the Vichy government found refuge during the last months of the war:

Maybe I shouldn't talk Siegmaringen up... but what a picturesque spot!... you'd think you were at an operetta... a perfect setting... you're waiting for the sopranos, the lyric tenors... for echoes you've got the whole forest... ten, twenty mountains of trees! Black Forest, descending pine trees... waterfalls ... your stage is the city, so pretty-pretty, and pink and green, semi-pistachio, assorted pastry, cabarets, hotels, shops all lopsided for the effect... all in the "Baroque *Boche*" and the "White Horse Inn" style... you can already hear the orchestra... the most amazing is the Castle... stucco and papier-mâché... like a wedding cake on top of the town. (C, 124)

The constellation of references in this passage serves to transform a historical moment into a theatrical representation. The first reference is to the operetta and, from this point on, the setting of the novel becomes almost indistinguishable from a theatrical set. Not only is history transformed into spectacle but also Céline borrows from numerous and varied genres. The operetta—the light musical comedy—serves as the primary reference, appearing in the form of the "lyric tenors" and the "White Horse Inn," a popular turn-of-the-century musical. Wagner, to be sure, is not entirely absent from this passage, and the presence of his works is inscribed both in the setting—the "Black Forest"—and in the voluntary misspelling of "Siegmaringen." The *sieg* morpheme might function as an ironic evocation of the German *sieg heil* but is also a reference to the Wagnerian hero Siegfried of the *Ring* tetralogy. The role of Siegfried is indeed sung by a tenor, and Wagner's work is often referred to as a *scherzo*, a light composition rather than a tragic opera.

The references to the operatic genres are complemented by a terminology that insists on the artificial aspects of the setting. Not only is the town a stage, but the castle is also described as if it were nothing more than a false front.

We might thus be tempted to agree with Llambias's statement that the town of Sigmaringen has been "removed from History" (1986, 99). This mixture of references and the transformation of Vichy's German headquarters into the setting of an operetta render unclear the precise semantic situation and ideological value of the passage. The geopolitical site of Sigmaringen has been transformed, it would seem, into the stage of an anodyne, even farcical, operetta. This type of reading, however, seems to rely on the belief that there is a stable, nonaesthetic reality behind Céline's aestheticized representations. Nor does Llambias attempt to account for the political ideology of the aesthetic vocabulary. By returning again to the historical archive, we see that Céline uses the language of the spectacle to elaborate a juridical argument and a description that is consistent in its apologetics of the French collaborationist refugees and the author's anti-Purge tendencies.

Céline, as it turns out, was not the first to use the language of simulation to depict Sigmaringen. If we look beyond the aesthetic field, we find the use of this same terminology in a 1948 collection of transcripts from the trials of three collaborators at the close of the war. All three, Fernand de Brinon, Joseph Darnand, and Jean Luchaire were tried for treason, convicted in Paris, and executed. Along with the accusation of having acted in collusion with the occupying forces, the flight of these three collaborators to Sigmaringen with the Vichy government, was, for the prosecution, further proof of their guilt. In his defense of Jean Luchaire attorney Jacques Floriot, answers this specific accusation: "Sigmaringen, you consider this operetta important? . . . Doesn't Sigmaringen make you smile? That there were some French in Germany to create a puppet government? . . . Didn't you have the feeling that it was an opera troupe?"[19] In an attempt to evacuate the political import of the Vichy government in exile, Floriot transforms the military troop into an opera troupe, thereby leaving only a caricature of power where the prosecution would attempt to locate political responsibility and discrediting the accusation of collaboration brought against his client.

Whether Céline had read the transcripts from the Luchaire trail is unknown, although we do know that he kept a close eye on the Purge trials while in exile in Denmark. The parallels between Luchaire's case and his own are remarkable: both men were accused of intellectual collaboration (Luchaire was a journalist on the Nazi payroll), and both men fled to Sigmaringen in 1944 to avoid the advancing Allied troops. Thus, when Céline uses both the operatic terminology and the direct address to an audience previously used in Floriot's defense plea, he inscribes his work within an existing juridical and political framework. Nowhere do Céline's responses to the trials of the Purge become more intense, if ultimately unpersuasive, than when he leaves the realm of the obviously political for the world of the spectacle. Céline's references to the operetta in *D'un Château l'autre*, his dependence on the language of simulation, and his eclectic and anachronistic historical borrowings, far from decontextualizing the novel and far from transforming history into spectacle, serve to reinscribe the novel into the historical context. And this context is not the military or diplomatic history of World War II, for example, or simply the chronicle of the Vichy régime by an impartial witness, but the history of the rhetoric of the postwar Purge in France. The language of simulation, as Floriot well knew, is precisely what permits the production of an ideological discourse.

The recuperation of an author's work by generations intent on developing a new aesthetic is certainly not a recent phenomenon. Any reflection on contemporary literature inevitably demands the discovery of sympathetic antecedents. Still, the recuperation of Céline poses problems. The postmodern critical reception of Céline served to canonize the author's novels through a simultaneous exaltation of their formal attributes and a silencing of their political implications. Certainly, one of the motivations for this new reception was a desire to break with the pattern of accusatory criticism exemplified by Sartre's work. Reading Céline, consuming Céline's texts, could even be construed as an act of resistance to totalizing institutional discourses. Unfortunately, Céline's texts themselves resist the attempt to read them as free from ideologies and political affirmations. It is also in the readings elaborated by these critics that we may find the most useful techniques for coming to terms with the politics of Céline's last novels. If we are to account for, rather than evacuate, the politics of Céline's novels, we must do so with an eye to precisely those unstable forms of discourse that seem to disengage his writing from the political field. If we are to keep reading Céline, we must maintain his texts within the historical archive that was, at least in part, responsible for their production. Political thinking may take on many widely dispersed and divergent forms; Céline's last novels teach us that political thinking may also depend on forms of representation that have as their basis dispersal, divergence, and instability.

Notes

▼

All short citations in the notes are referenced in full in the Works Cited.

Introduction

1. See especially Kristeva (1982); Blondiaux (1985); Godard (1985); Kaplan (1986); Hewitt (1987); Alméras (1987); Solomon (1988); Bellosta (1990); Winock (1990); and Llambias (1986).

2. For a thorough discussion of these institutional tensions, see Jonathan Culler's *Framing the Sign: Criticism and Its Institutions* (Norman: University of Oklahoma Press, 1988).

3. See Jacques Derrida's La Différance," in *Marges—de la philosophie* (Paris: Minuit, 1972), 1–29, and "La Structure, le signe et le jeu dans le discours des sciences humaines," in *L'Ecriture et la difference* (Paris: Seuil, 1967), 409–28.

4. See Derrida's *De la Grammatologie* (Paris: Seuil, 1967), *Marges—de la philosophie* (Paris: Minuit, 1972), *Positions* (Paris: Minuit, 1972), *Eperons* (1978); Luce Irigaray's *Ce Sexe qui n'en est pas un* (Paris: Minuit, 1977) and *Speculum de l'autre femme* (Paris: Minuit, 1974); Hélène Cixous and Catherine Clément's *La Jeune Née* (Paris: 10/18, 1975); and Cixous's influential essay "Le Rire de la méduse," *L'Arc*, 61 (1965): 39–54. For further contributions to the discussion of the excluded other(s) of European phallogocentrism, see *Europe and Its Others*, ed. Francis Barker, 2 vols. (Colcester: University of Essex, 1985); Edward Said's *Orientalism* (New York: Pantheon, 1978); Gayatri C. Spivak's *In Other Worlds* (New York: Routledge and Kegan Paul, 1987); Trinh T. Minh Ha's *Woman, Native, Other* (Bloomington: Indiana University Press, 1989); Chandra Mohanty et al., eds., *Third World Women and the Politics of Feminism* (Bloomington: Indiana University Press, 1990); and Robert Young's *White Mythologies: Writing History and the West* (New York: Routledge, 1991).

5. See Michel Foucault, *Folie et déraison: Histoire de la folie à l'âge classique* (Paris: Plon, 1961).

6. Young writes: "Everyone knows that [*De la Grammatologie*] is a critique of 'logocentrism'; what is less often recalled is that the terms of the critique with which it opens announce the design of focusing attention on

logocentrism's *'ethnocentrism'* which, Derrida suggests, is 'nothing but the most original and powerful ethnocentrism, in the process of imposing itself upon the world,'" *White Mythologies*, 18, Young's emphasis.

7. See Sartre, *Réflexions sur la question juive* (1946), and Céline's response to the accusations Sartre made in this essay in "A l'agité du bocal," CC7, 382–87).

8. See Mosse (1978; 1985) and Klaus Theweleit's *Male Fantasies: Women, Floods, Bodies, History* (Minneapolis: University of Minnesota Press, 1987).

9. See Robert Soucy's *French Fascism* (1986); Zeev Sternhell's *Ni Droite Ni Gauche: L'Idéologie fasciste en France* (Paris: Seuil, 1983); Robert Jackson's *The Popular Front in France* (1988); Philippe Bernard and Henri Dubief's *Le Déclin de la Troisième République, 1914–1938* (1985); Serge Klarsfeld's *Vichy-Auschwitz: Le Rôle de Vichy dans la Solution Finale de la question juive en France.* 2 vols. (Paris: Fayard, 1983/1986); Michael Marrus and Robert Paxton's *Vichy France and the Jews* (New York: Schocken, 1983); André Kaspi's *Les Juifs pendant l'Occupation* (Paris: Fayard, 1991); Diane Rubenstein's *What's Left* (1990); Jean-Pierre Azéma's *De Munich à la Libération* (Paris: Seuil, 1978); J.-P. Azéma, ed., *Le Régime de Vichy et les Français* (Paris: Fayard, 1992). See also Kaplan (1986) and R. J. Golsan, ed., *Fascism, Aesthetics and Culture* (Hanover: University Press of New England, 1992) for treatment of the political dimensions of the aesthetic practices of the period.

10. Henri Rousso, *Le Syndrome de Vichy* (Paris: Seuil, 1987).

11. Marguerite Duras takes de Gaulle to task precisely on this issue in *La Douleur* (Paris: P.O.L., 1985), where the General's postwar maneuvering to "cover up" the internal political tensions and cover over the society's collective grief is characterized as a "criminal" undertaking. Duras further draws attention to the specificity of class and gender oppression that has often been subsumed in official historical accounts of the period under the broader categories of national subjugation occasioned by the military defeat of June 1940. Duras's "rewriting" of that history in 1985 can surely be considered part of the return of the repressed effects and affect of the historical trauma which Rousso so persuasively formulates in *Le Syndrome de Vichy*.

12. Schlemilovitch reminisces: "Je ne passait pas sous silence ses pamphlets antisémites, comme le font les bonnes âmes chrétiennes. J'écrivais à leur sujet: 'Le docteur Bardamu consacre une bonne partie de son oeuvre à la question juive. Rien d'étonnant à cela: le docteur Bardamu est l'un des nôtres, c'est le plus grand écrivain juif de tous les temps. Voilà pourquoi il parle de ses frères de race avec passion'." See Patrick Modiano's *La Place de l'Etoile* (Paris: Gallimard, 1968); 13–16. For a discussion of Modiano's pastiche of Céline, see Ora Avni's "Narrative Subject, Historic Subject: *Shoah* and *La Place de l'Etoile*," *Poetics Today*, 12(3) (Fall 1991): 495–516, and her "A French Jew? Patrick Modiano," forthcoming in *Yale French Studies*.

13. I do not mean to suggest here that only European societies and their New World derivatives practice discrimination against those who are different for there are, quite obviously, human communities throughout the

world that erect barriers to the influence of outsiders. Notwithstanding, given the hegemonic role the West and its value systems have had in shaping global relations and dynamics in both the colonial and postcolonial eras, the discourses on difference we are analyzing here can be seen as meaningful both within the geographic bounds of Western societies and in relation to the expanse of non-European cultures we have historically ravaged. In the modern encounter between the West and its many subordinated others, these discourses have been widely disseminated and their repressive effects felt across the globe, thus making our enthnocentrism and racism much more than simply a European family affair.

14. See Marrus and Paxton's *Vichy France and the Jews*; David Weinberg's *A Community on Trial: The Jews of Paris in the 1930s* (Chicago: University of Chicago Press, 1977); Paula Hyman's *From Dreyfus to Vichy: The Remarking of French Jewry, 1906–1939* (New York: Columbia University Press, 1979); and Kaspi's *Les Juifs pendant l'Occupation*.

15. Germany, France, England, and the United States have all seen a heightening of racial and ethnic tensions over the last several years, and anti-Semitism appears once again to be asserting itself in numerous Eastern European countries. Serbian efforts to carry out wholesale "ethnic cleansing" of the Muslim presence in former Yugoslavia reverberates eerily not only with echoes of the Nazi's "Final Solution" of the "Jewish Problem" but also with the West's centuries-old orientalist discourses of domination that Edward Said and other scholars who have followed in his footsteps have rigorously documented and textually deconstructed. See especially Said's *Orientalism*.

Céline: A Clinical or a Critical Case?

1. One can read, for example, in the November 12, 1932, issue of *D'Artagnan* the following commentary: "All the pathological cowardice a man can have inside himself is analyzed here with unimaginable complacency. One might think it's the work of a deranged man. Yet we've been assured that, quite the contrary, the author is a physician. A poor man's doctor. Hailing from Marseille." Similarly, in the December 27, 1932, issue of *La Volonté* the following advertisement was published: "Mme Marcelle Vioux, the renowned woman of letters, will defend Louis-Ferdinand Céline's sensational work, *Journey to the End of the Night*, addressing the question: *Was it right or wrong not to award him the Prix Goncourt? A Work of Genius or of insanity?*"

2. *Editors' Note*: For a discussion of Céline's autofictional writing, see Spear (1991).

3. A noteworthy example of this can be found in Stephen Day's very self-assured assertion: "Céline is a neurotic. Yes, but only to the degree that *we who are normal* can enjoy nature, for example, without envisioning, as he does, the ceaseless slaughter of species taking place under every blade of grass and beneath each stone" (1974, 133; emphasis added).

4. Even if Nina Gourfinkel would have us believe that the utterance of the lunatic is synonymous with the lunatic himself (and her choice of Céline is, perhaps, not intentional), the diagnosis of paranoia—introduced

in her 1936 article "Les Thèmes scatologiques en littérature"—in fact, pertains to Ferdinand, the protagonist of *Mort à crédit*, not to the author. Her diagnosis of Ferdinand's paranoia competes, most notably, with her diagnoses of his mental imbalance, psychoneurosis, and hysteria.

5. It should be noted that if Hindus considered Céline a paranoid ("The sad truth appears to be that paranoia was for Céline what astigmatism and visual disorders may have been for other masters of modern art" [HER, 376]), the novelist countered such charges preemptively by accusing Hindus himself of hysteria: "Oh Hindus is a virgin asshole who imagined he was going to make a name for himself in Literaaaaatuure zip! zip! just like that!... Rot from America! He resented the hell out of me! as spiteful as a broad! frantic hysteria!" (CC6, 226).

6. In the second part of the 1951 version of *Céline tel que je l'ai vu* (1951), Hindus refers to Céline's "quasi-paternal malevolence" toward the critic, malice he sees as responsible for the degeneration of their relationship following the appearance of the first version of his manuscript: "From that point on Céline became increasingly hateful towards me. He continued to inveigh against me for having dared to record the literal truth, even though I responded to none of his insults. Day after day, as I received the little packages of filth his editor, lawyer, and friends would send me, my sensitivity was more and more dulled. I had needed the crowning lesson which his quasi-paternal malevolence was giving me in order to sever the last spiritual bonds tying me to him" (1951, 109–10).

7. Confidence for confidence, in a 1955 interview, Céline made reference to his experience as an "intern" (although it is well known that he in fact never took the psychiatry examinations). Speaking of the difference between emotional intensity and academic French parlance, he said he "frequented a good many asylums and you know in insane asylums, to what type of questioning the madman is subjected? The former!" Cited in the interview conduced in March 1955 by Robert Sadoul for Radio Suisse-Romande and published under the title "Céline: Au Début était l'émotion," *Magazine Littéraire*, 280 (September 1990): 94–103. Milton Hindus also makes mention of Céline's involvement with psychiatry in his reference to the novelist's "experiences in the madhouse" (1951, 39).

8. In his correspondence with Albert Paraz, Céline accused Hindus, among other things, of seeking through the publication of his book to "avenge Buchenwald now that there were no risks involved" (CC6, 64).

9. Hindus notes that Céline "has enough insight left to objectify his paranoid delusions, and he has sufficient power over an artistic medium to involve the public which acts as his confessor. He also has enough intelligence, prudence, caution, or cowardice to limit his violent fantasies to paper and not to confuse life with imagination" (1951, 59).

10. It is on this inability to play that Tzvetan Todorov, in an article dealing with psychotic discourse, establishes one of the fundamental characteristics of paranoid discourse, noting that: "The discourse of the paranoid is quite similar, as a discourse, to what is called normal discourse; the only important difference lies in the fact that the referants evoked do not, for us, necessarily exist in reality. It would suffice, however, for this discourse to be presented as a fiction, or as a way of saying something else,

indirectly (as an allusion, as a trope, as a joke) for the pathological character to vanish. This is precisely what the paranoid can never do: he cannot make this distinction" (1978, 79).

11. In addition to the personality traits that are specific to paranoia, such as grandiosity (in the form of conceit or arrogance), self-involvement, authoritarianism, intolerance of others, psychorigidity, suspiciousness, and irritability, Kretschmer's use of this term designates other manifestations associated with the disorder that are more sentient in nature, such as emotional anguish, hypersensitivity, petulance, abrasiveness, excitability, dissatisfaction, and punctiliousness—a broad range of affects that can bring on a depressive state.

12. Gibault makes the following comments about an anecdote concerning Céline's fictitious encounter with the emperor of Austria: "It underscores Céline's need to fabricate stories, less out of mythomania than out of the simple pleasure of recounting colorful events" (1977, 114). Céline's lover, Elizabeth Craig, essentially corroborates this view, noting:

[Céline] exaggerated things, yes! He exaggerated in order to generate his ideas, to see where his inventions would take him. He did this in a fanciful manner, the way that some women live their fantasies, but he did it through writing. He recounted things as if they had actually happened to him... sometimes I joined in the game... He acted exactly as if he were in the process of living it all... sometimes his fantastic constructions lasted two or three days... he was in full fantasy.... At first I let myself be taken in... I really believed him and then one day I said to myself... that can't be possible, is he inventing all this?... Then why not join in his game[?]... and I played my part in his fantasies for some time.... I don't know if he learned to do this to fill the void of solitude when he was alone or if it was merely a technique he devised to make himself feel better... or perhaps it was just a way of experimenting with ideas before committing them to paper... in order to develop the identity of his characters, to scrutinize them.... I don't know what techniques writers employ... I think many of them must do the same thing... create situations and invent characters and set it all in motion in order to be sure it all works the way they want it to. (Monnier, 1988, 60–61)

13. In an undated letter to Eugène Dabit, Céline wrote: "In the sphere of madness, it was also frankly necessary to intensify the whole tone. This naturally sets things off. I'm absolutely certain of it" (HER, 58); and elsewhere: "I've got to enter into a state of delirium, to accede to the realm of Shakespeare, because I'm incapable of constructing a story with the logical mentality of the French" (CC1, 51).

14. Céline declined Lucien Combelle's February 1941 request for an interview in much the same tone he used with Paraz: "I hate such exhibitionism far too much in others, those vampish come-ons, to indulge in it myself. It's all hysteria, narcissism in our craft, that, I'll accept, but then a certain decency is our only redemption, a certain transposition, our penance, excusing us somewhat. Other than that, what abjection!" (HER, 106).

15. My use of the notion of mythomania is taken from Ernest Dupré (to whom Céline refers repeatedly in *Journey* and *North*, as well as in his

correspondence), who presented it during the introductory lecture of his 1905 Seminar on Forensic Psychiatry:

> For general purposes of accurate construction and for the sake of clarity (*mythos*, imaginative narrative, fable), I propose the use of this neologism to designate *the pathological propensity, more or less intentional and conscious, for falsehood and the creation of imaginary tales.* It is not the various forms of lying and feigning which I propose we investigate here, but rather the study of a constitutional proclivity which compels certain categories of individuals, through pathological activity of the creative imagination, to lie, to pretend, and to invent tales and situations that have no basis in objective reality. (1905, 5, emphasis added)

16. "Whereas you want to create . . . to transmit messages to the world . . . you want . . . then you fall into grotesque play-acting, you know? So, at the bottom of what goes into being a writer and of everything that takes place on stage, you know, is largely a question of getting yourself talked about, and then you can be yourself, you are miraculously yourself. It's paranoia, isn't it? It's a sickness" (see interview cited in note 7). Contrary to lay usage in which the term *paranoia* is used to describe a feeling of persecution, Céline tends to exhibit both its megalomaniacal aspect and a form of vanity, attaining delusionary proportions. One can see this in the manner in which he illustrates paranoia in *Entretiens avec le Professeur Y*: "Take the theater for instance... there's not a single freshly-baked young dairymaid coming to the city to make it big as an actress, who, after three lessons at Brichantzky's, Elysée-des-Beaux-Arts, is not determined to toss out the whole repertory system! song, dance, diction! No arguing with her! that's it!... the slightest criticism!... what a reception you get! these young ladies, they no longer belong to this world!... they live in the world of *paranoia*!" (CY 41, emphasis added).

17. This problematic is not unique to Céline. In *The Gay Science* (1882) Friedrich Nietzsche sees the *histrion*, or joker, as an inferior form of the authentic genius. In the segment entitled "On the problem of the actor," Nietzsche writes: "The problem of the actor has troubled me for the longest time. I felt unsure (and sometimes still do) whether it is not only from this angle that one can get at the dangerous concept of the artist—a concept that has been treated with unpardonable generosity. [The 'artist,' the buffoon, the imposter, the fool, and the clown, even the classic example of a servant, Gil Blas: in such types we find the pre-history of the artist and even of the 'genius'" (1974, 316–17). *Editors' Note*: For further discussion of the problematic of the histrion, see note 22; see also Watts, Chapter 11, pp. 213–15.

18. I have borrowed the term *follittéraire* from Monique Plaza (*Ecriture et folie*, Paris: Presses Universitaires de France, 1986). *Translators' note*: The noun *follittéraire* has been rendered as the adjective *folliterate*, which collapses the French words *folie* (madness) with *littérature* to yield the notion of "follitérature" or a "literature of madness."

19. Gourfinkel's study is actually a series of articles that appeared in two, rather than "five or six issues" (as Céline had claimed), of the *Courrier d'Epidaure*.

20. In his correspondence with Albert Paraz, for instance, Céline writes: "hysteria is the vice of the Jew" (CC6, 64).

21. Freud, for instance, saw Otto Weininger's anti-Semitism and anti-feminism as the product of castration anxiety, explaining:

> The castration complex is the deepest unconscious root of anti-Semitism; for, even in the nursery, little boys hear that a Jew has something cut off his penis—a piece of his penis, they think—and this gives them a right to despise Jews. There is no stronger, unconscious root for the sense of superiority over women. In a chapter that attracted much attention, Weininger (the young philosopher who, highly gifted but sexually deranged, committed suicide after producing his remarkable book, *Geschlecht und Charakter (Sex and Character* [1903]), treated Jews and women with equal hostility and overwhelmed them with the same insults. Being a neurotic, Weininger was completely under the sway of his infantile complexes; from this standpoint, what is common to Jews and women is their relation to the castration complex. (Freud, 10: 36)

22. Nietzsche elaborates on this in fragment 361 of *The Gay Science* ("On the problem of the actor") in which he views the histrionic "instinct" as the sole means of "get[ting] at the dangerous concept of the 'artist'" (1974, 316), and as the trait that Jews, litterati, and women—all experts in feigning—have in common: "As for the *Jews*, the people who possess the art of adaptability par excellence, this train of thought suggests immediately that one might see them virtually as a world-historical arrangement for the production of actors, a veritable breeding ground for actors. And it is really high time to ask: What good actor today is *not*—a Jew?"; "the man of letters is essentially an actor: He plays the "expert," the "specialist"; "Finally, women. Reflect on the whole history of women: do they not have to be first of all and above all else actresses? . . . That they 'put on something' even when they take off everything" (317, Nietzsche's emphases). *Editors' Note:* Nietzsche's English translator, Walter Kaufmann, gives greater specificity to this last commentary on women in his note: "Dass sie 'sich geben,' selbst noch, wenn sie—sich geben." Literally: "That they 'give themselves' (that is, act or play a part) even at the very moment when they—give themselves" (317, German translation altered).

23. Cited in Derrida (1979, 71).

24. Derrida writes: "Not only is there the artist-histrion, or affirmative dissimulation, but there is also the artist-hysteric whose reactive dissimulation is that of the 'modern artist.' In fact, it is the latter that Nietzsche compares to 'our small women' [nos petites hystériques], and 'poor women . . . agitated and uncertain' [petites femmes hystériques]" (1979, 71).

Sources in Bagatelles pour un massacre

1. This essay is based on the research presented in my volume *Relevé des sources et citations dans* Bagatelles pour un massacre (Paris/Tusson: Editions du Lérot, 1987).

2. Céline's widow, Lucette Destouches, has continued to honor the author's request that his pamphlets not be reprinted. The possibility of publishing a new, annotated edition of these works has, however, been considered in recent years. See *Le Nouvel Observateur*, December 1991.

3. Georges Zérapha, an industrialist, philanthropist, activist with the International League Against Anti-Semitism (LICA), and admirer of the Popular Front, had offered his office and support staff in 1933 to the journal *Esprit*, which was then experiencing financial difficulties. In 1938, at the same time his article on Céline's *Bagatelles pour un massacre* appeared in *La Conscience des Juifs*, all of Zérapha's work documenting its sources — including their juxtaposition in columns with the text of *Bagagelles* — was published in *Esprit* without any indication of its origins. See Zérapha: "Probité celinienne," *La Conscience des Juifs*, 2–3 (February–March 1938): 14–18. See also Jeanine Roy's "Bagatelles pour un massacre," *Esprit*, 66 (March 1938): 959–61. Roy's article is reprinted in *Le Cahier de L'Herne* (HER, 466–67), where it has been mistakenly attributed to Emmanuel Mounier. Céline himself appears to refer to this *Esprit* article in a letter to Henry-Robert Petit (in the 1930s, Petit's first name appears with a "y" rather than an "i"): "I never responded to this piece of trash which smacked of 'provocation.' I was counting on you to see to it that it gets slobbered on appropriately" (LHP, 10). For information on Zérapha and the *Esprit* group, see Michel Winock's *Histoire politique de la revue "Esprit": 1930–1950* (Paris: Seuil, 1975). During the Occupation, Zérapha was a founding member of the underground network, Libération. He left France in 1943 for Spain and then took refuge in London where he had ties to the Independent Labour Party and the journal, *Left*. In the first post-Liberation issue of *Esprit* (December 1944: 34–55), Zérapha published a powerful polemical essay on fascism and the excesses of the liberation purges entitled "Le problème politique français, 1789–1944."

4. See Edouard Helsey, "Par le Fer et par le feu" (the sixth installment in a series entitled "Ceux de la Faucille et du Marteau") in *Le Journal*, July 15, 1937; 4.

5. Jean Fontenoy, *L'Ecole du renégat* (Paris: Gallimard, 1936). The book's printing was completed on October 16, 1936. Céline's trip to Leningrad took place between late August and September 25, 1936; *Mea Culpa*, suivi de *La Vie et l'œuvre de Semmelweis* (Paris: Denoël, 1936), was published at the end of December.

6. Maurice Thorez, *Le Fils du peuple* (Paris: Editions Sociales Internationales, 1937). The book's printing was completed on October 18.

7. See note 10.

8. Jérôme and Jean Tharaud, "Aux mains de Staline: Béla Kun, bourreau de la Hongrie," *Candide*, (December 9, 1937, 3a–e. Céline must have added this epigraph to the book's last proofs because *Bagatelles* came out just three weeks later, on December 28.

9. Céline summarizes in epigraph form an article on Roger Martin du Gard published in the December 3, 1937, issue of *L'Univers Israélite*: "Roger Martin du Gard: Prix Nobel de littérature 1937" (B, 217).

10. Jean Barois, "Hommes, Femmes et Secrets du Jour: La Carrière et les carrières," *Paris-Soir*, October 25, 1937, 2f, quoted in *Bagatelles*, 260–61.

11. Jean Barois, "Le Baron d'Erlanger ou le lyrisme dans les Finances," *Paris-Soir*, October 28, 1937, 2d, an article Céline refers to in *Bagatelles* with the title "Le Baron de Cahen ou le lyrisme dans les Finances" (B, 263–64).

12. In *Le Juif, Poison mortel* (Paris, Editions R.I.F./Collection Les Grandes Conférences de Combat, 1935), 30, Jean Boissel writes: "the princesse Lucinge-Faucigny (the Baron of Erlanger's daugher) [is] another Jewish Cahen." This publication was initially presented as a public lecture at Central Hall on January 4, 1935.

13. Céline's source here is Henry Coston's article "La Conspiration Juive," which appeared in an October 1937 issue of *Siècle Nouveau*.

14. "Sur la pierre de mon tombeau on osera pas graver mon blase" (R2, 311–12).

15. One of the many questions Céline attributes to *L'Univers Israélite*. I was able to locate nine source articles spanning the period from June 25 to December 3, 1937.

16. Maurice M. Feuerlicht, "Where the Jews Fail," *Forum Magazine*, September 1937, 99–104; "Children of the Martyred Race," *Readers Digest*, 31 (186) (October 1937): 21–23.

17. Marcus Eli Ravage, "A Real Case against the Jews," *The Century* (January 1928): 346–50; "Commissary of the Gentiles," *The Century* (February 1928): 476; reprinted in "Deux articles juifs du juif M. E. Ravage, at the 'Service Mondiale' [sic] Bookstore, Fascicule 5"; this pamphlet has not been recovered, but reference to it is made in the Service Mondial's newsletter of February 15, 1937.

18. These include an introduction to Auguste Rohling's *Le Juif talmudique*, written in 1936, a book that provided Céline with his Talmudic epigraphs; a Québécois pamphlet entitled *La Clé du mystère*, published in France in 1936 by Henry Coston's Office de Propagande Nationale; and finally De Vries de Heekelingen's *Israël: son passé, son avenir*, which was published in 1937 by the Librairie Académique Perrin. It was from this latter work that Céline drew the anti-Semitic epigraphs attributed to Wickham Stead, Cicero, Metternich, and so on.

19. John Grand-Carteret, *L'Histoire—La Vie—Les Mœurs et la Curiosité par l'Image, le Pamphlet et le Document (1450–1900)*, 5 vols. (Paris: Librairie de la Curiosité et des Beaux-Arts, 1927–28).

20. Attributed to John Grand-Carteret in "Extrait de l'Histoire des Gens de Finance."

21. Quoted by Grand-Carteret in *L'Histoire*, (2: 195). A letter from Joseph Scalinger informs us that "many copies [of d'Aubigné's work] were burned while the author's reputation for biting commentary saw to it that pamphlets he had never written were attributed to him."

22. The sources are "La Conspiration Juive," an essay published in the October 1937 issue of *Le Siècle nouveau*; Feuerlicht's article in the October 1937 *Reader's Digest*; (a review of the film *La Vie facile* in the Communist daily *L'Humanité*; *Paris-Soir* articles from late October 1937; and Henry-Robert Petit's *Le Règne des Juifs*, whose preface is dated late September). Céline also makes mention of the "last gathering" (B, 248) of the Ras-

semblement Universel pour la Paix, an antifascist organization that had in fact met in Paris in late September 1937.

23. See Zérapha, "Probité célinienne."

24. François Porché, "L.-F. Céline: *Bagatelles pour un massacre*," *L'Epoque*, February 28, 1938. Reprinted in *L'Univers Israélite*, March 11, 1938.

25. Henry Coston, "La Conspiration Juive," *Siècle nouveau*, October 1937, 4–21. The page layout is much denser in *Bagatelles* than in "La Conspiration Juive."

26. Terms used in his *Lettres à Henri-Robert Petit* (LHP) and in his second pamphlet, *L'Ecole des cadavres* (33).

27. The quotation in *Bagatelles* (259), said to have been taken from the newspaper *Le Moment*, is from an article entitled "For Freedom: Communism Unmasked by Dr. Goebbels," published in the May 1, 1936, issue of *Le Réveil du peuple*. The *Réveil du peuple*'s statement—"This Laser Moissejevitch is truly a *great* man; it is he who will one day reign supreme in the land of the Czars. . . . His daughter, who is going on 21 years of age, is now Stalin's wife. He is *good* for the Jews. . . . You see, there is an advantage in having one of our men *in the right place*"—is reformulated by Céline with hyperbolic supplement as: "This Laser Moissejevitch is truly a *very great* man... it is he who will one day reign supreme in the land of the Czars.... His daughter, who is going on 21 years of age, is now Stalin's wife. He is *excellent* for the Jews. . . . You see, there is an advantage in having one of our men *in the best place* [editors' emphasis added]."

28. German economist whose work *Les Juifs et la vie économique* was translated by S. Jankélévitch and published in 1923 by Payot, the publishers of Montandon and Grenier, both quoted in *Bagatelles*.

29. A 962-page manuscript that was placed on public sale at the Hôtel Drouot on November 20, 1984.

30. The error involved a misprint in a June 24, 1937, article in *L'Univers Israélite* by A. Mandel entitled "Où va l'Europe sans l'Esprit judéo-chrétien? Conférence du R.P. Dieux au théâtre des Ambassadeurs." Céline comments on this in *Bagatelles* (212). *Editors' note: Gode* suggests *godemiché*, "dildo," an instrument that could be linked to Gide, given his well-known homosexuality.

31. *Translator's note:* The historian Paula Hyman describes France's consistorial structure, established after the emancipation of French Jews during the Revolution of 1789, as "centralized religious institutions under state supervision, called upon to administer the Jewish community but also to serve the needs of the French state by preaching patriotism and recruiting soldiers." After the separation of Church and State in 1905, she adds, the consistories "remained quasi-governmental bodies . . . and served as a model for the voluntary organizational structure of French Jewry in the period following the separation." See Hyman's *From Dreyfus to Vichy: The Remaking of French Jewry, 1906–1939* (New York: Columbia University Press, 1978), 5–6.

32. *Service Mondial*, 4.4, February 15, 1937, 10.

33. André Gide writes:

And when he plays the role of the Jew responsible for his misfortunes, it is obviously a joke. And if this were not a joke, then Céline would be completely loony. Just as when he includes willy-nilly Cézanne, Picasso, Maupassant, Racine, Stendhal and Zola among the Jews of his massacre. What more do you need? How can you show any better that you're kidding. Like when he presents shocking statistics as the "declaration of the Grand Rabbi"; or when he plays the martyr, or someone who's been plagiarized, etc. . . . He does his best not to be taken seriously. In this case, if you are outraged, it is you commiting the error, the one made so frequently by critics: that of not understanding books for what they are.

See "Les Juifs, Céline et Maritain" (1938, 630–34).

34. *Translator's note:* The *Décret Marchandeau* was legislation passed on April 21, 1939, that prohibited publication of materials deemed to defame and injure groups "belonging by origin to a specific race or religion when th[e] aim [of these materials] is to incite hatred against citizens and residents" of France. This legislation was promptly repealed by the Vichy government after France's defeat by Nazi forces in June 1940.

35. Darquier's quotation is reported in the *Bulletin de Vigilance*, 30: 4–5. The relationship between this appeal and the title Céline chooses for his first pamphlet is not as direct as it would appear and might well be misinterpreted. In Céline's mind, the French are being massacred *by* the Jews ("Affreuses massacreuses de Juifs!" [B, 89]) and a renewal of the 1914–18 hostilities is a result of "Jewish policy." The massacre of the Jews in war is proposed by Céline as an imaginary solution: "If I were dictator" — 'All Jews to the front lines'" (B, 91).

36. *Bulletin de Vigilance,* 59: 4.

37. Dean of the anti-Semitic press who had begun his career as a sidekick of Edouard Drumont at the *Libre Parole*.

38. See Céline's *Lettres à Henri-Robert Petit* (LHP). One of these first letters was a subscription request for *Le Pilori*, dated July 8, 1938.

39. Céline sends Montandon's address to Petit. The subsequent letter from Petit to Montandon, now in the archives of the Centre de Documentation Juive Contemporaine, is dated September 5. The letter begins: "Your friend, L.-F. Céline, has send me your address requesting I contact you with regard to the anti-Jewish struggle." See CDJC, Montadon archives, Document #XCV-27.

40. *La France enchaînée*, published at Darquier de Pellepoix's *centre* on the rue Laugier, supplanted *L'Anti-Juif* as the official organ of the "French anti-Jewish Mobilization." See Robert Dubard's "Having a Drink with Céline," in *La France enchaînée*, December 15–31, 1938 (rpr. in *Le Bulletin Célinien* December 28, 1984), for testimony confirming Céline's presence at the meeting.

41. See Norman Cohn, *Warrant for Genocide* (1967). *Editors' note:* For additional details on the *Protocols*, see Solomon, Chapter 3, pp. 61-62.

42. It should be noted that *Bagatelles* had quite the opposite effect: with its designer-label publisher (Denoël) and sales comparable to those of *Voyage au bout de la nuit, Bagatelles* circulated massively in the literary

world material that would normally have remained within the confines of minor pamphlet literature.

Céline's Review of La Grande Illusion

1. *Pamphlet* refers to the polemical nature of the work, not to its length; all three are book-length volumes.

2. For the writing and publication of *Bagatelles*, see Frederic Vitoux (1988, 307–10) and the chronology provided by Henri Godard (R1, lxxii).

3. See the Renoir filmography in Christopher Faulkner (1979, 101–05).

4. *Editors' note*: See Kaplan's essay, Chapter 2.

5. For the history of the Popular Front government, see Bernard and Dubief (1985), Jackson (1986), and Soucy (1986).

6. Quoted by Gauteur (1980, 30).

7. I have furnished my own translation of the film's dialogue. The text of the film appears in English in Jean Renoir, *Grand Illusion*, trans. Mariane Alexander (New York: Simon & Schuster, 1968). It is available in French, with frame-by-frame shots, in Renoir and Spaak (1974).

8. The film was later banned and lost at the end of the war. See Faulkner (1979, 106) and Durgnat (1974, 157).

9. See Alméras (1987, 45–131), McCarthy (1975, 139–59), and Hewitt (1987, 148–65).

10. *Editors' note:* For a more extended discussion of *L'Eglise*, see Alméras, Chapter 4, pp. 67–68, and Krance, Chapter 5, pp. 86–90.

11. The Freemasons, a secret society, are frequently described by anti-Semites as allies of the Jews.

12. An alliance between the Soviet Union and France was initially signed in May 1935 but was not ratified until March 1936, before the Popular Front assumed power.

13. See Genette (1966, 207–11).

Céline's Masquerade

1. *Journal*, February 13, 1900.

2. *Journal*, December 11, 1907.

3. *Translators' note: The Nouvelle Revue Française* (N.R.F.) was a preeminent literary journal founded in 1909 by André Gide, Jacques Rivière, Jean Paulhan, and Gaston Gallimard that had close ties to the Gallimard publishing house. For a discussion of the journal's history and prevailing aesthetic norms and values, see Pierre Hebey, ed. *L'Esprit N.R.F., 1908–1940* (Paris: Gallimard, 1991).

4. *Editors' note:* Eugène Labiche (1815–1888), was a nineteenth-century French playwright known for his lighthearted middle-class dramas. In *Les Beaux Draps*, Céline defines Labiche Communism as "petty bourgeois Communism, with home ownership and inheritance allowed, that can't be confiscated under any circumstances, with a small garden, and insurance for everything. Everyone is a small property owner" (BD, 136).

5. *Editors' note:* For a more extensive discussion of this episode in Céline's literary career, see Krance's essay, in Chapter 5.

6. *Je Suis Partout*, February 1933. *Editors' note:* The expletives were clearly marked by elision in the original French text.

7. See LJG for the correspondence between Céline and Joseph Garcin; see also Elisabeth Porquerol, "Propos recueillis" (CC1, 44–49), and de St.-Jean (1974).

8. *Editors' note:* see Krance, Chapter 5, pp. 86-87.

9. *Le Canard Enchaîné*, 27 September 1933.

10. *Commune*, November 1933.

11. *Editors' note:* The Paris Commune was a popular uprising that lasted from March 18 to May 28, 1871, in which the Parisian working classes attempted to establish an automonous, worker-controlled municipal government. The initiative was brutally repressed during the week of May 21, 1871, by reactionary forces united in the National Assembly that had formed at Versailles after the routing of the French army in the Franco-Prussian war of 1870–71.

12. *Editors' note:* For the complete reference, see Kaplan, 226, note 33.

13. During the campaign of May–June 1940, the French Army did, however, suffer more fatalities than the American forces did on all fronts between 1941 and 1945.

14. *Translators' note:* Located on the outskirts of Paris, Achères is the site of a sewage treatment plant.

15. "A Lüneburg il y avait des poufs, pas que des charniers." *Puf* means "brothel" in German.

16. Along with "Palestines" and "Fuzz-heads" (Frizous), "morbac," a deformation of *morpion* (a parastic crab), is one of Céline's favorite postwar slurs for insulting Jews.

17. In his use of the name Esther Loyola, Céline is actually referring to Anne Frank whom he obviously believed had been elevated to the status of a Jesuit cult figure.

L.-F. Céline: "Just an Individual"?

1. Subsequent references to Contat and Rybalka's critical commentary accompanying the Pléiade edition of Sartre's *Œuvres romanesques* (Paris: Gallimard, 1981) will be included in the body of my text followed by the abbreviation *OR*.

2. See Contat and Rybalka's account (OR, lii). *Vendredi*'s co-founder was Jean Guéhenno, whom Sartre targeted for bitter sarcasm in *La Nausée* (in the "tête-à-tête" with the Autodidacte).

3. According to Contat and Rybalka (OR, 1665), whereas Céline's *Voyage* vented a desperate recrimination against life itself, Sartre's *La Nausée* undertook a systematic demystification of the reigning bourgeois *épistémè*; thus, although both novels seemed steeped in the same antisocial and antihumanist enterprise, Céline's self-proclaimed anarchism was of the right-wing variety whereas Sartre's partook of the left-wing brand of anarchy.

4. It is worth noting here that the song's composer, Shelton Brooks, was, in Sophie Tucker's own words, "a colored writer," rather than a Jew.

Roquentin's "recognition of otherness" thus seems to be less factual than mythical. See Hollier (1986, xxiii).

5. *Editors' note:* see Alméras, 3–4, Chapter 4, pp. 71-72.

6. *Editors' note:* The League of Nations, in French the SDN or the *Société des Nations*, was the precursor to today's United Nations.

7. Sartre's postwar statement about the venality of Céline's collaboration first appeared in his 1945 essay "Portrait de l'Antisémite" published in *Les Temps Modernes*. An expanded version of this piece entitled *Réflexions sur la question juive* was published by Morihien in 1946 and was reprinted by Gallimard in 1955.

8. Jacques Lecarme, "Sartre et Céline: Deux violents dans le siècle," *Magazine littéraire*, 282 (November 1990): 41. *Editors' note:* One might argue that Céline's response to Sartre in "A l'agité du bocal" effectively silenced Sartre's criticism of Céline. See Spear, Chapter 6, pp. 100-101.

9. On exhibit at the Anne Frank House Museum in Amsterdam.

10. Texts such as Léon Bloy's anti-Semitic tract *Le Salut par les Juifs* ("Salvation by the Jews" [1892]), typify this kind of writing.

11. In *L'Ecole des cadavres*, Céline himself refers to *Bagatelles pour un massacre* as a "simple vulgarization," characterized by its "stylized virulence," and as falling short of a systematic exposure of "la judéologie" (33).

12. Nesta Helen Webster, *Secret Societies and Subversive Movements* (1924); cited in Alméras (1987, 376).

13. Bernard Steele, the American Jew, who, together with Robert Denoël, was Céline's first publisher, posits Céline's anti-Semitism as a reaction to his own sense of personal vulnerability (Alméras, 1987, 117).

Virility and the Jewish "Invasion" in the Pamphlets

1. An earlier version of this essay was included in my Ph.D. thesis, "The Narrator and the Narratee in Céline's Autofiction" (New York University, 1988). In addition to the advice from Professors Erika Ostrovsky and Ernest Sturm for the 1988 version, I would particularly like to acknowledge my coeditor, Rosemarie Scullion, for her careful editing of the reformulated essay.

2. H. E. Kaminski was, incidentally, one of the first critics to take Céline to task for the ideas expressed in the pamphlets, publishing his *Céline en chemise brune* just two months after *Bagatelles pour un massacre* appeared in print (February 1938 and December 1937, respectively). *Editors' note:* for further discussion of Kaminski's work, see Blondiaux, Chapter 1, p. 13.

3. Alluding quite possibly to the French national anthem, *La Marseillaise*, ("le jour de gloire est arrivé"), the original reads: "le jour de bander enfin nous arrive!" (EC, 22).

4. For purposes of clarity, I will use narrational terms ("narrator," "narratee," "narration") in my discussion of Céline's pamphlets, not without acknowledging the ambiguity of such terminology when applied to texts that are an amalgam of racist, anti-Semitic diatribes (directly pilfered from various external sources) and Céline's original material that, although successfully marketed in the same format as his previous novels and by the same publisher (Denoël), never make a claim to fictionality. On the

contrary, Céline's use of his civil and professional names (Destouches and Céline), to say nothing of his numerous references to current events and personalities, has typically led critics to categorize these works generically as (polemical) pamphlets. My use of narrational terminology is thus principally an attempt to facilitate recognition of the distinction between text (as representation, or *mimesis*) and (extratextual) reality, a critical claim that does not necessarily correspond to Céline's authorial intention.

5. Soviet leader Joseph Stalin, for example, was rumored to have kept his Russian edition of *Voyage au bout de la nuit* at his bedside (R1, 1265).

6. It is interesting to note that Céline's characterization of Roosevelt and the Pope as Jewish was considered too disrespectful and was therefore expunged from the German translation of *Bagatelles*, entitled *Die Juden-verschwörung in Frankreich (The Jewish Conspiracy in France)*. In a very informative essay, Christine Sautermeister (1989) compares Céline's original text with the translation approved by Nazi authorities. The German version deleted Céline's punctuation, neologisms, crude language, and any passages that criticized Aryan decadence (except where applicable solely to France), the Nazi conception of war, and, of course, Hitler. Sautermeister notes that the passage in which Céline imagines Hitler making sexual advances toward him (B, 83)—of particular interest for my study here—was stripped of its promiscuous connotations and rendered as an expression of homage to the Führer. See Sautermeister, 1989.

7. See *L'Express*, June 14, 1957, 16. These "reservations" do not necessarily square with the unmistakably anti-Semitic portraits he sketches in, for example, his play *L'Eglise*, composed in 1927. See Alméras (1987), 9–10, 32–35.

8. Because, for Céline Jews are synonymous with blacks, Gutman is linked with Jewish identity because he calls himself a "nigger" (moi nègre [B, 227]). Gutman also is said to have "Jewish eyes" (B, 33).

9. *Editors' note:* See Kaplan, Chapter 2, p. 35.

10. This citation (B, 179) can be compared with the epigraph of *Les Beaux Draps*—"A la corde sans pendu" (To the rope without someone to be hanged"—which does not specify who the victim will be. *Editors' note:* See, Kaplan, Chapter 2, p. 45.

11. *Editors' note:* see Kaplan, Chapter 2.

12. In *L'Ecole des cadavres*, Céline unequivocally calls for a Franco-German pact consolidating a "Confederation of Aryan European States" (EC, 287); see also B, 221, the text in question here.

13. Information provided to me by Frédéric Vitoux, one of Céline's biographers.

14. Quoted in CC5, 249. Céline had already asserted that all women want to "fuck the yids" (B, 33). To render the full force of Céline's racism, I have chosen to translate the French term "nègre" as the English "nigger" instead of "black," which it also signifies.

15. George Mosse cites a 1937 issue of *Das Schwarz Korps*, an SS newspaper stating that "Jews and homosexuals were working hand in hand to destroy all that was creative in man and so undermine his virility" (1985, 141).

16. *Editors' note:* Céline's call for the return of "emotion" in art (his

famed *métro émotif*) is a curious entreaty when one considers the fact that constructions of the feminine in Western culture have typically resulted in the diminished worth of women precisely because of their presumed "emotional" excesses. For further discussion of this problematic, see Mosse (1985, 146) and Scullion, Chapter 8.

17. Milton Hindus's translation in "Rereading *Voyage and Bagatelles*. Paper read at The MLA Convention, New York, December 1986.

18. *Editors' note:* For a definition of "Labiche Communism," see Alméras, Chapter 5, note 4.

19. Céline tongue-lashes Jean Paul Sartre in his essay "A l'agité du bocal," stating: "Dirty little devil full of shit, I yank you from my ass and you sully me on the outside!" (CC7, 383).

20. Ultimately a humanist, though surely "à rebours" (as Erika Ostrovsky notes [1967, 88ff.]), Céline's statements regarding homosexuality are typically brief, often comical anecdotes and mockery of a general sort that is very much akin to his derision of the rest of the human race. His comments on Proust are especially telling of his general disinterest in this particular mark of difference, which he considers thoroughly banal as it affects, or so he claimed, "20% of the population" (CC2, 155).

The (Con)Quest of the Other in Voyage

1. For a discussion of the interrelations of biography, gender problematics, and literature in Céline's *Voyage*, see Montaut (1985) and Alméras (1976).

2. In 1503, Amerigo Vespucci wrote: "It was to us a matter of astonishment that none was to be seen among them who had a flabby breast, and those who had borne children were not to be distinguished from virgins by the shape and shrinking of the womb" (cited in Tiffany and Adams, 1985, 78).

3. *Editors' note:* For an extended psychoanalytic discussion of voyeurism, see Scullion, Chapter 8.

4. Dijkstra writes: "She floated, because to walk is to act, and to beckon a form of invitation, a way of taking charge. And to the late nineteenth-century male nothing was as unwelcome as the thought of woman—even woman as the embodiment of nature—taking charge. He wanted to be in charge, it was his right to be in charge. . . . It was woman's appointed role, even as the personification of nature, to float weightlessly in the breeze" (1986, 87).

5. Ralph Manheim's translation of *pardon* as "all-forgiving" and of the verb *plonger* as "bathing" deemphasizes the powerful coupling of religious and erotic imagery in this passage, in which Céline's gaze passes from the organ pipes (likened to a woman's thighs) to the screen during the dimming of the lights, which is associated simultaneously with absolution and sexual penetration (R1, 201).

6. For a discussion of the problematics of the male gaze in the cinematic experience, see E. Ann Kaplan, *Women and Film: Both Sides of the Camera* (New York: Methuen, 1983).

7. "When anybody mentioned France to me, I instantly thought of my guts, so I wasn't nearly so open to patriotic ardor" (J, 42).

8. "The moment I stopped kissing her, I was in for it, she'd start on the war and her fritters" (J, 42).

9. During his passage to Africa, Bardamu projects that the continent will have "nothing in common with the emasculated Africa of travel agencies and monuments, of railways and candy bars. Certainly not! We'd be seeing Africa in the raw, the real Africa!" (J, 95).

10. Consider young Ferdinand's far less medically marked assessment of the derrière in *Mort à crédit*: "I'd caught on, believe me, I knew the score with women. Ass is a rat race, a sucker's caravan! An abyss, a bottomless pit, and that's that" (D, 239).

11. The term *la garcerie* is a Célinian neologism that defies translation. Although this term contains the noun *la garce*, the first definition of which is "bitch" and the second "prostitute," there is no single word in English that conveys the notion of "bitch" (in a moral sense) and "prostitute" (which is also linked to animality, *chienne* in a biological sense) and also refers to the general category of "woman." Nor does the English translation offered by Ralph Manheim, "bitchery" cover the conceptual terrain of a degenerative female sexuality.

12. *Editors' note:* For Céline's definition of Labiche Communism, see Alméras, Chapter 4, note 4.

13. Should there be any doubt that medical language is at work semantically well before the protagonist's return to France, we need only look at the final conversation between Lola and Bardamu in New York. It is during this meeting that we learn that Bardamu had started his medical studies prior to leaving France, had temporarily put them aside, and intends to resume his training on returning to his homeland. In the final analysis, Lola is defeated in the symbolic battle between hero and Amazon for she is ultimately obliged to submit to Bardamu who acts in this episode as the purveyor of medical and anatomical knowledge, expertise that he sadistically deploys in tormenting this "garce" with predictions that her mother will not recover from cancer and will soon perish.

14. Michel Collomb comments on the prevalence of standardization in cultural consumerism: "Music-hall spectacles, identical from one end of the Union to the other, seemed to celebrate the application of the laws of standardization onto man. Forty showgirls' absolutely identical legs raised at the same time imitate the perfection of mechanical operations" (1987, 94).

15. The power of the masculine gaze to transform is illustrated near the end of the novel in Bardamu's description of Sophie. He must first identify the qualities that lend themselves to petrification such as the muscular body and the hardness in her corporeal features. Bardamu classifies her as of the American sort: "Sophie had the winged, elastic, precise gait that is so frequent, almost habitual, among the women of America, the gait of heroic creatures of the future, whom life and ambition carry lightly toward new kinds of adventure... Three-masters of joyful warmth, bound for the Infinite" (J, 408). The process of petrification sets in as he sneaks unannounced into her room and watches her sleeping. He may claim that his gaze works

to "humanize" her, but it is clear that it also reflects a will to mastery: "Wishing to take her by surprise, to ravish a little of her pride, of the prestige and power she had acquired over me, to diminish her, in short to humanize her a little and reduce her to our paltry proportions, I would go into her room when she was sleeping" (J, 40).

16. See Solomon (1988), 54–56.

17. "Living under clouds and surf that seem like steam rising from the boiling cauldron of the elemental sea, these [New Women] represent that unabashed independence and elemental sense of freedom the men of 1900 feared, and found most fascinating, in the viragoes of their day. In the very directness of their passion and strength, these women embodied the paradox of the self-possessed and therefore hated, yet so very delectable and admirable New Woman, she who had thrown off the trappings of the household nun and had toppled her weak and fainting mother's pedestal" (Dijkstra, 1986, 265).

18. "To the American Metropolis—Fritz Lang's film is from 1926— European intellectuals contrast the myth of the symmetrical European city, 'scaled to the size of man,' warm, welcoming, and peaceful with its immutable hierarchies, transcribed onto the urban landscape" (Collomb, 1987, 93).

19. I am referring to the narrators in the novels that follow *Voyage*.

Choreographing Sexual Difference

1. Julia Kristeva's *Pouvoirs de l'horreur* (1980a) makes important (psycho)analytic strides in this area. Although the analysis that follows is conceptually indebted to Kristeva, its focus on the dynamics of male spectatorship raises issues of gender domination and oppression that are, I would argue, critically sidestepped or at least woefully understated in Kristeva's reading of Céline.

2. For notable exceptions to this general critical indifference to gender problematics in Céline, see Alméras (1974; 1976). See also Montaut (1985). In my present analysis, I am much indebted to Philip Solomon's *Night Voyager* (1988), which effectively underscores the relationship between gender configurations and Céline's textual binarism and which initially sparked my interest in this much-neglected aspect of Céline's writing.

3. Most references to the Hindus correspondence are taken from *The Crippled Giant: A Literary Relationship with Louis-Ferdinand Céline* (Hanover: University Press of New England, 1986), which contains selections from the Céline-Hindus exchange. The remaining citations are drawn from Céline's letters to Hindus published in the 1972 edition of the *Cahier de L'Herne* HER). Unless otherwise indicated, translations are my own.

4. The discussion that follows focuses solely on Céline's implicitly heterosexual male spectatorship and the ballerina. Both the female spectator's and the male homosexual's relationship to the ballet spectacle raise a quite different set of psychocultural issues that remain beyond the scope of this analysis.

5. For an account of the circumstances surrounding Céline's imprison-

234 ▾ *Notes to Pages* 143–44

ment in Denmark, his extradition proceedings, and the trial that followed, see Gibault (1981, 91–234).

6. See Metz (1982, 42–57) and Silverman (1983, 194–236).

7. See Bartky (1988) for a Foucauldian discussion of the modernization of patriarchy and its regimentation of the female body within the contemporary Western cultural setting. Bartky observes that

there are significant gender differences in gesture, posture, movement and general bodily comportment: women are far more restricted then men in their manner of movement and in their spatiality. . . . A space seems to surround women in imagination that they are hesitant to move beyond: this manifests itself both in a reluctance to reach, stretch, and extend the body to meet resistances of matter in motion . . . and in a typically constricted posture and general style of movement. Women's space is not a field in which her bodily intentionality can be freely realized but an enclosure in which she feels herself positioned and by which she is confined (66).

8. The ballerina has not always occupied center stage in ballet. In its earliest courtly forms, male dancers were considered the art's virtuosos and the moves they executed were interpreted as signs of male accomplishment. Céline in fact alludes to the male-centered origins of ballet in the Hindus correspondence when he states that "Louis XIV had faith in ambassadors only if they were perfect dancers" (107). The fall of France's *Ancien Régime* put an end to aristocratic patronage of ballet, which gradually came to be seen in the post-revolutionary period as an unsuitable occupation for men. From the early nineteenth century to the early 1960s, women dancers far outnumbered their male counterparts, who were relegated to a secondary status often described as that of a *porteur*. With the ascendence of Soviet dancer Rudolph Nureyev and later, his compatriot Mikhail Baryshnikov, male dancers were brought once again to the performative fore. For a discussion of the historical shifts of gender emphasis in Western theater dance, see Hanna (1988, 121–48).

9. Hanna notes that although women have both founded ballet companies (in many instances, later taken over by men) and been recognized for their choreographic and directorial achievements, these successes have generally failed to garner the name recognition of their male counterparts such as George Balanchine, Robert Joffrey, and Arthur Mitchell. Hanna further emphasizes the statistical significance of male dominance in ballet, reporting that in 1984, out of 75 American ballet companies, nearly three-quarters were run by male directors, with the largest and most prestigious (the New York City Ballet, American Ballet Theater, San Francisco Ballet, and Boston Ballet) all under male direction (1988, 127–28).

10. For a discussion of the gender-marked "prestige hierarchy" in Western theater ballet, see Hanna's chapter "Patterns of Dominance: Men, Women and Homosexuality" (1988, 119–49).

11. Hanna is quoting Suzanne Gordon's *Off Balance: The Real World of Ballet* (New York: Pantheon, 1983), 155, 173. For a discussion of the cultural influences on the development of the anorexic aesthetic, see Susan Bordo's

"Anorexia Nervosa: Psychopathology as the Crystallization of Culture," in *Feminism and Foucault: Reflections on Resistance*, ed. I. Diamond and L. Quinby (Boston: Northeastern University Press, 1988), 87–117.

12. I would like to thank Natasha Lesser, a graduate student in Comparative Literature at the University of Iowa, for sharing her experiences with and insights into the ballet world and its professional culture.

13. For a discussion of the heterosexist foundations of this hierarchy see Hanna, 1988, 119–49).

14. Proust's actual "esquisse," or sketch, of this passage is included in the appendix to the Pléiade edition of *A la Recherche du temps perdu* (2: 1151–59).

15. I emphasize the term *adult* here, for in another passage of the Hindus correspondence, Céline openly acknowledges what can only be considered his pedophilic propensities: "[I'm] a pagan for my complete worship of physical beauty, health. I hate sickness, penitence, anything morbid. Completely Greek in that respect. I admire the wholesomeness of childhood. It makes me swoon—could easily fall in love, madly—I mean love—with a little four-year-old girl in full bloom of youth, health and beauty" (1950, 119).

16. See Lacan's "The Mirror Stage as formative of the function of the I as revealed in the psychoanalytic experience" in *Ecrits: A Selection* (1977). For an introductory discussion of the terms of Lacanian psychoanalysis, see Elizabeth Grosz's *Jacques Lacan* (New York: Routledge, 1990). See also Jane Gallop's "The Mirror Stage: Where to Begin," *SubStance*, 37/38 (1983): 118–28.

17. See especially Heath (1978), (1982), Mulvey (1986), and Silverman (1983, 1990).

18. *Editors' note:* For a discussion of Céline's literary representation of the seductions of cinema in *Voyage au bout de la nuit*, see Forrest, Chapter 7.

19. For a discussion of cinema's scopic regime, see especially the chapters entitled "Identification, Mirror" and "The Passion for Perceiving" in Metz (1982).

20. For an analysis of the problem of sexual difference in Freud and Lacan and its relevance to film theory, see Heath (1978).

21. For a fascinating critique of the manner in which Freud's own castration anxiety projects itself into his analysis of sexual difference, see Luce Irigaray's "La Tâche aveugle d'un vieux rêve de symétrie" in *Spéculum de l'autre femme* (Paris: Minuit, 1974). For a critique of the Freudian notion of fetishism as a purely male phenomenon, see Naomi Schor's "Female Fetishism: The Case of George Sand," in Susan R. Suleiman, ed. *The Female Body in Western Culture* (Cambridge: Harvard University Press, 1985), 363–72.

22. For a discussion of the difference between "having" and "being" the phallic signifier, see Jacques Lacan's "The Meaning of the Phallus" (1977, 281–91) and Judith Butler's critique of Lacan's essay (1990, 35–78). It is worth noting that several of Céline's critics have drawn attention to the author's own feminine physical and personality traits. Hindus, for example, noticed that "[t]he upper part of Céline's arms are white, hairless, delicate,

almost feminine" (34), that there was "something almost feminine about certain lines in his face" (9) "what he says is true of women is certainly true of himself" (36) and that he often "repeat[ed] things eight or nine times like a primitive person, like my grandmother for example" (10). Maurice Bardèche asserts that Céline was "hysterical" and often fell prey to the "capriciousness, mood swings and blubbering [which is characteristic] of a feminine disposition" (1986, 258), a view of the author that Elizabeth Craig seems to corroborate in her statement that "he was extremely excitable" (Monnier, 1988, 24).

23. Jacques Derrida pithily defines the deconstructionist term *phallogocentrism* as "the complicity of Western metaphysics with a notion of male firstness" (1979, 69).

24. All speaking subjects are, Lacanian psychoanalysis demonstrates, subject to symbolic castration on entering into signification, and no one actually "has" the phallus, which makes such demonstrations of phallic force a veritable charade. Lacan writes:

Let us say that those relations will turn around a "to be" and a "to have", which, by referring to a signifier, the phallus, have the opposed effect, on the one hand, of giving reality to the subject in this signifier, and, on the other, of derealizing the relations to be signified. This is brought about by the intervention of a "to seem" that replaces the "to have" in order to protect it on the one side, and to mask its lack on the other, and which has the effect of projecting in their entirety the ideal or typical manifestations of the behaviour of each sex, including the act of copulation itself, into the comedy [of sexual difference]. (1977, 289)

25. These three ballet scenarios, along with *Van Bagaden* and *Voyou Paul, Brave Virginie*, are included in CC8. *La Naissance d'une fée*, *Voyou Paul, Brave Virginie*, and *Van Bagaden* are all included in *Bagatelles pour un massacre*.

26. See note 6. Hanna further points out that "Louis XIII danced and took on women's parts," whereas "Louis XIV of France (1643–1715), dancing in his roles as milkmaiden, king, or god Apollo, was glorified as the 'Sun King,' the epithet coming from a role he danced at age fifteen. The nobility acclaimed male peer dancing" (1988, 122–23).

27. Pierre Birnbaum lends further credence to this claim in his account of the racist imagery political adversaries disseminated in attacking Léon Blum, the Socialist leader who in 1936 became France's first Jewish prime minister: "Blum was a 'great hysteric, a great maniac, already ripe for a padded cell and straight jacket,' a hysteric who took after camels or serpents, an individual struck with 'delirium tremens,' who expressed his sadism by constant use of the whip. Doriot saw him as an 'intellectual sadist,' and in the Salle Wagram, before 10,000 people . . . Jean Renaud, head of *Solidarité française*, described him as 'Valentine the acrobat of *danses macabres* brandishing the whip' in order to conquer power." *Anti-Semitism in France: A Political History from Léon Blum to the Present*, trans. Miriam Kochan (Cambridge, Mass.: Blackwell, 1992), 153.

28. Although the demonic imagery Céline introduces here in his construction of earthly evil is decidedly unimaginative, it is identical to that

which Adolf Hitler and Julius Streicher invoked in vilifying Europe's Jewish population in the weeks proceeding the January 20, 1942, Wannsee Conference where the Third Reich's "Final Solution" (Endlösung) to the "Jewish Problem" was formulated. In *Why Did the Heavens Not Darken: The "Final Solution" in History* (New York: Pantheon, 1988), the historian Arno Mayer writes: "in *Der Stürmer* of December 25 [Julius] Streicher declared that he saw no solution other than the 'extermination' (Ausrottung) of the '[Jewish] people, whose father is the devil,' if the 'curse of God, lodged in its blood' was to be exorcized. Three days later . . . the führer defended Streicher against some of his detractors. . . . Hitler asserted that 'the Jew is much meaner bloodthirstier, and more satanic' even than Streicher portrayed him in *Der Stürmer*" (296–97).

29. In this reference to the ingestion of body fluids, Céline is obliquely resuscitating one of the most galvanizing images and enduring myths in traditional Christian anti-Semitic demonology: that of Jews ritually murdering Christian children and drinking their blood during Passover ceremonies. For the history of this legend, see George L. Mosse's "The Jews: Myth and Counter-Myth" (1978).

30. Karalik's limp is quite similar to that of the physically impaired mother Clémence who obsequiously hobbles around the family dwelling in *Mort à crédit*. Describing his father Auguste's fits of rage, the narrator recalls: "In his bad spells he used to turn purple and swell up all over, he rolled his eyes like a dragon. It was horrible to look at. My mother and I were scared stiff. Then he broke a dish and went to bed. 'Turn toward the wall, you little pig! Don't turn around.' I had no desire to... I knew... I was ashamed... it was my mother's legs, the skinny one and the fat one... She continued to limp about from one room to the next... He was trying to pick a fight... she insisted on finishing the dishes" (D, 53–54). Along with its perfectly normative display of male sadism and female masochism, this passage succinctly illustrates the negative affect ("I had no desire to,' "I was ashamed") the missing maternal phallus can generate in the male subject. Here, I would argue, that deficiency is displaced on to the lower extremities of the mother's body ("my mother's legs, the skinny one and the fat one").

31. For a discussion of the origins of the notion of "suture" in Jacques-Alain Miller's psychoanalytic thought and of the development of the concept in film theory, see Heath (1977–78) and Silverman (1983, 194–236).

32. See Julia Kristeva's analysis in *Pouvoirs de l'horreur* (1980a) of borderline discourse and "abject" narration in the modernist text of which Céline's writing is, she persuasively argues, exemplary.

Franks and Gauls *in the German Trilogy*

1. For the text of and commentary on Article 75, see Assouline (1985, 158).

2. "The extreme right oscillates between a definition of nation understood as a legacy of centuries and an organicist vision. The same ambivalence presides in the conception of Europe either as an ensemble of peoples

who share the same values or as an alliance of ethnic groups" (d'Appollonia, 1988, 50–51).

3. Gregory of Tours and other early chroniclers claim that the Franks got their name, as François Hotman writes in *Francogallia* (1586 edition), "from their freedom and ferocity (the latter being a play upon words [*a libertate, et... a ferocitate*] by these authors), because they refused to be hired by the Emperor Valentinian and to pay tribute as was the custom of other nations" (1972, 202–03). Hotman, a professor of law, argues that the Franks and Gallo-Romans mixed very early on and that the first kings were chosen by election, not by heredity.

4. Abbé de Vertot: "France is the name of a nation rather than of a country." From the *Dissertation sur la véritable origine des Français*, published in 1705, quoted in Barzun (1932, 150). Like d'Appollonia's definition of extreme-right nationalism cited in note 2, "nation" designates a people more than a political body.

5. For example: "Physically from the North, he [Céline] got his tall height"; "In very different tones, according to his humor, the Celt [Céline] lets himself digress on his own end"; "A mental boundary mysteriously allowed him, however, to distinguish France from Brittany" (Perugia, 1987, 22, 558, 647).

6. *Astérix* is about a Gallic village and its inhabitants' exploits. It has been argued that Goscinny and Uderzo's presentation of the inhabitants corresponds to popular notions of the "Nordic" type. Characters wear the Frankish winged helmet and have blond or red hair worn long (James, 1988, 242). The village itself is also located in the northernmost part of Armorique (Brittany). Surrounded by Roman camps, this village is the last outpost of nonsubjugated Gauls (Celts?), who fearlessly defend their freedom with the help of their Druid's magical potion. Barbarian invasions are always committed by Goths or Anglo-Saxons, but never by Franks. Their absence in the comic strip suggests that they are always already assimilated to the village's "Gallic" inhabitants. Léon Poliakov writes:

> Let us therefore give credit to Henri Martin, father of a Celtic myth, which was popularized by the "Our ancestors the Gauls" in Third Republic manuals, but which one only dares admit to through the figures of Astérix and Obélix. Astérix is, moreover, not a negligible character. There would be a lot to say about his clownishness which is in keeping with a certain tradition of Gallic humor, for beneath this veil, he continues to titillate an underlying streak in the small and the big, the same streak which a short while ago prompted grand collective resolutions and served as a relay between the great carnage and political doctrines.' (1971, 47).

In general, there appears to be a certain confusion between Gauls (and/or Celts) and Franks in the popular imagination. The most striking example of this is the popular brand of French cigarettes, *Gauloises*, which is emblematized by the Frankish helmet.

7. In "FRANÇOIS ou FRANÇAIS," Voltaire distinguishes the Franks from the Gauls by what he calls the "génie français." The special genius of the Gauls survived Frankish subjugation to reemerge many centuries later as

"la politesse" because "the nation's foundation is made up of Gallic families, & the character of the old Gauls still existed." Caesar and others had found that "of all the barbarians the Gauls were the most polite" (1779, 338, 339).

8. In an interview Céline goes so far as to claim that the Hohenzollern castle is "the nest of Europe's mother dynasty" (CC2, 64).

9. *Editors' note:* Céline's "ils promettent, ils rient, tout est dit" (R2, 548) ridicules the inscription displayed at Caeser's Pontic triumph: "Veni, vidi, vici."

10. "I established, from one time period to another, the dominant national idea and class or party opinions about French society's origins and its revolutions" (Thierry, 1840, 9).

11. " 'I do not want to steal the honor of others in telling what I have done. I believe that historians, who only write about princes and the great, say enough about these personages and pass over in silence those who are not of such great stature' " (cited in Courteault, 1907, 86. See also 70, 76).

12. The chroniclers often had good reason for writing defenses of their pasts. Monluc was accused of having collaborated with the king's enemies, of having dipped into the king's finances, and of having extorted goods and monies from the people. In his preamble, he states explicitly that he writes his life so as to reestablish the truth of his innocence (8). Commynes, an earlier chronicler, was accused of having taken advantage of Louis XI's largesse and, after eight months of solitude in the Conciergerie tower, he found himself decrepit and confined by court order to his only remaining château. It was here that he wrote his *Mémoires* to defend himself for posterity's sake and to console himself during the immense legal battle over his seized property, which was not to conclude until fifty years after his death.

13. The captive court analogy must have been commonly recognized because it also appears in the form of a limerick composed by a collaborationist refugee for the amusement of his fellow refugees: "Le burg enfin n'est pas si mal,/C'est du roi Pétain la cour; / Mais pourquoi avoir dit un jour; / 'Mon royaume pour un Laval!' " (cited in Saint-Pauline, 1966, 485).

14. Paul Broca, founder of the Société d'Anthropologie in 1859, measured skulls for the purpose of determining ethnic ancestry and of establishing white superiority. Countless gadgets, methods, interpretations, and valorizations grew out of this field, culminating in the person of the infamous Dr. Montandon, an acquaintance of Céline's, who was a professor of anthropology before the war and, during the Occupation, the much-feared official racial theorist for the Commissariat Général aux Questions Juives (Commissioner General for Jewish Affairs) in 1943. For information on Montandon's dubious clinical "methodology," see Paxton and Marris (1983, 300–301).

15. Camus was involved in the Resistance and was, for a short time, a member of the Comité National des Ecrivains (National Committee of Writers), a group of writers who, toward the end of the Occupation, drew up a blacklist of compromised and collaborationist writers and journalists. The Comité and its list were influential in the severe reprisals taken against

these blacklisted writers by the Liberation authorities. Camus, as well as other writers, spoke out strongly against the purge tactics of the Liberation.

16. Céline would side with Maurice Bardèche's opinion of the war's final outcome stated in his infamous book, *Nuremberg: ou la terre promise.* Writing against the Nuremberg trials, Bardèche comments: "All nations, all parties that recall the soil, tradition, occupation, race are suspect. . . . There are no more boundaries, no more cities [cités]. From one end of the continent to the other, the laws are the same, as well as the passports, the judges and the currencies" (1948, 55–56).

17. "I don't know if Froissart (I'm citing immense names not to distinguish myself but because they come to mind), Joinville, or Commynes deliberately got involved in the events they describe... They found themselves there through the fault of historical circumstances. Me too, I found myself in a history" (CC2, 25).

Postmodern Céline

1. I wish to thank Rosie Sarah Reiss and Jody Enders for their knowledgeable and helpful comments on reading a first draft of this essay.

2. For the characterization of Céline as a problematic modernist, see Kaplan (1986, 109). See also Huyssen, who associates Céline with "modernists such as Marinetti, Junger, Benn, Wyndham Lewis" all of whom ascribe to a "powerful masculinist mystique" (1986, 55). For the designation of Céline as a precursor to postmodernism, see, for example, McCaffery (1986, xiv).

3. In much the same way Ihab Hassan presents the "disjunctive and indeterminate forms" of the postmodern as inevitably leading to a " 'white ideology' of absences and fractures" (1982, 271).

4. See also Callinicos (1970), who, in an attempt to recuperate the Enlightenment project of emancipation, calls postmodernism's rejection of Enlightenment ideology "reactionary."

5. At the time, the currency of the term *postmodern* was more frequent in the United States than in France. Still, behind Kristeva's phrases, the "decentering of subjective identities," stands Deleuze and Guattari's schizophrenic subject, first outlined in *L'Anti-Oedipe* (1972), and now directly associated with the elaboration of a postmodern subjectivity. What is more, although Kristeva uses the terms *avant-garde* and *modern* in her 1977 article, three years later she turns to the term *postmodern* to characterize the very same linguistic activity. See Kristeva (1980b, 136–41).

6. The opposition between Sartre and Céline found in Kristeva's essay is all the more significant as it reiterates a debate between the two writers in the years following the war.

7. Céline's last novels are loaded with declarations such as the following, from *Rigodon*: "politics, speeches, bullshit!... only one truth! biology!" (R, 107).

8. My critique of Kristeva follows Alice Yaeger Kaplan's, who sees Kristeva's *Powers of Horror* as an ahistorical reading, intent on saving Céline from fascism by invoking modernist aesthetic and symbolic categories. See Kaplan (1986, 109).

9. Céline makes this explicit in an interview with Madeleine Chapsal in which he describes his writing as "a little music [une certaine petite musique] introduced into the style" (CC2, 20).

10. *Editors' note*: Céline himself was fully aware of his role as chronicler of apocalyptic events. *Féerie pour une autre fois, II* is dedicated to Pliny the Elder (23–70 A.D.), witness to and victim of the eruption of Mount Vesuvius.

11. Two source studies in particular have demonstrated the extent to which Céline relies on preestablished forms of representation. See Kaplan's Chapter 2, and Bellosta (1990). Both works are essential for demonstrating that Céline's transcendental style is caught in the web of contemporary political attitudes.

12. See for example Winston Churchill's downplaying of the destruction in *The Second World War*. Churchill writes, "Throughout January and February our bombers continued to attack, and we made a heavy raid in the latter months on Dresden, then a center of communications of Germany's Eastern Front" (1953, 540).

13. Of Bardèche's book, Céline wrote to his friend Albert Paraz in a letter dated January 13, 1949: "The ending is stupid, but the development is solid" (CC6, 123). *Editors' note*: see note 19 and Loselle, Chapter 10, pp, 200–202.

14. Along with Bardèche, Paul Rassinier turns to a denunciation of Allied bombing raids when he attempts to put into doubt the horrors of the death camps. See, for example, the introduction to the second edition of *Le Mensonge d'Ulysse* ("Ulysses's Lie"). Rassinier attacks those who would condemn Nazi war crimes and make no mention of victims of "Leipzig, Hamburg . . . Nagasaki and Hiroshima" (1955, 29). In my view, the best refutation of the arguments and rhetoric of Rassinier and the negationists have been presented by Vidal-Naquet, (1980), Fresco (1980), and Finkielkraut (1982).

15. For example, in the following passage from *D'un Château l'autre*, he writes: "the Volga... Buchenwald... the Great Wall of China... Nasser and the Pyramids... the same racket! swift kicks in the ass are nothing new!" (C, 241). Or again, in Céline's critique of mercantilism in *Nord*, we read: "in the Russian labor camps, in Buchenwald, in the darkest dungeon, or under the atomic ashes, Mercury is right there!" (N, 5).

16. The effectiveness of litotes for condemning the horror of war is evident in Vonnegut (1969). Vonnegut recovers from Céline the aesthetic terminology, the ironic understatement, and the condemnation of the bombing of Dresden. Transmission from novel to novel takes place both on a stylistic and an ideological level.

17. That Céline's public pronouncements are founded on revisionist impulses is also demonstrated by private declarations in his correspondence. In letters to Albert Paraz and Roger Nimier, the postwar Céline manifests both his revisionist tendencies and his continued anti-Semitism. Regarding Paul Rassiner, Céline writes to Paraz: "[Rassinier] tends to cast doubt on the magical gas chamber. That's quite something!" (CC6, 276). And shortly after the release of *D'un Château l'autre* in 1957, Céline writes to Nimier: "Jews and their whining pis[s me off]... If they hadn't made

France declare war, they wouldn't have known Buchenwald and all the rest" (L, 373).

18. Even when using Bakhtin as a model, Godard's reading of Céline coincides with the postmodern's elaboration of an eclectic referential system as described, for example, by Jim Collins who states that "the simultaneous presence of traditionally contradictory discourses epitomizes Post-Modern textuality" (1989, 64).

19. Cited in *Les Procès de la Collaboration (The Collaboration Trials* [Paris: Albin Michel, 1948]), 627.

Works Cited

Primary Texts: Louis-Ferdinand Céline

Principal French editions

Dates in parentheses are those of first publication.

Bagatelles pour un massacre. Paris: Denoël, 1937. Also cited in rpt. 1943 (Denoël).

Les Beaux Draps. Paris: Denoël, 1941; Nouvelles éditions Françaises, 1941.

D'un Château l'autre (1957). In *Romans, I*, 1–299.

Castle to Castle. Trans. Ralph Manheim. New York: Delacorte Press, 1968 (rpts., New York: Penguin, 1976; New York: Carroll & Graf, 1987).

Entretiens avec le Professeur Y (1955). Paris: Gallimard, 1981.

Conversations with Professor Y. Trans. Stanford Luce. Hanover, NH: University Press of New England, 1986.

L'Ecole des cadavres. Paris: Denoël, 1938.

L'Eglise. Paris: Denoël, 1933. Rpt. in *Œuvres complètes*, 1: 335–47; and Paris: Gallimard, 1952.

Féerie pour une autre fois, I. Paris: Gallimard, 1952.

Féerie pour une autre fois, II: Normance. Paris: Gallimard, 1954.

Guignol's Band, I (1944). In *Romans, III*, 81–310.

Guignol's Band. Trans. Bernard Frechtman and Jack T. Nile. London: Vision Press, 1950.

Guignol's Band, II. Le Pont de Londres. In *Romans, III*, 311–759.

Cahier de l'Herne: L.-F. Céline. Ed. Dominique Le Roux, Michel Beaujour, and Michel Thélia. Paris: L'Herne, 1972. [This single volume compiles much of: *L'Herne* 3 (1963) and *L'Herne* 5 (1965).]

Lettres à la N.R.F., 1931–1961. Ed. Pascal Fouché. Paris: Gallimard, 1991.

Lettres à son avocat. Ed. F. Monnier. Paris: La Flûte de Pan, 1984.

Lettres à Henri-Robert Petit, 1938–1942. Paris: Collin Maillard, 1986.

Lettres à Joseph Garcin. Texte établi et présenté par P. Lainé. Paris: Monnier, 1987.

Mea Culpa, suivi de *La Vie et l'œuvre de Semmelweis.* Paris: Denoël, 1936. Rpt. in *Oeuvres complètes*, I: 335–47, and in CC3, 15–109.

Mea Culpa and *The Life and Work of Semmelweis.* Trans. R. A. Parker. New York: Fertig, 1937 (rpt. 1979).

Maudits soupirs pour une autre fois. Une version primitive de Féerie pour une autre fois. Etabli. et présenté par H. Godard. Paris: Gallimard, 1985.

Mort à crédit (1936). In *Romans, I,* 507–1104.

Death on the Installment Plan. Trans. Ralph Manheim. New York: New Directions, 1983.

Nord (1960). In *Romans, II,* 301–707.

North. Trans. Ralph Manheim. New York: Delacorte, 1972 (rpt. 1975).

Oeuvres complètes, 5 vols. Ed. J. A. Ducourneau. Paris: André Balland, 1966–69.

Rigodon (1969, posthumous). In *Romans, III,* 709–927.

Rigodoon. Trans. Ralph Manheim. New York: Delacorte, 1974 (rpt. 1975).

Romans, I. Ed. Henri Godard. Bibliothèque de la Pléiade. Paris: Gallimard, 1981.

Romans, II. Ed. Henri Goddard. Bibliothèque de la Pléiade. Paris: Gallimard, 1981.

Romans, III. Ed. Henri Godard. Bibliothèque de la Pléiade. Paris: Gallimard, 1988.

Voyage au bout de la nuit (1932). In *Romans, I,* 1–506.

Journey to the End of the Night. Trans. Ralph Manheim. New York: New Directions, 1983.

"Cahiers Céline"

Céline et l'actualité, 1933–1961. Textes réunis et présentés par J.-P. Dauphin et P. Fouché. Paris: Gallimard, 1986.

Céline et l'actualité littéraire, 1932–1957. Textes réunis et présentés par J.-P. Dauphin et H. Godard. Paris: Gallimard, 1976.

Céline et l'actualité littéraire, 1957–1961. Textes réunis et présentés par J.-P. Dauphin et H. Godard. Paris: Gallimard, 1976.

Lettres à Albert Paraz. Edition établie et annotée par J. P. Louis. Paris: Gallimard, 1980.

Lettres à des amies. Textes réunis et présentés par C. W. Nettelbeck. Paris: Gallimard, 1979.

Lettres et premiers écrits d'Afrique. 1916–1917. Textes réunis et présentés par J.-P. Dauphin. Paris: Gallimard, 1978.

Progrès, suivi de Oeuvres pour la scène et l'écran. Textes réunis et présentés par Pascal Fouché. Paris: Gallimard, 1988.

Semmelweis et autres écrits médicaux. Textes réunis et présentés par J.-P. Dauphin et H. Godard. Paris: Gallimard, 1977.

Works on *Céline*

Alméras, Philippe. 1974. "Du sexe au texte avec arrêt raciste." *La Revue des lettres modernes,* 398–402: 81–103.

———. 1976. "L'Amérique femelle ou les enfants de Colomb." *The Australian Journal of French Studies,* 13.1/2: 97–109.

———. 1987. *Les Idées de Céline.* Paris: Bibliothèque de Littérature Française Contemporaine.

Bardèche, Maurice. 1986. *Louis-Ferdinand Céline.* Paris: La Table Ronde.
Bellosta, Marie-Christine. 1983. *Le Système de références de L.-F. Céline dans* Voyage au bout de la nuit. Thèse (3ᵉ cycle), Paris VII.
————. 1990. *Céline ou l'art de la contradiction: Lecture de* Voyage au bout de la nuit. Paris: Presses Universitaires de France.
Bleton, Paul. 1978. "L'Impossible Portrait de l'antisémite ou l'impossible, portrait de l'antisémite." *Etudes littéraires,* 11: 313–31.
Blondiaux, Isabelle. 1985. *Une Ecriture Psychotique: Louis-Ferdinand Céline.* Paris: Nizet.
Chesneau, Albert. 1971. *Essai de psychocritique de Louis-Ferdinand Céline.* Paris: Minard.
————. 1974. *La Langue sauvage de L.-F. Céline. Essai de stylistique thématique.* Thèse de doctorat d'Etat, Paris III, Sorbonne. Lille: Atelier de reproduction des thèses.
Crapez, Marc. 1991. "Le Communisme Labiche. Céline au fil de certains courants du socialisme." Mémoire, Ecole des Hautes Etudes Politiques et Sociales, Académie de Paris.
Dauphin, Jean-Pierre, and Pascal Fouché. 1985. *Bibliographie des écrits de Louis-Ferdinand Céline.* Paris: BLFC.
Day, Stephen. 1974. *Le Miroir allégorique de Louis-Ferdinand Céline.* Paris: Klincksieck.
Debrie, Nicole. 1990. *Il Etait une Fois . . . Céline.* Paris: Aubier.
Durette, Dominique. 1972. *Louis-Ferdinand Céline (1894–1961). Contribution à l'étude du médecin et de l'écrivain.* Thèse de doctorat en médecine, Université de Lyon.
Gibault, François. 1977. *Céline. 1. Le Temps des espérances (1894–1932).* Paris: Mercure. Rpt. 1985.
————. 1985. *Céline. 2. Délires et persécutions, (1932–1944).* Paris: Mercure.
————. 1981. *Céline. 3. Cavalier de l'Apocalypse (1944–1961).* Paris: Mercure.
Gide, André. 1938. "Les Juifs, Céline et Maritain." *NRF,* 295 (avril): 630–34. Rpt. *Cahier de l'Herne: L.-F. Céline,* 468–70.
Godard, Henri. 1974. "Un Art poétique." *Revue des Lettres Modernes,* 398–402: 7–40.
————. 1985. *La Poétique de Céline.* Paris: Gallimard.
Hewitt, Nicholas. 1983. "*Voyage au bout de la nuit*: Voyage imaginaire et histoire de fantômes." *Céline: Actes du Colloque International de La Haye, 25–28 juillet 1983.* Paris: Bibliothèque L.-F. Céline de l'Université Paris-VII, Bulletin 8: 9–19.
————. 1987. *The Golden Age of Louis-Ferdinand Céline.* Leamington Spa, Eng.: Berg.
Hindus, Milton. 1950. *The Crippled Giant.* Hanover, NH: University Press of New England (2nd edition, 1986).
————. 1951. *L.-F. Céline tel que je l'ai vu.* Paris: L'Arche.
Ifri, Pascal. 1989. "Le Livre rédempteur: *Féerie pour une autre fois* et *Le Temps retrouvé.*" *Céline: Actes du Colloque International de Londres, 5–7 juillet 1988.* Tusson: Editions du Lérot; Paris: Société des Etudes Céliniennes.

———. 1991. "Céline et Proust: Un parallèle au niveau stylistique." *Céline: Actes du Colloque de Toulouse, 5–7 juillet 1990*. Tusson: Editions. du Lérot; Paris: Société des Etudes Céliniennes.

Kaminski, H. E. 1983. *Céline en chemise brune ou le mal du présent* (1938). Paris: Champ libre.

Kaplan, Alice Yaeger. 1987. *Relevé des sources et citations dans Bagatelles pour un massacre*. Tusson: Du Lérot.

Knapp, Bettina. 1974. *Céline: Man of Hate*. University, Alabama: University of Alabama Press.

Kristeva, Julia. 1977. "Actualité de Céline." *Tel Quel*, 71/73: 45–52.

———. 1980a. *Pouvoirs de l'horreur: Essai sur l'abjection*. Paris: Seuil. *Powers of Horror: An Essay on Abjection*. Trans. L. S. Roudiez. New York: Columbia University Press, 1982.

Llambias, Robert. 1986. "Guerre, histoire et langage dans le récit célinien." *Revue des Sciences Humaines*, 204: 89–105.

Luce, Stanford. 1979. *A Glossary of Céline's Fiction*. Ann Arbor: University Microfilms International.

McCarthy, Patrick. 1975. *Céline: A Critical Biography*. London: Allen Lane.

Monnier, Jean. 1988. *Elizabeth Craig raconte Céline. Entretien avec la dédicataire de* Voyage au bout de la nuit. Paris: BLFC.

Montaut, Annie. 1985. "Le 'Méchant' Voyage: Masculin/féminin." *Etudes littéraires*, 18(2) (Fall): 301–13.

Morand, Jacqueline. 1972. *Les Idées politiques de Louis-Ferdinand Céline*. Paris: Librairie Générale de Droit et de Jurisprudence.

Muray, Philippe. 1981. *Céline*. Paris: Editions du Seuil.

Nettelbeck, Colin. 1972. "Journey to the End of Art: The Evolution of the Novels of L.-F. Céline." *PMLA*, 87 (1): 80–89.

O'Connell, David. 1976. *Louis-Ferdinand Céline*. Boston: Twayne.

Ollivier, Jean-Claude. 1970. *Céline et le docteur Destouches*. Thèse de doctorat en médecine, Paris V.

Ostrovsky, Erika. 1967. *Céline and His Vision*. New York: New York University Press.

———. 1972. *Voyeur Voyant: A Portrait of Louis-Ferdinand Céline*. New York: Random House.

Pagès, Yves. 1991. "The 'Modest Proposal' of Doctor Destouches." *Actes du Colloque International de Toulouse, L.-F. Céline, 1990*. Tusson: Editions du Lérot, pp. 195–214.

Perugia, Paul del. 1987. *Céline*. Paris: Nouvelles Éditions Latines.

Poulet, Robert. 1971. *Mon Ami Bardamu: Entretiens familiers avec L.-F. Céline*. Paris: Plon.

Robert, P. E. 1991. *Céline et les Editions Denoël, 1932–1948*. Paris: IMEC.

Roussin, Philippe. 1987. "Céline: Les tirages d'un auteur à succès entre 1932 et 1944." *Actes du Colloque International de Paris, L.-F. Céline, 1986*. Tusson: Editions du Lérot.

Sautermeister, Christine. 1989. "La Traduction allemande de *Bagatelles pour un massacre*." *Actes du Colloque International de Londres, L.-F. Céline*. Tusson: Editions du Lérot, pp. 209–221.

Sollers, Philippe. 1986. "Le Rire de Céline." In *Théorie des Exceptions*. Paris: Gallimard, pp. 112–14.

Solomon, Philip H. 1988. *Night Voyager: A Reading of Céline*. Birmingham, AL: Summa.

Spear, Thomas C. 1991. "Céline and 'Autofictional' First-Person Narration." *Studies in the Novel*, 23(3) (Fall): 357–70.

Stromberg, Robert. 1961. "A Talk with Louis-Ferdinand Céline." *Evergreen Review*, 5(19) (July–August): 102–07.

Trotsky, Leon. 1989. "Novelist and Politician." In *Critical Essays on Louis-Ferdinand Céline*. Ed. William K. Buckley. Boston: G. K. Hall, pp. 30–34.

Vitoux, Frédéric. 1988. *La Vie de Céline*. Paris: Grasset.

Winock, Michel. 1990. "Le Scandale Céline." In *Nationalisme, antisémitisme et fascisme en France*. Paris: Seuil.

Other References

d'Appollonia, Ariane Chebel. 1988. *L'Extrême-droite en France: de Maurras à Le Pen*. Questions au XXᵉ siècle. Brussels: Editions Complexes.

Armstrong, Carol M. 1985. "Edgar Dégas and the Representation of the Female Body." In *The Female Body in Western Culture*. Ed. Susan R. Suleiman. Cambridge: Harvard University Press, pp. 223–42.

Assouline, Pierre. 1985. *L'Epuration des intellectuels*. Questions au XXᵉ siècle. Brussels: Editions Complexes.

Bardèche, Maurice. 1948. *Nuremberg ou la Terre promise*. Paris: Les Sept Couleurs.

Bartky, Sandra Lee. 1988. "Foucault, Femininity and the Modernization of Patriarchy." In *Feminism and Foucault: Reflections on Resistance*. Eds. I. Diamond and L. Quinby. Boston: Northeastern University Press, pp. 61–86.

Barzun, Jacques. 1932. *The French Race: Theories of Its Origins and Their Social and Political Implications*. New York: Columbia University Press.

———. 1937. *Race: A Study in Superstition*. New York: Columbia University Press. Rpt. Harper & Row, 1965.

Baudrillard, Jean. 1983. *Simulations*. New York: Semiotext(e).

Bernard, Philippe, and Henri Dubief. 1985. *The Decline of the Third Republic, 1914–38*. Trans. Anthony Forster, Vol. 5 of *The Cambridge History of Modern France*. Cambridge: Cambridge University Press.

Brandt, William J. 1966. *The Shape of Medieval History: Studies in Modes of Perception*. New Haven: Yale University Press.

Braudel, Fernand, and Ernest Labrousse., eds. 1979. *Histoire économique et sociale de la France*. Tome IV, vol. I. Paris: Presses Universitaires de France.

Broca, Paul. 1871. *Mémoires d'anthropologie*, Vol. 1 Paris: C. Reinwald et Cⁱᵉ.

Butler, Judith. 1990. *Gender Trouble: Feminism and the Subversion of Identity*. New York: Routledge.

Callinicos, Alex. 1990. "Reactionary Postmodernism?" In *Postmodernism and Society*. Ed. Roy Boyne and Ali Rattansi. New York: St. Martin's Press, pp. 97–118.

Caron, François. 1979. *An Economic History of Modern France.* Trans. Barbara Bray. New York: Columbia University Press.

Churchill, Winston. 1953. *The Second World War,* Vol. 6. Boston: Houghton Mifflin.

Cixous, Hélène. 1981. "Castration or Decapitation?" Trans. Annette Kuhn. *Signs,* 7(1): 36–55.

Clapham, J. H. 1961. *The Economic Development of France and Germany: 1815–1914.* Cambridge: Cambridge University Press.

Cohn, Norman. 1967. *Warrant for Genocide: The Myth of the Jewish World-Conspiracy and the Protocols of the Elders of Zion.* London: Eyre and Spottiswoode.

Collins, Jim. 1989. *Uncommon Cultures: Popular Culture and Post-Modernism.* New York: Routledge.

Collomb, Michel. 1987. *La Littérature art-déco.* Paris: Klincksieck.

Courteault, Paul. 1907. *Blaise de Monluc historien: Etude critique sur le texte et la valeur historique des* Commentaires. Paris: Alphonse Picard et Fils.

Debord, Guy. 1967. *La Société du spectacle.* Paris: Buchet-Chastel.

Daley, Jean. 1956. "Névrose et création." Discours inaugural du *Congrès des médecins aliénistes et neurologistes (1954).* Paris: Masson.

Deleuze, Giles, and Felix Guattari. 1972. *L'Anti-Oedipe: Capitalisme et schizophrénie.* Paris: Editions de Minuit.

Derrida, Jacques. 1979. *Spurs: Nietzsche's Styles / Eperons: Les Styles de Nietzsche.* Trans. Barbara Harlow. University of Chicago Press.

———. 1982. "Choreographies: An Interview with Jacques Derrida." *Diacritics,* 12(2): 66–76.

Dijkstra, Bram. 1986. *Idols of Perversity: Fantasies of Feminine Evil in Fin-de-Siècle Culture.* New York: Oxford University Press.

Doane, Mary Ann. 1985 "The Clinical Eye: Medical Discourses in the 'Woman's Film' of the 1940s." In *The Female Body in Western Culture.* Ed. Susan R. Suleiman. Cambridge: Harvard University Press, pp. 152–74.

Dupré, Ernest. 1905. *La Mythomanie. Etude psychologique et médico-légale du mensonge et de la fabulation morbide.* Paris: Jean Gainche.

Durgnat, Raymond. 1974. *Jean Renoir.* Berkeley: University of California Press.

Faulkner, Christopher. 1979. *Jean Renoir: A Guide to References and Resources.* Boston: G. K. Hall.

———. 1986. *The Social Cinema of Jean Renoir.* Princeton: Princeton University Press.

Felman, Shoshana. 1978. *La Folie et la chose littéraire.* Paris: Seuil.

Finkielkraut, Alain. 1982. *L'Avenir d'une négation: Réflexions sur la question du génocide.* Paris: Seuil.

Fresco, Nadine. 1980. "Les Redresseurs de morts." In *Les Temps Modernes,* 407 (June 1980): 2150–2211.

Freud, Sigmund. 1953. *The Standard Edition of the Complete Psychological Works.* Trans. James Strachey. 23 vols. London: Hogarth Press.

Froissart, Jehan. 1972. *Chroniques.* Ed. George T. Diller. Geneva: Droz.

Gauteur, Claude. 1980. *Jean Renoir: La Double Méprise.* Paris: Les Éditeurs Français Réunis.

Gavronsky, Serge. 1979. "Proust dans l'appareillage célinien." *Céline: Actes du Colloque International de Paris, 17–19 juillet 1979*. Paris: Bibliothèque L.-F. Céline de l'Université de Paris-VII, Société des Etudes Céliniennes, 3: 57–71.

Genette, Gerard. 1966. *Figures I*. Paris: Seuil.

Gide, André. 1936. *Retour de l'U.R.S.S.* Paris: Gallimard.

Gilman, Sander L. 1985. *Difference and Pathology: Stereotypes of Sexuality, Race, and Madness*. Ithaca, NY: Cornell University Press.

Gourfinkel, Nina. 1936. "Les Thèmes scatologiques en littérature." *Le Courrier d'Epidaure*, 9–10: 26–37, 51–59.

Habermas, Jürgen. 1987. *Lectures on the Philosophical Discourse of Modernity*. Cambridge: MIT Press.

Hamilton, Edith 1969. *Mythology: Timeless Tales of Gods and Heroes*. New York: Mentor.

Hanna, Judith Lynn. 1988. *Dance, Sex and Gender: Signs of Identity, Dominance, Defiance, and Desire*. Chicago: University of Chicago Press.

Harvey, David. 1989. *The Condition of Postmodernity*. Cambridge: Basil Blackwell.

Hassan, Ihab. 1982. *The Dismemberment of Orpheus*. Madison: University of Wisconsin Press.

Heath, Stephen. 1977–78. "Notes on Suture." *Screen*. 18(4): 48–76.

———. 1978. "Difference." *Screen*, 19(3): 51–112.

Hindus, Milton, 1967. *The Proustian Vision*. Carbondale and Edwardsville: Southern Illinois University Press.

Hodgens, Pauline. 1988. "Interpreting the Dance." In *Dance Analysis: Theory and Practice*. Ed. J. Adshead. London: Dance Books, pp. 60–89.

Hollier, Denis. 1986. *The Politics of Proof: Essay on Sartre*. Trans. J. Mehlman. Minneapolis: University of Minnesota Press.

Hotman, François. 1972. *Françogallia*. Ed. Ralph E. Geisey. Trans. J. H. M. Salmon. Cambridge: Cambridge University Press.

Huyssen, Andreas. 1986. *After the Great Divide: Modernism, Mass Culture, Postmodernism*. Bloomington: Indiana University Press.

Jackson, Robert. 1988. *The Popular Front in France: Defending Democracy, 1934–38*. Cambridge: Cambridge University Press.

James, Edward. 1988. *The Franks*. Oxford: Basil Blackwell.

Jameson, Fredric. 1991. *Postmodernism or The Cultural Logic of Late Capitalism*. Durham: Duke University Press.

Kaplan, Alice Y. 1986. *Reproductions of Banality. Fascism, Literature and French Intellectual Life*. Minneapolis: University of Minnesota Press.

Kelly, Donald R. 1964. *"De Origine Feudorum:* The Beginnings of an Historical Problem." *Speculum: A Journal of Medieaval Studies*, 39(2) (April): 207–28.

Kindleberger, Charles P. 1964. *Economic Growth in France and Britain: 1861–1950*. Cambridge: Harvard University Press.

Kingston, Paul J. 1983. *Anti-Semitism in France during the 1930s: Organizations, Personalities and Propaganda*. Hull: University of Hull Press.

Kristeva, Julia. 1980b. "Postmodernism?" In *Romanticism, Modernism, Postmodernism*. Ed. Harry R. Garvin. Lewisburg: Bucknell University Press, pp. 136–41.

Lacan, Jacques. 1977. *Ecrits: A Selection*. Trans. Alan Sheridan. New York: Norton.

Langmuir, Gavin. 1990. *Toward a Definition of Anti-Semitism*. Berkeley: University of California Press.

Lombroso, Cesare. 1889. *L'Homme de génie* (1864). Trans. Fr. Colonna D'Istria. Paris: Alcan.

Lyotard, Jean-François. 1984. *The Postmodern Condition: A Report on Knowledge*. New York: Minneapolis: University of Minnesota Press.

Marny, Jacques. 1968. *Le Monde étonnant des bandes dessinées*. Paris: Editions du Centurion.

Mauron, Charles. 1963. *Des métaphores obsédantes au mythe personnel. Introduction à la psychocritique.*Paris: Corti. Rpt. 1983.

McCaffery, Larry, ed. 1986. *Postmodern Fiction: A Bio-Bibliographical Guide* Westport, Conn.: Greenwood.

Metz, Christian. 1982. *The Imaginary Signifier: Psychoanalysis and the Cinema*. Trans. C. Britton et al. Bloomington: Indiana University Press.

Monluc, Blaise de. 1964. *Commentaires*. Ed. P. Courteault. Paris: Gallimard (Pléiade).

Mosse, George L. 1978. *Toward the Final Solution: A History of European Racism*. Madison: University of Wisconsin Press.

———. 1985. *Nationalities and Sexuality: Respectability and Abnormal Sexuality in Modern Europe*. New York: Howard Fertig.

Mulvey, Laura. 1975. "Visual Pleasure and Narrative Cinema." *Screen*, 16(3): 6–18. Reprinted in *Narrative, Apparatus, Ideology: A Film Theory Reader*. Ed. P. Rosen. New York: Columbia University Press, 1986.

Nietzsche, Friedrich. 1974. *The Gay Science*. Trans. Walter Kaufman. New York: Random House.

Paris, Gaston, and A. Jeanroy, eds. 1892/1927. *Extraits des chroniqueurs, Français: Villehardouin, Joinville, Froissart, Comines*. Paris: Hachette.

Paxton, Robert O., and Michael R. Marras. 1983. *Vichy France and the Jews*. New York: Schocken.

Poliakov, Léon. 1971. *Le Mythe aryen: Essai sur les sources du racisme et des nationalismes*. Paris: Calmann-Lévy.

Proust, Marcel. 1987–89. *A la Recherche du temps perdu*. Ed. Jean-Yves Tadié. Paris: Gallimard. (Pléiade) 4 vols. *Remembrance of Things Past*. Trans. C. K. Scott Moncrieff and Terence Kilmartin. New York: Random House, 1982. 3 vols.

Ragache, Gilles, and Jean-Robert Ragache. 1988. *La Vie quotidienne des écrivains et des artistes sous l'Occupation 1940–1944*. Paris: Hachette.

Rassinier, Paul. 1955. *Le Mensonge d'Ulysse*. Paris: La Librairie Française.

Renard, Jules. 1965. *Journal, 1887–1910*. Paris: Gallimard.

Renoir, Jean. 1968. *Grand Illusion*. Trans. Mariane Alexander. New York: Simon & Schuster.

———. 1974a. *Ecrits, 1926–1971*. Ed. Claude Gauteur. Paris: Belfond.

———. 1974b. *My Life and My Films*. Trans. Norman Denny. New York: Atheneum.

Renoir, Jean and Charles Spaak. 1974. *La Grande Illusion*. Paris: Balland.

Retz, Cardinal de. 1956. *Mémoires*. Eds. Maurice Allen, Edith Thomas. Paris: Gallimard.

Reynold, Gonzague de. 1939. *D'où Vient l'Allemagne?* Paris: Plon.

Robert, Pierre E. 1979. "Marcel Proust et Louis-Ferdinand Céline: Un contrepoint." *Bulletin de la Société des Amis de Marcel Proust et des Amis de Combray*, 29: 34–46.

Rubenstein, Diane. 1990. *What's Left? The Ecole Normale Supérieure and the Right.* Madison: University of Wisconsin Press.

St. Jean, Robert de. 1974. *Journal.* Paris: Grasset.

Saint-Paulien [Maurice-Ivan Sicard]. 1964. *Histoire de la Collaboration.* Paris: L'Esprit Nouveau.

Sartre, Jean Paul. 1945. "Portrait de l'antisémite." *Les Temps Modernes,* 1: 442–70.

———. 1946. *Réflexions sur la question juive.* Paris: Morihien.

———. 1948. *Portrait of an Anti-Semite.* Trans. G. J. Becker. New York: Schocken Books.

———. 1976. "L'Autoportrait à 70 ans." In *Situations X.* Paris: Gallimard.

———. 1981. *Oeuvres romanesques.* Ed. Michel Contat and Michel Rybalka. Paris: Gallimard (Pléiade).

Silverman, Kaja. 1983. *The Subject of Semiotics.* New York: Oxford University Press.

———. 1988. *The Acoustic Mirror: The Female Voice in Psychoanalysis and Cinema.* Bloomington: Indiana University Press.

Sipriot, Pierre. 1985. *Montherlant sans masque.* Paris: Laffont.

Soucy, Robert. 1986. *French Fascism: The First Wave, 1924–1933.* New Haven: Yale University Press.

Tacitus, Cornelius. 1939. *Dialogus, Agricola, Germania.* Trans. Sir William Peterson. Cambridge: Harvard University Press.

Tallemant des Réaux, Gédéon. 1960–61. *Historiettes.* 2 vols. Paris: Gallimard.

Thierry, Augustin. 1840. *Récits des temps mérovingiens.* 2 vols. Paris: Garnier Frères.

Tiffany, Sharon W., and Kathleen J. Adams. 1985. *The Wild Woman: An Inquiry into the Anthropology of an Idea.* Cambridge: Schenkman Publishing.

Todorov, Tzvetan. 1978. "Le Discours psychotique." *Les Genres du discours.* Paris: Seuil, pp. 78–85.

Tournier, Michel. 1981. "Qu'est-ce que la littérature: Un entretien avec Michel Tournier." *Magazine Littéraire,* 179: 80–6.

Trotignon, Y. 1985. *La France au XXe siècle. Tome 1: Jusqu'en 1968.* Paris: Dunod.

Vidal-Naquet, Pierre. 1980. "Un Eichmann de papier." *Esprit,* 45: 8–52.

Voltaire [François Marie Arouet]. 1779. "FRANCHISE," "FRANÇOIS ou FRANÇAIS." *Encyclopédie ou dictionnaire raisonné des sciences, des arts et des métiers.* Eds. Diderot and d'Alembert, vol. 15, 3rd ed. Geneva: Pellet. 17 vols, pp. 323–24, 338–42.

Vonnegut, Kurt. 1969. *Slaughterhouse-Five.* New York: Delta.

Weber, Eugen. 1986. *France, Fin de Siècle.* Cambridge: Belknap.

Woolf, S. J. 1981. "Introduction." *Fascism in Europe.* Ed. S. J. Woolf. London: Methuen, pp. 1–18.

Index

260 ▼ *Index*

UNIVERSITY PRESS OF NEW ENGLAND publishes books under its own imprint and is the publisher for Brandeis University Press, Brown University Press, Dartmouth College, Middlebury College Press, University of New Hampshire, University of Rhode Island, Tufts University, University of Vermont, Wesleyan University Press, and Salzburg Seminar.

Library of Congress Cataloging-in-Publication Data
Céline and the politics of difference / Rosemarie Scullion, Philip
    Solomon, Thomas C. Spear, editors.
        p.   cm.
    Includes bibliographical references and index.
    ISBN 0–87451–697–8
        1. Céline, Louis-Ferdinand, 1894–1961—Political and social views.
    2. Politics and literature—France—History—20th century.
    3. Literature and society—France—History—20th century.
    I. Scullion, Rosemarie. II. Solomon, Philip H. III. Spear, Thomas
    C.
PQ2607.E834Z626   1995
834'.912 — dc20   94–29452